The Drama of Memory in
Shakespeare's History Plays

This book analyses the drama of memory in Shakespeare's history plays. Situating the plays in relation to the extradramatic contexts of early modern print culture, the Reformation and an emergent sense of nationhood, it examines the dramatic devices the theatre developed to engage with the memory crisis triggered by these historical developments. Against the established view that the theatre was a cultural site that served primarily to salvage memories, Isabel Karremann also considers the uses and functions of forgetting on the Shakespearean stage and in early modern culture. Drawing on recent developments in memory studies, historical formalism and performance studies, the volume develops a vocabulary and methodology for analysing Shakespeare's mnemonic dramaturgy in terms of the performance of memory that results in innovative readings of the English history plays. Karremann's book is of interest to researchers and upper-level students of Shakespeare studies, early modern drama and memory studies.

ISABEL KARREMANN is professor of English Literature at Würzburg University, Germany. She is the co-editor of *Forgetting Faith? Negotiating Confessional Conflict in Early Modern Europe* (with Cornel Zwierlein and Inga Mai Groote, 2012), *Shakespeare in Cold War Europe: Conflict, Commemoration, Celebration* (with Erica Sheen, forthcoming, 2015) and *Forms of Faith: Literary Form and Religious Conflict in Early Modern England* (with Jonathan Baldo, forthcoming, 2016).

The Drama of Memory in Shakespeare's History Plays

ISABEL KARREMANN

CAMBRIDGE
UNIVERSITY PRESS

CAMBRIDGE
UNIVERSITY PRESS

University Printing House, Cambridge CB2 8BS, United Kingdom

Cambridge University Press is part of the University of Cambridge.

It furthers the University's mission by disseminating knowledge in the pursuit of
education, learning and research at the highest international levels of excellence.

www.cambridge.org
Information on this title: www.cambridge.org/9781107117587

© Isabel Karremann 2015

First published 2015

Printed in the United Kingdom by Clays, St Ives plc

A catalogue record for this publication is available from the British Library

Library of Congress Cataloguing in Publication data
Karremann, Isabel.
The drama of memory in Shakespeare's history plays / Isabel Karremann.
   pages cm
Includes bibliographical references and index.
ISBN 978-1-107-11758-7 (hardback)
1. Shakespeare, William, 1564–1616–Histories.   2. Memory in literature.   I. Title.
PR2982.K37 2015
882.3′3–dc23   2015022568

ISBN 978-1-107-11758-7 Hardback

Contents

Contents

Figures

Acknowledgements

I have incurred many debts of gratitude in writing this book. One of them predates its conception by almost a decade, when Ina Schabert hired me, still a student then, as assistant on the editorial team of the *Shakespeare-Jahrbuch*. Ina Schabert inspired me with her fascination for early modern drama, her passion for research and her insistence that methodology be both rigorous and creative. This book is dedicated to her.

I would like to thank, first of all, Jonathan Baldo for being a wonderful colleague and fellow-oblivionist. Among my colleagues at Munich University, my very special thanks go to Tobias Döring for so generously sharing his ideas on early modern oblivion with me, and to Andreas Höfele for making things possible. The research network 'Pluralisation and Authority in the Early Modern Period' provided critical feedback and intellectual companionship; I thank in particular Susanne Friedrich for drawing my attention to the title engraving with which I open my introductory chapter. I received support and advice from Ingrid Hotz-Davies, Ulrich Pfisterer and Susanne Scholz, who gave me important feedback on earlier versions of this book, as well as from Michael Dobson, Ewan Fernie, Kate McLuskie and Laurie Maguire, who generously supported my applications for funding. I would like to thank James Simpson for running a workshop on iconoclasm and memory with me during his stay at Munich University, and for his enthusiastic encouragement.

I am very grateful to Freya Sierhuis and Brian Cummings, who gave me the opportunity to develop my ideas on nostalgia on the Jacobean stage in two workshops at the Centre for Advanced Study in Munich and to publish a part of Chapter 5 in their volume *Passions and Subjectivity in Early Modern Culture*. My gratitude also goes to Peter Holland for accepting earlier versions of Chapters 2 and 5 for *Shakespeare Survey*, and for generously granting permission to reprint them in revised form here. Special thanks are due to Gordon McMullan for inviting me to present my work on Falstaff at the

London Shakespeare Seminar and for encouraging me to approach Cambridge University Press in the first place. Sarah Stanton has been the most supportive editor possible, and Rosemary Crawley has seen me patiently and efficiently through the final stages of copy-editing. I would like to thank them as well as the two anonymous readers for helping me to turn a manuscript into a book.

My greatest debt of gratitude belongs to Eberhard Roske, as always.

Note on the text

All Shakespearean texts are cited according to the following edition:

The Norton Shakespeare. Based on the Oxford Edition.
Eds. Stephen Greenblatt, Walter Cohen, Jean E. Howard,
Katharine Eisaman Maus. New York: W.W. Norton, 1997.

Quotations from Shakespeare's plays are references according to
this edition, with act, scene and line numbers given in parentheses in
the text.

All other references are given in the Bibliography section at the end.

Introduction: forms of remembering and forgetting in early modern England and on the Shakespearean stage

The title engraving to Johann Philipp Abelin's second volume of his European history, the *Theatrum Europaeum* (1633), depicts early modern attitudes to the historiographical project of reconstructing the past in terms that are also at the core of this study about the drama of memory in Shakespeare's theatre. The centre of the picture is occupied by a rectangular stone table bearing the elaborate subtitle of the work: *The Continuation of Historical Chronicles or True Description of all Memorable Stories Having Occurred in Europe and other Places in the World, from the Year of Our Lord 1629 to 1633* (my translation). The engraved stone, a visual reference to the written nature of historical memory as well as to its durability, is surrounded by allegorical figures representing history, time and truth. Directly above it we see a winged stag carrying the figure of Time, a North European adaptation of Greek mythology, where the winged horse Pegasus carries the muses from Parnassus, among them Clio, the muse of historiography.[1] To the left, the figure of Historia as an old woman is teaching a child, her feet resting on a piece of marble inscribed 'Magistra Vitae'; on the right, the beautiful young figure of 'Lux Veritatis' is seen with a torch, bringing the light of Truth. This ensemble was a familiar topos in the iconography of early modern historiography. The title engraving to Sir Walter Ralegh's *History of the World* (1614), for example, features a similar pairing of History, Experience and Truth as opposed to Death and Oblivion, whose supine figures at the bottom of the picture provide the stepping-stones for a triumphant History, again addressed as 'Life's Mistress'. The engraving to Abelin's *Theatrum Europaeum* is likewise separated by a horizontal line: the lower part of the picture

---

[1] The mother of Clio was Mnemosyne, from whom the mnemonic art derives its name. Stuart Hampton-Reeves discusses depictions of Clio in early modern paintings and texts in his contribution to Cavanagh et al. (eds.), *Shakespeare's Histories and Counter-Histories*, 'Staring at Clio', pp. 1–5.

1

is occupied by a subterranean cave in which several figures crouch, half
obscured by shadows, representing the enemies of historical truth. The
sleeping female figures on the right-hand side embody oblivion, or forgetfulness.[2] In the middle background, cowering in the shadow, we see
two half-naked, hirsute male figures in chains and with asses' ears on
their heads, representing Inscitia, ignorance. An owl, the bird of wisdom,
is perched – mockingly? – on a bough above them. On the left sit two
female figures, also in chains, and wearing masks. The subscription identifies them as Mendacium, the lie. Their accessories, however, would invite
yet another identification: they look similar to the masks that were used
in ancient Greek drama. A European audience would have been familiar with such theatrical masks from medieval mystery plays or from the
commedia dell'arte that originated in Renaissance Italy. If these masked
figures recall the theatre – to its attackers nothing but an art of lying –
then this raises the question of their specific relation to the figures mirroring them in the spatial arrangement of the picture, the embodiments
of oblivion. The engraving implies that history and truth are opposed to
forgetting and theatricality, an assumption that was often voiced also in
antitheatrical tracts and as often refuted by defences of the stage, which
habitually praised the theatre as a site of memory, truth and virtue.[3]

[2] On the early modern iconography of oblivion as a sleeping or dead figure, see
William E. Engel's essay 'The decay of memory', where he discusses, among
other examples, the title engraving to Ralegh's *History of the World*.
[3] John Northbrooke, for example, associates the theatre with forgetfulness when
he writes in *A Treatise wherein Dicing, Dauncing, Vaine playes or Enterluds ...
Are Reproved* (1577) that playgoers 'have no mind of any reformation or
amendment of [their] life' (p. 25), and Stephen Gosson's *Playes Confuted in
Five Actions* (1582) calls for plays to 'bee banished, least ... little and little
we forget God' (p. 193). The definitive study of antitheatrical literature is
still Jonas Barish's *The Antitheatrical Prejudice* (1981); the essays by Garrett
A. Sullivan Jr. and Zachariah Long in C. Ivic and G. Williams (eds.), *Lethe's
Legacies*, pp. 41–52 and pp. 151–64 respectively, discuss early modern attacks
on the stage specifically from the perspective of forgetting. The best-known
defences of the stage in terms that identify it as a medium of memory (as well
as morality) can be found in Thomas Nashe's *Pierce Pennilesse* (1592), where
history plays are praised for raising 'our forefathers valiant acts ... from the
Graue of Oblivion', inspiring the audience to follow their model (p. 86). Thomas
Heywood's *Apology for Actors* (1612) likewise insists that plays help to form
ideal, obedient subjects through teaching them England's history, a lesson
directly conducive to 'exhorting them to allegiance, dehorting them from all
traitorous and felonious stratagems' (p. 494). For a more detailed discussion of
antitheatrical literature and the language of memory, see chapter 3 of this study.

Figure 1 Johann Philipp Abelin, *Theatrum Europaeum*, title engraving to vol. II (1633)

There was a third opinion available, however, articulated not in the register of polemic but of performance, by the plays themselves. It is one of the basic assumptions of this study that the stage provides us with a more complex notion of the workings of oblivion than either its attackers or its defenders. Proceeding from the premise that all memory is formed and transformed through acts of remembering as well as through acts of forgetting, in an ongoing process of recall and reinscription, it examines a number of Shakespeare's history plays with the aim to explore how these plays both provided and changed the subterranean structures of what would be acknowledged as history. As I will show, the relation between memory and oblivion on the early modern stage was not one of opposition but of a creative interplay – creative in the two-fold sense that this interplay is constitutive of both history and theatre. Taking the cue from Abelin's title engraving, I will highlight the proximity of theatricality and forgetting throughout in the hope of redressing a certain imbalance in scholarship toward treating the early modern stage solely in terms of memory. Only recently has critical attention been devoted to the workings of cultural forgetting, both in early modern scholarship and in memory studies. This introductory chapter will trace the 'oblivionist' turn in both fields and bring them into dialogue in order to chart the ways in which the early modern theatre can be thought of as an important site of cultural forgetting as well as of remembering.

Traditionally, the relation between memory and oblivion has been thought of as an oppositional one. This view, familiar since antiquity and rendered visually in the engraving just examined, still informs the often-quoted essay by Umberto Eco that considers the possibility of an art of forgetting only to dismiss it categorically in its very title: 'An *ars oblivionalis*? Forget it!' While he readily admits that it is possible to forget by accident, as a natural event, because of an illness or old age, to forget deliberately, let alone through use of linguistic or material signs, is utterly impossible. Eco's model can comprehend forgetting only as a negative power, as a failure of memory, as absence. It is deduced from and stands in the tradition of antique and medieval mnemonic practice which, in his view, rightly treats oblivion as a destructive force of nature, an involuntary process against which a recuperative, intentional *ars memorativa* is pitched.[4] Because for Eco all mnemotechniques are by definition semiotic systems, he deduces that there can be no equivalent art of forgetting: 'If the arts of memory are semiotics, it is not possible to construct an arts of forgetting on their model, because a semiotics is by definition a mechanism that presents something to the mind and therefore a mechanism for producing

---

[4] It thus carries the seeds not only of one but of two elaborate sets of mnemonic practices, the rhetorical *ars memorativa* and the ritual commemoration of

intentional acts'.[5] This is borne out by the founding myth of mnemo-techniques as told by Cicero in *De Oratore*. The Greek poet and rhet-orician Simonides of Ceos attended a symposium that was cut short by the collapse of the building in an earthquake. Only Simonides escaped and was able to identify those killed and mutilated beyond recognition by remembering exactly the order in which the participants had been seated. In this episode, the destruction of the building equals the destruc-tive force of oblivion, while Simonides' mnemonic art restores order and identity as well as the very possibility of performing proper funeral rites.

   The relation between forgetting and memory is more complicated, however, than this oppositional model of catastrophic suffering and purposeful art, of obliteration and preservation, of nature and culture suggests. In fact, theorists and practitioners of the *ars memorativa* con-sidered oblivion not only as its enemy and a source of anxiety but as an integral part of the cognitive process: since a memory clogged with images becomes inoperable, an important part of mnemonic prac-tice is their deletion. There was a 'deliberate or selective forgetting' at work in the memory arts, Mary Carruthers states in the preface to the second edition of her ground-breaking study of medieval mne-motechniques, *The Book of Memory*, 'a kind of forgetting that itself results from an activity of memory'.[6] A case in point is John Willis's *Mnemonica; or, The Art of Memory* (Lat. 1618, Engl. 1661), which fig-ures simultaneously as rhetorical handbook and dietary regimen. Here the discussion of mnemotechniques systematically includes the 'Art of Oblivion' as an integral part of regulating the memory.[7] Willis differ-entiates between the two complementary operations of 'Reposition' and 'Deposition'. Reposition is 'the manner of charging Memory with Note-worthy things', and thus corresponds to the process of storing images in the memory. Before this can happen, however, it is necessary 'to drown all unnecessary thoughts in oblivion, that he may perfectly intend the thing he is to learn'. Not only a preparatory act, forgetting is also a part of the artful process of recollection: '*Deposition* is when we recollect things committed to memory; and having transcribed or

---

the dead, which both in their different ways serve to uphold social order and identity against their obliteration by death and oblivion; see Goldmann, 'Statt Totenklage Gedächtnis', 43–66, and Assmann, *Cultural Memory*, pp. 23–8.
[5] Eco, 'An *ars oblivionalis*?', 259.
[6] Carruthers, *The Book of Memory*, p. xi.
[7] Willis, *Mnemonica*, p. 31.

transacted them, discharge our memories of them.' This must always happen at the earliest opportunity, lest irrelevant memories clutter and impede the brain. Willis concludes that this 'is not unlike expunging writings out of Table-Books: If therefore there be any Art of *Oblivion* (as some affirm[8]) it may be properly referred hither'.[9] In employing the traditional metaphor of the memory as a set of wax-tablets, which need to be cleared before and after something has been inscribed, Willis firmly establishes artificial forgetting as a regulative and purposeful technique integral to the art of memory.

John Willis may be better known to students of early modern mnemonic culture as the most likely English source for Robert Fludd's concept of 'memory theatres', developed in his *Utrisque Cosmi ... Historia*, which was published only one year after Willis's *Mnemonica*.[10] Willis had described a memory system consisting of several sets of 'theatres' or 'repositories' that are strikingly similar to the more elaborate ones that Fludd developed, which were enriched with Hermetic concepts of the microcosm to form a *theatrum orbi*. While the idea for a memory theatre probably came from Willis's text, Fludd drew on the architecture of a real theatre to establish his mnemonic locus. That theatre, as Frances Yates persuasively argued, was in all likelihood none other than the Globe theatre.[11] Fludd explicitly pointed out that he was employing an existing place, not a fictitious one, and the Globe theatre was the one he probably had in mind since he dedicated the first volume of his work to James I, the patron of the King's Men to whom Shakespeare belonged and whose home was the Globe. Given that Willis and Fludd employed the image of a theatre to perform acts of 'reposition', that is of recollection, it seems likely that a similar image was used to effect the kind of 'deposition' that constitutes an '*Art of Oblivion*'.

---

[8] This tantalising parenthesis simultaneously asserts and elides the existence of an *ars oblivionalis*. While there is no corresponding body of medical or philosophical literature on an art of forgetting as there is on remembering, the possibility, and indeed the necessity of a technique of forgetting has accompanied the art of memory from the start: the politician and general Themistocles, a contemporary of Simonides of Ceos who according to Cicero invented the ancient mnemotechniques, rejected Simonides' offer to teach him the art of memory and wished instead for the art of forgetting to counterbalance his naturally prodigious memory (Weinrich, *Lethe*, pp. 23–4).

[9] Willis, *Mnemonica*, pp. 28–30.

[10] See Yates, *Art of Memory*, pp. 324–6.

[11] *Ibid.*, pp. 330–54.

Since it took only a very small step to link such imagined memory theatres with real places like the Globe theatre, this raises the urgent question whether we have to consider the stage on which Shakespeare's histories were performed as a site of not only 'reposition' but also of 'deposition', as a medium of *forgetting* as well as of remembering. From this possibility follows the equally urgent question of whether we can identify and describe the theatrical practices that would enable such acts of deposition. My study seeks to do precisely that: it analyses how both memory and oblivion were enacted in the early modern theatre through the use of stage images or, to be more precise, through the use of verbal, visual and material signs. What I am interested in is, specifically, how oblivion was both represented and enacted, not through the absence of signs but by employing signs. This necessitates a theatrical semiotics of forgetting, which I will outline in the following.

The starting point for such a semiotics of forgetting is the insight that remembering and forgetting are complementary forces rather than mutually exclusive opposites. They do not work against each other but are integral aspects of the process through which cultural memory is formed and transformed.[12] This entails a perspective on forgetting as a purposeful, constructive cultural act. Such a view seems to require that we distinguish for the moment between individual forgetfulness and collective forgetting, between cognitive and cultural processes. In everyday life, personal forgetfulness may indeed be largely involuntary, the result of old age, an illness, or a traumatic experience; in this sense, it is a matter for medical treatment or psychiatric therapy. Collective forgetting, on the other hand, like collective remembrance, can be deliberate, purposeful and regulated. 'Therein', explains David Lowenthal, 'lies the art of forgetting – art as opposed to ailment, choice rather than compulsion or obligation, [an] astute judgement about what to keep and what to let go, to salvage or to shred or shelve, to memorialize or anathematize'.[13] However, my aim is not to draw a rigid line between personal and collective memory since both are, as we will see in a moment, formed through social practices and institutions.

A second step toward a semiotics of forgetting comes with acknowledging that what is forgotten is not irretrievably gone but rather

[12] Krämer, 'Das Vergessen nicht vergessen!', 251–2 and 268–9.
[13] Lowenthal, 'Preface', p. xi.

purposefully overlooked, put aside as insignificant or as an obstacle to signification. Renate Lachmann proposes a model of culture as a semiotic system which accommodates forgetting as a necessary process of cultural semiosis itself – not, as Eco claimed, as opposed to it.[14] For Lachmann, cultural memory is not a site of passive storage but rather a dynamic, continuous process of remembering and forgetting. In the economy of cultural signs and meanings, forgetting is an important instrument of regulation.[15] A memory which continually accumulates experiences, knowledge and meaning quickly becomes a hypertrophy of singularities; it is shaped and kept operable only by the selection of certain experiences as meaningful and the deletion of others as insignificant. In Lachmann's semiotic terminology, forgetting can be considered as a temporary designification of signs rather than their material deletion or destruction. 'Designification' means that a sign loses the semantic and pragmatic value it had while circulating within a cultural system and its institutions. In contrast to, for example, the destruction of monuments in Reformation iconoclasm, it is not the material vehicles of signs that are deleted, but their value as currency. Because this is so, the devalued sign can also be reintroduced into the circulation of culturally validated, meaningful signs. In such a process of 'resignification', vacant or disused signs are re-included in active memory and charged anew with meaning – but their new value typically differs from the meaning they had before. This difference can be seen as a form of cultural forgetting.

The relation of memory and the past is therefore not simply one of storage and retrieval but of a reconstruction of the past under conditions and constraints determined by the present. 'Remembering is basically a reconstructive process', Aleida Assmann points out: 'it always starts in the present, and so inevitably at the time when the memory is recalled, there will be shifting, distortion, revaluation, reshaping.'[16] And forgetting is always part of this reconstruction since, as John Frow observes, 'rather than having a meaning and a truth determined once and for all by its status as event, [the past's] meaning and its truth are constituted retroactively and repeatedly ... Data are not stored in

---

[14] Lachmann, 'Kultursemiotischer Prospekt', pp. xvii–xxvii.
[15] As David Lowenthal concurs: 'To forget is as essential as to keep things in mind, for no individual or collectivity can afford to remember everything. Total recall would leave us unable to discriminate or to generalize.' ('Preface', p. xi).
[16] Assmann, *Cultural Memory*, p. 19.

already constituted places but are arranged and rearranged at every point in time. Forgetting is thus an integral principle of this model, since the activity of compulsive interpretation that organizes it involves at once selection and rejection.'[17] The concept of inclusion and exclusion, or of selection and rejection, however, is not only a matter of the cultural economy of signs, where forgetting means that some signs are not activated in communication and thus simply drop out of circulation. It also begs the urgent question of who determines what gets included and what is excluded from the realm of meaningful signs.

One possible answer to this question can be found in the work of the French sociologist Maurice Halbwachs, especially in his concept of the social frames of memory, which he developed in *Les Cadres sociaux de la mémoire* (1925, published posthumously 1952). Halbwachs claims that there is no memory, be it individual or collective, which is not social. There is no clear-cut boundary between my own memories and those of others because they develop in the process of everyday interaction and within common frames of reference or significance. Even the most private memories are created and recreated in interaction with others and with shared social frames. In Halbwachs's view a society remembers of its past only what each epoch can reconstruct within its given frames of reference. These frames have the status of cultural fictions and are subject to historical change. Experiences thus become meaningful memories only insofar as they can be inserted into active frames. Forgetting can be understood as the result of a change in reference frames, in the process of which some memories become meaningless, insignificant and hence expendable. At the same time, a change in frame means that other pieces of information, knowledge or experience are included in the new set of frames and, by being reinvested with significance (resignified), become memories.[18]

The repeated, refracted waves of the plural 'English reformations', to borrow the title of Christopher Haigh's study, formed such a series of shifts in the frames of reference that determined what could be remembered and revered as meaningful and true. This example also makes it immediately clear that cultural frames of memory do not, as

---

[17] Frow, 'Toute la mémoire', p. 229.
[18] For a more detailed discussion of Halbwachs's frames of memory as a model for conceptualising the formation and transformation of cultural memory, see Assmann, *Cultural Memory*, ch. 6.

Halbwachs's teleological model suggests, peacefully follow one after the other, but that they constitute simultaneous, competing claims to authority and truth, claims that are sometimes staked violently. One way of describing the alteration of interpretive frames in terms of power and struggle is offered by Raymond Williams, who described the internal dynamic of the cultural process in terms of the 'emergent', 'dominant' and 'residual' features of societies.[19] The dominant is embodied in the majority of the society or by its ruling and most powerful class. It is not a natural given but results from an ongoing series of selections, and hence also exclusions, from the full range of human skills, practices, relationships and perceptions. Williams terms such excluded forms of knowledge as 'the residual' and 'the emergent'. The residual (in our case, the beliefs and practices of Catholicism) is usually still active in the cultural process (clandestinely observed in private or transferred, for example, to the realm of literature[20]), yet it is divested of its validity and authority, merely available as idealised, nostalgic memories. Often, these elements of the past are subjected to a process of, in Lachmann's words, designification and resignification so that they can be safely incorporated into the dominant culture. If a residual feature proves too oppositional, however, the dominant tries to suppress or marginalise it, another act of forgetting which in early modern England was performed, for instance, through censorship or iconoclasm. There are also emergent elements – new meanings and values, new practices, new kinds of relationship – that are being developed out of new frames of reference as societies change. In time, they may themselves eventually become incorporated into the dominant way of thinking, as was the case with the proto-Protestant ideals of the Lollards that developed from heresy in the fourteenth century to become part of the orthodox theology in the sixteenth century.[21]

Williams's model has the advantage of adding the question of power as well as a notion of the simultaneous plurality of cultural values to Halbwachs's, in which frames of reference too neatly succeed each other in time. Echoing the extensive body of work by Marxist criticism and discourse analysis, Renate Lachmann, too, points out that the mechanism of semiotic inclusion and exclusion is controlled by the

---

[19] Williams, *Literature and Marxism*, pp. 121–7.
[20] See Mazzola, *The Pathology of the English Renaissance*.
[21] See Strohm, *England's Empty Throne*, ch. 2.

hegemonic or the dominant social group. Yet even so, the realm of culture and society is far from homogenous; it consists of subgroups, each of which might have their own standard of what memories count as meaningful or as insignificant.[22] What Lachmann adds here merely in parenthesis is, in fact, of great importance for the analysis of the political uses of remembering and forgetting, for this plurality of memory values may itself trigger acts of oblivion on the side of the dominant group: memories that deviate from the official version are subjected to acts of silencing such as censorship, taboo, or iconoclasm. By the same token, forgetting an official version of historical events and providing a set of counter-memories allows for the constitution of alternative accounts and legitimations of authority, and can thus also be seen as a strategy of resistance to structures of violent suppression.[23] We must therefore be aware of the fact that remembering and forgetting are not only complementary processes in society, but that they are also instruments of domination or of resistance to its underlying power structures.

In the face of such power structures, one may well ask why we should speak of 'forgetting' at all. 'Silencing', with its connotations of the suppression and subjugation of dissenting voices, might be deemed the more appropriate term by many, as well as more readily accessible to a broader audience. It has indeed been the term privileged by many studies seeking to account for the suppression of the memories of a vanquished population in the aftermath of a war.[24] However, I believe that 'forgetting' is the better term for describing how cultural memory is shaped more generally, for at least two reasons. The first is strategic. The term 'forgetting' situates projects like mine firmly in the field of memory studies: to explore the forms and functions of forgetting is an important contribution to our thinking about how cultural memory works, not a detraction or exception from it. The second reason is methodological. Forgetting is, by comparison with silencing, the

---

[22] Lachmann, 'Kultursemiotischer Prospekt', p. xviii.

[23] Several essays in the volume edited by Cavanagh et al., *Shakespeare's Histories and Counter-Histories*, explore such counter-histories in early modern England.

[24] See for example G. Adrian's *The Silence of Memory: Armistice Day 1919–1945* (1994); M. Richards' *A Time of Silence: Civil War and the Culture of Repression in Franco's Spain* (1999); or F. Stewart (ed.), *Silence to Light: Japan and the Shadows of War* (2001), an essay collection whose title recalls the early modern iconography of history as 'the light of truth' and the shadowy cave in which forgetting, lying and ignorance lie huddled together.

more inclusive term.[25] To speak of 'silence' means to identify memory exclusively with discursive practices, with its articulation in language. Memories can, however, also be shared without words, as the commemorative practice of keeping a minute of silence shows.[26] Likewise, forgetting encompasses discursive as well as non-discursive practices, as I will show in Chapter 3. 'Remembering' and 'forgetting' are therefore better suited for describing the whole ensemble of practices that form and transform cultural memory. 'Silencing' is also too restrictive a term in that it identifies forgetting exclusively with suppression, absence and erasure, whereas forgetting is in fact a constructive force and deliberate practice in the constitution of individual and collective memory, as we will see.

In contrast with what we might call the 'oppositional' or 'compensation model' and a concomitant 'suppression hypothesis' that has dominated memory studies until recently, I intend to argue here that forgetting is a constitutive part of cultural semiotics and that it operates through a range of practices that form and transform cultural memory. In the early modern period, one of the most important of these signifying practices was the theatre. Before I identify the ways in which the theatre employed verbal, visual and material signs to perform acts of 'deposition' as well as of 'reposition', to take up Willis's words, we need to look at the larger socio-political context that enabled, indeed necessitated, the erasure of certain memories. During the sixteenth and seventeenth centuries, at least three interrelated cultural developments crucial to social memory occurred and brought about a large-scale mnemonic crisis: a shift from oral to print culture; a shift from medieval feudal structures to what would eventually become the modern nation-state; and a shift from the ritual-centred liturgy of Roman Catholicism to the Protestant focus on word and book.[27] These shifts can

---

[25] Thus Connerton in 'Seven types of forgetting' and Assmann in 'Formen des Vergessens' discuss silence as one possible form of cultural forgetting among others (Assmann even distinguishes further between the defensive silence of the guilty, the symptomatic silence of traumatised victims, and the complicit silence of society). Identifying seven different forms of forgetting each (although their categorisation is not identical), they do offer alterative terms for forgetting, such as repressive erasure, structural amnesia or, indeed, silencing, but they emphasise that neither can substitute the important umbrella term and its constitutive role for cultural and individual memory.

[26] Passerini, 'Memories between silence and oblivion', p. 248.

[27] Pfister, 'Shakespeare's memory', p. 219.

be usefully described in terms of Halbwachs's social frames of memory, which determine what is included and what is excluded from the store of meaningful signs, practices and memories.

'[W]ith the changing nature and development of the various media', Aleida Assmann states, 'the constitution of the memory will also be continually changing', both as regards its contents and the access to them.[28] The impact of media shifts on memory culture became particularly clear with the spread of the printing press. The traditional *ars memorativa*, as part of classical rhetoric, was aimed primarily at oral communication between individuals or groups. Although it employed writing both as an ancillary practice and as a powerful metaphor for the process of remembering, it was firmly situated in oral culture. The spread of the printing press and the mass-circulation of the printed word profoundly altered the conditions under which collective memory was constituted and communicated. While the practices of an older, oral-performative memory culture continued to exist alongside the book, the advent of print culture dramatically expanded the storage capacities of early modern culture as well as the access to written memory. The proliferation of the written and printed word made the past widely available in different material forms, ranging from cheap broadside pamphlets retailing folklore, ballads or myths, to expensive folio prints of respectable chronicle histories.[29]

The spread of print culture in the vernacular went hand in hand with the emergence of the early modern nation fostered through a sense of a shared past. The increasing number of written records and the growth of literacy were key factors in the creation of the nation as an 'imagined community', in Benedict Anderson's influential formulation. This community was imagined in the sense that it included too many people for them to have ever met in person, as well as – what is less often remarked on – in the sense that it furnished itself with the narrative of an 'antiquity', or an 'invented tradition' in Hobsbawm's

---

[28] Assmann, *Cultural Memory*, pp. 10–11.

[29] This does not mean that mnemotechniques became entirely obsolete. As Lina Bolzoni has shown in *The Gallery of Memory*, the cognitive and rhetorical practices of the *ars memorativa* continued to provide powerful models for conceptualising and communicating knowledge and memory in the age of the printing press. It also continued to provide 'magically powerful images' for the theatre (as well as models for translation and historiography, those other two formative genres of the Renaissance), as William Engel demonstrates in *Death and Drama in Renaissance England*, p. 26. More recently Andrew Hiscock has traced the legacies of traditional memorial culture and its continuing

sense, that served to legitimise nationalist claims in the present and future.[30] Three qualifications are important here. First, Anderson's account, written with an eye firmly on the establishment of nationalism in the nineteenth century, needs to be historicised in order to acquire explanatory power for the early modern period. This has been undertaken by, among others, Richard Helgerson, who sees Tudor England positioned between 'an essentially dynastic conception of communal identity' and a 'postdynastic nationalism'.[31] To reconstruct an early modern sense of nationhood entails more than seeing it as a mere precursor of modern nationalism, however, Andrew Hadfield claims: 'It seems perverse that historians of nationalism have been so keen to stress only the recent history of the concept of the nation, as if the pre-history (in their terms) only led to a current state of affairs.' Instead of a teleological development toward a unified sense of nationhood, Hadfield sees a process of reimagination and renegotiation at work that is 'predicated upon the existence of a public space – geographical and conceptual – which will always include competing voices desiring to speak for the "nation" and fashion it according to their particular designs'.[32]

The most important and readily available public space for imagining a community, in early modern London at least, was not the printed text but the theatre. Peter Womack has argued that the new commercial theatres constituted their audiences in a way that differed markedly from either the exclusive, homogenous entity of noble audiences at private houses and at court, or the inclusive, communal ones of the medieval Corpus Christi plays which tended to address a whole urban

impact on the articulation of collective and individual identities across a wide range of early modern literary texts. His study explores how the theories and techniques of *ars memorativa* were interrogated as well as transformed in the process of articulating 'radically changing formulations of subjectivity' (*Reading Memory in Early Modern Literature*, p. 3) in the discursive fields of politics, religion, erotics or authorship. My study can be regarded as a complementary enterprise: while it also recognises the importance of both continuity and change in the formation of collective and individual identities, it follows a different trajectory. Apart from our different text corpus (Hiscock does not consider dramatic writing), my focus is on cultural memory rather than memorial culture, and on the interplay of remembering and forgetting rather than on the enduring power of recall.

[30] Anderson, *Imagined Communities*, pp. xiv, 5–6.
[31] Helgerson, *Forms of Nationhood*, p. 3.
[32] Hadfield, *Literature, Politics and National Identity*, pp. 2–3.

community. While those audiences attended plays as a pre-existing community – of the court, of a town – the new playhouses attracted 'a casual grouping of individuals, whose coherence must come, if at all, from the show itself'. This necessitates that the theatre find its own ways of creating an imagined community through generating an 'idea of England' that exists beyond localised and personalised affiliations.[33]

The competing notions of 'the nation', to return to Hadfield's point, and their respective appropriations of a legitimising past were circulated in different media: while indeed increasingly united by a shared vernacular that nevertheless continued to be inflected by regional dialects, different 'ideas of England' were created in chronicle histories, in chorography and map-making, in the realms of law and imaginative literature as well as in the performative modes of royal pageants, court entertainments and on the public stage; they all provided different 'forms of nationhood', as Richard Helgerson has shown. A second qualification that needs to be added to Anderson's concept is therefore that the expanding range of media did not necessarily lead to a unification of national memory but rather to a pluralisation of histories. The result was often a struggle between competing versions of the national past, whose rivalling claims could lead to veritable wars of memory, Phyllis Rackin points out: 'Alternative accounts of historical events and opposed interpretations of their causes and significances now threatened each other's credibility, a process intensified by the development of the printing industry and the spread of literacy.'[34] The emergence of an elaborate system of censorship can be taken as evidence of this plurality of stories, as well as of the ideological significance of specific versions as a point of identification (or as a point of

---

[33] Taking Shakespeare's first tetralogy as example, Womack demonstrates how this idea is performatively enacted as the throne and the common people, which serve as focus and stand-in for the imagined community of the audience respectively, come increasingly into view in *2 Henry VI* and the following history plays ('Imagining communities', pp. 96, 109, 136–8). Ralf Hertel's recent study *Staging England in the Elizabethan History Play* is dedicated to the question of how the national community was imagined around 1600 and how the theatre shaped this imagination. Going beyond a new historicist approach by foregrounding also the performative surplus of the theatre event, but focusing on imagination rather than memory and on mental frameworks rather than theatrical dramaturgy, his study complements mine in useful ways.

[34] Rackin, *Stages of History*, p. 13.

resistance to the hegemonic view) in generating an imagined national community.[35]

Finally, this censorship worked not only at the institutional level but also at the level of the political unconscious. Creating an imagined community through reimagining its past entailed a partial erasure of that past, and in particular of past atrocities that would impede a peaceful co-existence as one people, as the French historian Ernest Renan observed already in the late nineteenth century.[36] The community-enabling act of forgetting past violence is not a singular event that consigns irrevocably to oblivion what would disrupt the fragile unity, however. Rather, the act of forgetting must be performed over and over again, and consequently what must be forgotten must also be kept in view, however obliquely: 'Having to "have already forgotten" tragedies of which one needs unceasingly to be "reminded" turns out to be a characteristic device in the later construction of national genealogies', Anderson himself points out in his reading of Renan.[37] Past violence must be forgotten and simultaneously recalled for an imagined national community to emerge. Thus the contested, never entirely successful act of creating a unified national identity through a shared memory of the past emphatically relies on forgetting.

In the case of early modern England, one period of past violence that had to be forgotten for the English nation to emerge was the civil war between the houses of Lancaster and York in the fifteenth century. The Wars of the Roses were ended in 1485 by the first Tudor monarch, Henry VII, who ushered in a time of peace and unity. The Tudor myth, which functioned as a founding fiction of the nation under his successors, was re-enacted again and again in history plays by Shakespeare and his contemporaries, thus keeping the nation's violent past in view at the same time as it was overwritten by the myth of unity it had served to bring about in the first place. Another violent rupture

---

[35] On the system of censorship with regard to historiography and historical drama alike, see Clegg, *Press Censorship in Elizabethan England*; Dutton, *Mastering the Revels* and *Licensing, Censorship and Authorship in Early Modern England*; and Patterson, *Censorship and Interpretation*.

[36] Renan, 'What is a nation?', p. 11. Assmann concurs that 'the link between memory and identity ... entails cultural acts of remembrance, commemoration, eternalization, past and future references and projections, and, last but not least, forgetting, which is integral to all of these actions' (*Cultural Memory*, p. 18).

[37] Anderson, *Imagined Communities*, p. 201.

in the history of the English nation was the Protestant Reformation. As a political event, it both supported and countermanded the forging of national unity. On the one hand, it fostered 'a sense of national identity, constructed largely in opposition to international Catholicism'.[38] On the other, it proved in itself a divisive force since confessional conflict threatened to undercut the desired national unity. As a cultural process, the Reformation triggered multiple shifts in the social frames of memory. In less than thirty years, the official religion in England changed four times: from Catholicism to a form of 'Anglo-Catholicism' under Henry VIII (1533/38), to a militant Protestantism under Edward VI (1547), back to Catholicism under Mary (1553) and finally to the more moderate, conciliatory theology of the Elizabethan Settlement (1559). Each shift meant that one of the rivalling faiths was declared valid while the others became invalid, and with them, the beliefs, practices and memories they had supported. In their stead, 'Reformation theology required a radically different interpretive framework to hold in place sacred meanings and values', Elizabeth Mazzola argues.[39] Different frameworks enable different memories: what was formerly fondly and actively remembered, such as the saints whose statues were worshipped on their holidays, was now just as actively consigned to the grave of oblivion, at least from the point of view of official theology, through practices of forgetting such as iconoclasm.[40]

Moreover, the shift toward print culture took on specific relevance in this context of the Protestant Reformation. The reformed Church, with its sole reliance on the word and the book, sought to oust the elaborate Catholic rites that were rooted in the medium of orality and the ritualised repetition of fixed phrases in prayer, liturgy and rituals.[41] To the reformers, such faithful repetition did not signal memory but oblivion. They distrusted the increasingly formalised and thus, it was feared, automatised nature of Catholic ritual, which was thought to promote forgetfulness instead of an authentic, deeply felt remembrance. The abolition of many rituals during the Reformation necessitated alternative

---

[38] Baldo, *Memory in Shakespeare's Histories*, p. 2.

[39] Mazzola, *The Pathology of the English Renaissance*, p. 9.

[40] Eamon Duffy, whose classic study *The Stripping of the Altars* still provides the most thorough history of Reformation iconoclasm, even goes a step further when he claims that 'Iconoclasm was the central sacrament of the reform' (p. 480), a statement that I will develop further in my chapter on the theatrical use of ceremony in bringing about oblivion.

[41] Schneider, 'Liturgien der Erinnerung', 677.

forms of remembrance. Reading scripture and writing spiritual autobiographies became privileged practices of pious recollection, made possible by the new medium of print. The fear of oblivion arising from ritual practices based in oral culture was not necessarily alleviated by the turn to print, however; rather, the new medium's heightened capacity for storing and circulating information seems to have produced mnemonic anxieties of its own since one effect of such technically enhanced memory is forgetting.[42]

Given these historical changes in the social frames of memory, it is no coincidence that some of the most interesting work on cultural forgetting has emerged in the field of early modern studies. Recent years saw the publication of several articles, essay collections and two monographs that have begun to shed light on the cultural work oblivion performed at the time.[43] In particular the essay collection edited by Christopher Ivic and Grant Williams in 2004 marks a new stage in the critical discourse about cultural forgetting in early modern England. In keeping with the reconceptualisation of oblivion in memory studies outlined above, the articles turn away from the notion of forgetting as a lack or failure of memory and acknowledge instead the constitutive role of forgetting in cultural processes: 'Memory is not a totalizing field, and forgetting is neither the outside nor a lack within such an idealized field', the editors state in their introduction, adding that 'Forgetting, too, must circulate within culture, possessing its own

---

[42] *Ibid.*, 681. This is the old argument against externalising memory in media, which Plato had already recounted in the *Phaedrus*: the Egyptian King Thammuz rejected Thoth's gift of writing, which Thoth claimed to be a 'recipe for memory and wisdom' because he feared that men might begin to rely on script instead of truly learning things by imprinting them in memory (Plato, *Collected Dialogues*, p. 520). However, Assmann warns against such an equation of automatised, externalised memory with oblivion, since it obscures the different forms of forgetting and banalises its vital functions for individual as well as collective memory (*Cultural Memory*, p. 22).

[43] Articles on forgetting in Shakespeare vary considerably in theoretical sophistication: Jonas Barish's 'Remembering and forgetting in Shakespeare' examines a broad section of Shakespeare's oeuvre in search of oblivion but does little more than to list scenes of forgetting and assess their moral implications within the immediate textual context. Adrian Poole's essay 'Laughter, forgetting and Shakespeare' points out the relation between laughter and forgetting as providing cathartic moments in an increasingly disciplined society. Aleida Assmann's 'The battle of memories in Shakespeare's histories' (Ger. 1994; Engl. transl. published 2011) discusses the functional connections between memory, identity and history. Jonathan Baldo's truly groundbreaking

discourse and practices; it can no longer remain the negative space of an obsolete model of memory.'[44] From this insight, they articulate the aim of a theoretically informed inquiry into cultural forgetting: 'Not only does forgetting struggle and collude with remembering to produce culture but it also forms its own images, places, materialities and practices. To recover these sites in early modern literature helps to reconceptualize the archive and complicates a totalizing representation of mnemonic culture, and, as a result, problematize easy scholarly and historiographical access to what that culture and our culture consider to be worthy of remembering.'[45] This differs emphatically from previous attempts at recovering the counter-memories of the marginalised, the disenfranchised and the silenced, as well as from trauma studies which typically examine the passage from psychological pain to full remembering, since those approaches conceptualise forgetting as 'a violence, as a negative cultural force subordinate to memory'. Rather, Ivic and Williams maintain that forgetting 'performs vital and complex cultural work, at times ideologically suspect, at other moments subversive, yet not restricted to a single political valence'.[46] It is undeniable that where it was discussed in early modern culture, oblivion was often pathologised or considered a sin. At the same time, however, various states of oblivion could also be ascribed a positive value, in the sense of non-destructive, if not necessarily the morally good. Discussions of memory in contexts ranging from physiology over religion and education to statecraft, Ivic and Williams point out, tended to stress the complementary nature of remembering and forgetting rather than pitching them against each other.[47] If we do not want to make the mistake of turning a blind eye to a significant part of early modern culture, we, too, should recognise the constitutive force of oblivion.

The two monographs by Garrett A. Sullivan Jr. and Jonathan Baldo take up this challenge and demonstrate the formative role forgetting

---

'Wars of memory in *Henry V*' (1996; rev. version in 2012) by contrast provides a more carefully historicising approach and explores the memory politics in the play and in the context of Elizabeth's reign. His excellent articles 'Exporting oblivion in *The Tempest*', 'Forgetting Elizabeth in *Henry VIII*' and '"A rooted sorrow": Scotland's unusable past' on *Macbeth* follow similar argumentative trajectories, examining these plays in terms of the Jacobean project of forging a sense of national unity through memory.

[44] Ivic and Williams (eds.), *Lethe's Legacies*, p. 1.
[45] *Ibid.*, p. 16.   [46] *Ibid.*, p. 3.   [47] *Ibid.*, pp. 4–9.

played in early modern ideas of subjectivity and national identity. Self-forgetfulness, Sullivan argues, was understood not as an absence either of selfhood or of memory, but as a source of agency and subjectivity. This is not to say that forgetting is identical to subjectivity; rather, forgetting is a form that subjectivity frequently takes on the early modern stage. His readings of plays by Marlowe, Shakespeare and Webster explore different somatic phenomena and non-normative behaviour associated with self-forgetfulness: idleness, excessive sleeping, or inordinate sexual desires are often the undoing of the dramatic figures. But the 'identity crisis' in which they thus find themselves is typically also a moment in which the characters find a new sense of selfhood. Opening up an opportunity for reimagining and reconceptualising notions of the self, oblivion does not so much spell a loss of identity but rather provides an opportunity for experimenting with alternative forms of selfhood outside of the parameters and dictates of normative behaviour.[48]

It is the merit of Jonathan Baldo to have placed cultural forgetting on the research agenda of Shakespeare studies. Since the publication of an article on the 'Wars of Memory in *Henry V*' in 1996, Baldo has repeatedly traced the cultural, political and psychological importance of forgetting in Shakespeare's plays, culminating recently in a monograph on *Memory in Shakespeare's Histories: Stages of Forgetting in Early Modern England* (2012). That study examines the dynamics of remembering and forgetting in the second tetralogy, demonstrating forcefully its central hypotheses 'of the centrality of historical erasure in the ongoing process of reform in Elizabeth's reign, of the utility of forgetting in responding to the traumatic effects of the Reformation, of the importance of a collective amnesia for enhancing national unity, and of the power of the stage in contributing to the reshaping of English historical memory'.[49] Offering incisive readings of how the theatre participated in and at the same time offered a critical perspective on the memory politics in early modern England, Baldo's work has provided important impulses for my own study.

While my book engages with a similar corpus of texts and draws on insights offered by both Baldo and Sullivan, it develops them into a different direction, adding to their questions of power, sovereignty

---

[48] Sullivan, *Memory and Forgetting*, pp. 1, 12, 20–1.
[49] Baldo, *Memory in Shakespeare's Histories*, p. 132.

and national unity, interpellation of the subject, and the dynamic of subversion and containment, a concern with theatrical semiotics and dramatic form. In redirecting the focus from statecraft back to stage-craft, this study participates in a recent return to concerns with literary form that Stephen Cohen has called 'historical formalism'.[50] Historical formalism emerges from a certain discontent with new historicism's insistence on reading all cultural practices and artefacts as texts, thus effectively eliding the specific nature of literary texts. In spite of asserting the continuing importance of analysing genre and form in its exploration of a 'poetics of culture', new historicist readings have in practice tended to treat Renaissance works as 'bundles of historical or cultural content, without much attention to the ways that their meanings are shaped and enabled by the possibilities of form'. Paradoxically, this constitutes a profoundly ahistorical gesture, since early modern writers, readers and, I would like to add, theatre-goers were 'very much aware of the distinctive, meaning-producing power of "poesy"'.[51] This does not mean that new formalist readings wish to return to an unexamined assertion of the 'greatness' and autonomy of literary texts or to a state of innocence regarding the ideological impact of extratextual, historical contexts. On the contrary, Cohen argues, 'The formal characteristics that distinguish literature from other cultural modes are neither innate nor immutable but rather historically produced and historically productive; consequently, any thoroughly historicist criticism must account for form, even as any rigorous formalism must be historical.' This means that 'Rather than focusing primarily on the historical content of a text, historical formalism insists on attention to the shape and composition of the text-as-container

---

[50] See Cohen (ed.), *Shakespeare and Historical Formalism* and his earlier essay 'Between form and culture'. Alternatively, terms like 'new formalism' (Dubrow, *A Happier Eden* and 'Guess who's coming') and 'new aestheticism' (Joughin and Malpas (eds.), *The New Aestheticism*) have been put forward; Mark Rasmussen rightly criticises the first for its claim to innovation (while it is actually a return to a moment when new historicism emerged from a struggle with formalism), the latter for eschewing questions of history and power in its focus on the relation between literature and philosophy (*Renaissance Literature and Its Formal Engagements*, p. 3). Hugh Grady greets the turn to form as akin to the project of 'presentism' as practised by Terence Hawkes, Evelyn Gajowski, Ewan Fernie and himself (*Shakespeare and Impure Aesthetics*, p. 233).

[51] Rasmussen (ed.), *Renaissance Literature and Its Formal Engagements*, pp. 1, 4.

and the impact they may have on the meaning and functioning of that content.'[52]

As Jean E. Howard remarks, questions of genre and form, or of the intertextual and intratextual dimensions of meaning-making, have over the last two decades been unduly neglected in favour of the discursive links between a play and a range of extradramatic contexts. Moreover, historicist readings have often tended to concentrate on 'moments in a text, rather than its overall narrative structure'.[53] Taking the cue from Howard, I will devote the rest of this introduction to specifying the formal features through which the genre of the Shakespearean history play partakes in a mnemonic economy of signs that is organised and shaped by acts of remembering as well as forgetting. In so doing I will re-examine established terms (topicality, *locus* and *platea*, metatheatricality) and introduce others of more recent coinage (ghosting, intertheatricality, mnemonic dramaturgy) with a view to how the history plays can be understood as a specific convergence of formal features and the relations between play and context, as well as stage and audience, that I deem central to the process of making memory.

Topicality is a critical term for describing the relations between a play and its contemporary extradramatic context. Reading for such topical references is a method of new historicism, but it was also the dominant way of perceiving history in the early modern period. Historians, poets and playwrights looked to the past to understand the present, focusing 'on historical figures and situations that provided instructive analogues for contemporary persons and predicaments'.[54] While the rapid and traumatic changes which England underwent in the course of the sixteenth century generated an increasing sense of alienation from the past, the exemplarity of history and its relevance for the present remained an important mode of writing and reading history. Topicality can and should also be seen as a specifically theatrical mode, as Warren Chernaik has suggested: 'the very nature of historical drama is that it seeks out analogies between the past and the present'.[55] This function was enabled not only by the subject matter of the history plays but also by the co-existence of two temporal-spatial frames of reference for a play,

---

[52] Cohen (ed.), *Shakespeare and Historical Formalism*, p. 2.
[53] Howard, 'Shakespeare, geography, and the work of genre', p. 50.
[54] Rackin, *Stages of History*, p. 11.
[55] Chernaik, *Cambridge Introduction to Shakespeare's History Plays*, p. 14.

the *locus* and the *platea*. Robert Weimann demonstrated in his magisterial study of medieval and early modern popular drama that these were
constitutive for the audience's experience of a play and their perception
of its meaning.[56] For Weimann, the *locus* refers to a historical or symbolic location – the world of the characters, in particular of the noble
characters that constitute the agents of historical events, set off from
the common crowd by a scaffold. This play-world is removed from the
audience's world through its symbolic character as well as, usually, its
temporal and geographical distance (although the latter is often reduced
to a minimum in the English history plays). The contemporary *platea*,
by contrast, refers to the here and now of the audience, both in a literal
and a broader sense. The *platea* is the material place of acting, performatively highlighted whenever characters, especially fools or clowns,
interact with the audience, in asides or by entrances through the pit. By
thus involving the spectators in the play, the shared space of the *platea*
draws attention to the here and now of the audience in the playhouse,
making them aware that they are watching a play and thus disrupting momentarily the spell of the *locus*. In a broader sense, it may also
include the public space outside the theatre – originally, *platea* meant the
public space between houses, in the streets or on the village commons,
which often were quickly converted into makeshift theatre venues – as
well as the events, concerns and discourses of contemporary society.
The perception of a play's meaning may indeed have been informed to a
greater extent by the factual conditions of the audience's life-world than
by the fictional ones of the theatrical play-world. Nevertheless, a play's
topicality does not exist in spite of the action presented on the scaffold,
but is rather strengthened by it since particular historical events were
viewed as symbolic, exemplary lessons the past holds for the present.

Weimann regarded the interplay between *locus* and *platea*, rather
than their mere juxtaposition, as characteristic of the early modern
stage. This interplay is one way in which we can understand historical
drama as an intervention in the mnemonic economy of early modern culture. For if, as John Frow has argued, memory is a construction of the past under conditions and constraints determined by the
present, and this construction necessarily involves acts of selection
and rejection,[57] then the contemporary *platea* is not only a possible

---

[56] Weimann, *Shakespeare und die Tradition des Volkstheaters*, pp. 121–39.
[57] Frow, 'Toute la mémoire', p. 228.

reference point of the play's historical *locus*, but also determines what is presented as history on the stage in the first place. Historical drama reconstructs the past according to the views and needs of the present; following Frow, that past is shaped by acts of recall as well as of erasure, which are motivated by contemporary concerns. Topicality, in other words, works both ways: if the function of history was to serve as an example or a mirror for the present, the present in turn shaped the perception of history. In this perspective, the theatre itself accordingly appears as a medium not only of remembering but also of forgetting. By the same token, forgetting is written deeply into the dramatic practices of the early modern stage. As the chapters in this study will demonstrate, again and again the plays under discussion explore oblivion as a constitutive dimension not only of historical memory, but also as a condition of historical drama itself. Topicality is therefore closely related to metatheatricality, a feature certainly not only of the history plays but of early modern theatre as a whole. As Brian Walsh perceptively points out, the very 'newness' of the public theatre generated – all familiarity with historical subject matter notwithstanding – a habit of self-reflection concerning the new medium.[58] In the case of historical drama, such theatrical consciousness became a source of historical consciousness, as metadramatic scenes, according to Phyllis Rackin, 'encourag[ed] their audiences to meditate on the process of historical representation rather than attempting to beguile them into an uncritical acceptance of the representation as a true mimesis of past events'.[59]

My analysis of the plays therefore operates on three interrelated levels: first, the referential level of the *locus*, that is, the historical events and their agents, who are presented as engaging in struggles over memory and performing acts of remembrance and forgetting. The referential level constitutes the mnemonic project *in* the plays. This is complemented (sometimes corroborated, sometimes contradicted) by the mnemonic project *of* the plays. It becomes evident when we focus on the second level of the *platea*, that is, on the question of how contemporary issues informed a play's representation of the past as well as the audience's reception of that representation. Historical scenes lend

---

[58] Walsh, *Shakespeare, the Queen's Men and the Elizabethan Performance of History*, p. 3.
[59] Rackin, *Stages of History*, p. 29.

themselves to topical readings, and in so doing the plays both draw on the spectator's knowledge (however unarticulated) of current issues and shape the collective memory of the audience and, by extension, of early modern society. Finally, the metadramatic level foregrounds the mnemonic work of the theatre as medium itself. Theatrical practice operates in the condition of 'as if',[60] and this condition of a double consciousness manifests itself as a genuinely theatrical practice in the simultaneous discrepancy and interplay of *locus* and *platea*, resulting in an awareness of the contingency of 'historical truth'. Shakespearean theatre as a mnemonic practice proceeds by making its spectators aware of both the potential and the limits of the stage in the production of cultural memory. These possibilities and limits are not congruent with remembering (as the promise of the theatre) and forgetting (as the limit of what theatre can do). On the contrary, forgetting itself is a property and condition of the theatre, and theatricality may actively consign memories to oblivion. Hamlet's prep-talk to the players is a case in point. When Hamlet urges the players to remember and deliver their lines faithfully while at the same time worrying about the many distractions that might interfere with 'the purpose of playing' (3.2.18) in performance, his speech suggests that theatrical practice can be viewed as a form of forgetting: the actors' deliverance of lines and modes of embodiment may divert from rather than support remembrance of events from history or myth. One argument I will advance in the following chapters is that while 'the purpose of playing' in the sense of content (both as regards subject matter and its ideological implications) may be quite clear, the forms of staging it may quite distract an audience from that purpose. At other times, the delivery of lines, sequencing and overall mnemonic dramaturgy may actively promote oblivion as the very purpose of a play. In other words, forgetfulness is not only a product of theatrical practice, it is also its very condition.[61]

Self-reflexive scenes thus highlight the mediated character of historical memory along with the process of selection, representation and transformation that produces it, thus creating an awareness of the role that forgetting, too, plays in making history (as well as in making

---

[60] Döring, *Performances of Mourning*, p. 194.
[61] On forgetfulness as a condition of theatrical practice in a quite different sense, see Peter Holland's 'On the gravy train'.

theatre). Another source of this awareness would have been the familiarity many early modern theatre-goers had with the historical subject matter presented on stage, which they might have read about in, for example, Holinshed's *Chronicles*, Fox's *Book of Martyrs*, or Thomas North's translation of *Plutarch's Lives*.[62] The less affluent or less educated would have been acquainted with historical events and figures through 'a still largely oral popular culture, such as ballads, songs and stories incorporating legends, folk-tales, fairy-stories, myths', or indeed through other plays staged on marketplaces, in inns, or the public theatres.[63] Such familiarity would have added to the attractions of a play rather than signalled a lack of novelty or dramatic effect. When the epilogue to *Henry V* alludes to the losses of French territory under the weak Henry VI as matter 'Which oft our stage hath shown' (Epilogue. 13), or when Thomas Nashe claims that the death of the heroic Talbot was greeted with 'the tears of ten thousand spectators at least, (at seuerall times)',[64] these statements testify to the pleasures of familiarity and recognition. While this meant that the playwright could not alter historical facts – in a story about Richard II, he has to be deposed and replaced by Henry IV – it opened up the possibility that specific deviations from the familiar facts of English history would have been noticed as meaningful. It also meant, as William N. West notes, that such moments in early modern plays 'call on their audiences to witness for them, making the audiences, as it were, responsible for elaborations or explanations that the plays omit'.[65] In this way, spectators

[62] I. G. [John Greene], for instance, claimed such a familiarity with historical subject matter in his antitheatrical work *A Refutation of the Apology for Actors*: 'But these that know the Histories before they see them acted, are euer ashamed, when they haue heard what lyes the Players insert amongst them, and how greatly they depraue them.' (p. 42) I. G. assumes that the only proper reaction to realising the discrepancy between historical 'fact' and dramatic representation is shame; I concur with Brian Walsh who stresses instead the sense of pleasure derived from such discrepant historical consciousness (Walsh, *Shakespeare, the Queen's Men and the Elizabethan Performance of History*, pp. 1–2). On the pleasures of early modern playgoing and their possible sources, see Jeremy Lopez's *Theatrical Convention and Audience Response in Early Modern Drama* and, focusing specifically on the spectators' emotional responses, Allison P. Hobgood's *Passionate Playgoing in Early Modern England*.
[63] Holderness *Shakespeare's History*, p. 33.
[64] Nashe, *Pierce Pennilesse*, p. 87.
[65] West, 'Intertheatricality', p. 156.

became active participants in the construction of the meaning and shape that history took in the early modern playhouse. This awareness of meaningful alterations, transformations and omissions from one theatrical articulation of historical memory to another, and the individual as well as collective acts of recall among the audience that enables it, has recently come under discussion in terms of 'ghosting' and 'intertheatricality'.

'Every play is a ghost', claims Marvin Carlson in his study *The Haunted Stage: The Theatre as Memory Machine* (2003). For him, the theatre is characterised by a structure of return and repetition, an 'uncanny sense of something coming back in the theatre'. This quality of 'ghosting' is what links the theatre with memory: 'The retelling of stories already told, the reenactment of events already enacted, the reexperience of emotions already experienced, these are and have always been central concerns of the theatre in all times and places'. This is not only an effect of content (stories already told, events already enacted) but of form and medium, 'the particular production dynamics of theatre: the stories it chooses to tell, the bodies and other physical materials it utilises to tell them, and the places in which they are told'.[66] Carlson identifies the following formal dimensions of ghosting in the dramatic text: the playtext itself, which is always a palimpsest, in the sense of Roland Barthes, haunted by intertextual echoes; the body of the actor, whose former roles may walk the stage with him like shades; and the places of performance, both geographical setting and theatrical venue, that recall earlier events and other productions.[67] The possibility or, in Carlson's view, the structural necessity of such ghostly recollections generates a stage crowded with rivalling memories, echoes that interfere with each other, drown each other out or create a mnemonic palimpsest that generates new meanings.

Jonathan Gil Harris's study of such hauntings in Shakespeare's theatre is helpful to specify the potential of ghosting to obliterate and create new memories. *Untimely Matter in the Time of Shakespeare* (2008) suggests, too, that we attend to 'the bodies of actors, their costumes, and their techniques of movement, gesture, and verbal delivery' in order to determine 'the working and reworking of theatrical

---

[66] Carlson, *The Haunted Stage*, p. 3.
[67] *Ibid.*, p. 9. Carlson also examines the material dimension of costume, props and lighting, a dimension my readings can neglect for the greatest part as

matter' between performances of the same play or between different plays.[68] He calls this phenomenon 'intertheatricality' because although it is modelled on the notion of intertextuality, it seeks to describe specifically the relations between theatrical performances that go beyond words and texts. Intertheatricality is a matter of gestures, phrases, costumes, props, or situations remembered from previous performances and other plays.[69] More interesting for our topic is Harris's contention that intertheatricality allows us to note and describe the extent to which theatre performances 'rework the past to produce new theatrical possibilities – possibilities that also have political applicability. Shakespearean intertheatricality thus strives for the future-oriented temporality of supersession.'[70] This claim deserves some comment. Taking his cue from the co-presence of historical *locus* and contemporary *platea* described by Weimann, Harris posits a co-presence of historical figures and their different re-enactments on the stage, with the latter framing our interpretation of the former. Theatrical performance draws on and in the process supersedes historical memory. This produces 'new theatrical possibilities': through performative embodiment – including the style of acting, the body of the actor and material

this is already admirably covered by Lina Perkins Wilder's recent study *Shakespeare's Memory Theatre: Recollections, Properties, and Character*, which examines the objects on the early modern stage – including the bodies of the actors – as creating a remembrance environment that is activated in performance.

[68] Harris, *Untimely Matter*, p. 68.

[69] On the dimensions of intertheatricality and how this approach urges us to read the theatre of early modern England as an interrelated 'system of playing' rather than a canon of individual plays, see the excellent article by William N. West, 'Intertheatricality'. Examples of such intertheatrical criticism are Philip Schwyzer's essay 'Shakespeare's arts of reenactment: Henry at Blackfriars, Richard at Rougemont', which carefully reconstructs the echoes between plays, actors and places (both geographical settings and theatrical venues) evoked in and through *Richard III* and *Hamlet* and the moments of 'scenic memory' thus created; Hester Lees-Jeffries's subchapter 'Haunting history', which also deals with *Richard III* (Lees-Jeffries, *Shakespeare and Memory*, pp. 78–84); and Brian Walsh's chapter on '*Henry V* and the extra-theatrical historical imagination' in which he explores how that play invokes the others of the second tetralogy as well as *3 Henry VI*, and demonstrates how it employs not only topical but also topographical references to turn specific loci within the city of London into memory seats (*Shakespeare, The Queen's Men and the Elizabethan Performance of History*, pp. 178–213).

[70] Harris, *Untimely Matter*, p. 69.

props – the stage appropriates historical figures and turns them into theatrical property. One of my chapters explores such a process through the figure of Falstaff, whose specific corporeality and theatricality supersede the memory of the historical figure Sir John Oldcastle. Supersession, however, does not mean complete obliteration, but rather the production of a palimpsest through partial erasure and reinscription. Thus the memory of the historical figure keeps informing the meaning of the theatrical figure. When Harris claims that this also has 'political applicability', I take this to mean that the direction of such appropriations runs not only from the state to the stage, but also the other way round. The supersession of meanings and memories effected in the theatre can highlight such appropriations in the political arena or even replace historical memories with theatrical ones. Again, the figure of Falstaff is a case in point: Falstaff, the fat, witty knight has become an indelible part of popular memory, while the historical figure Oldcastle is remembered merely in specialised scholarly discourse.

The audience's cognitive and affective experience of the past performed on stage is thus another dimension in which the early modern theatre intervenes in historical and cultural memory. Shakespeare's histories are a particularly good example, considering the cyclical structure of the two tetralogies that keep referring back to each other.[71] The cyclical structure of Shakespeare's histories highlights the interplay between remembering and forgetting at work in all reconstructions of history, including those enacted on the stage, thus activating the spectators' mnemonic capacities. That the plays were not written in historically chronological sequence does not invalidate this argument but, on the contrary, strengthens it, in the view of Nicolas Grene. He argues that Shakespeare's two tetralogies had indeed been written and should be read and staged in sequence (rather than the chronology of events represented), bringing out their intertheatrical relations: 'each sequent play is written with a full consciousness of what has gone before, and this awareness of previous

---

[71] In pointing out this cyclical sequence, I do not mean to reintroduce Tillyard's claim that the first tetralogy, culminating in *Richard III*, 'display[ed] the working out of God's plan' (*Shakespeare's History Plays*, p. 205), or that 'Shakespeare conceived his second tetralogy as one great unit' (p. 240). Where Tillyard placed the emphasis on unity, order and coherence – structural as well as ideological – I agree with Paola Pugliatti who, while she acknowledges integral relations between, for instance, the two parts of *Henry IV*, sees

history shared by characters and audience becomes part of the substance of the drama'. The mode of historical drama thus is a 'retrospective mode' in the double sense, 'both as it figures the sense of time in history and as theatrical experience for audiences'. What emerges from a non-chronological sequential arrangement is the very pattern of recall and reconfiguration, 'the distortion of truth that is one of the dramatic features' of historical drama itself, constantly enacted and sometimes explicitly explored in the dramatic action.[72]

The cyclical structure also alerts the audience to the possibility that the plays may themselves have performed such distortions in their re-enactment of the past. One pertinent example is the deposition of Richard II, that traumatic event to which the plays of the second tetralogy keep returning, and which they keep reshaping according to the changed circumstances in which that story is being told again and again in the play-world. The early modern theatre had a propensity to 'answer trauma with drama', in Jonathan Baldo's formulation.[73] Returning again and again to definitive moments in history that haunt the collective imagination but approaching them from different angles, these plays also reproduce the political bias of history, the selection and erasure of historical 'facts' in making history. In so doing, they highlight that there is no such thing as historical truth and that the theatre is not simply a mirror held up to nature but rather an institution and practice that actively participates in the shaping of cultural memory. Moreover, by referring to earlier theatrical instantiations of that primal scene, these haunting references also highlight

this relationship as one of increasing recapitulation and a 'progressive disfigurement' of themes, rather than their fulfilment in a meaningful closure (Pugliatti, *Shakespeare the Historian*, pp. 108, 130).

[72] Grene, *Shakespeare's Serial History Plays*, pp. 164–5, 172.

[73] Baldo, *Memory in Shakespeare's Histories*, p. 46; for a reading of *Richard II* as a play which dramatises traumatic loss as the source of historical consciousness and national identity, see *ibid.*, pp. 10–50. Paul Strohm's study *England's Empty Throne* examines the regicide of Richard II as the formative trauma of early modern politics and historiography. Thomas Anderson's *Performing Early Modern Trauma* explores the different traumatic events that shaped early modern historical consciousness, in particular the ways in which the historical imagination emerging from contemporary drama, as well as prose texts and poetry, 'does battle with the memory of a traumatic past that insistently presses its claim on the present' (p. 1). Patricia Cahill claims in *Unto the Breach: Martial Formation, Historical Trauma and the Early Modern Stage* that it was the experience of war, re-enacted especially in historical drama after 1587, that gave rise to a 'traumatic historicity' (pp. 2, 9).

the extent to which the audience's memory is formed and transformed in performance.

Janet Dillon's recent study of *Shakespeare and the Staging of English History* (2010), while not explicitly concerned with the workings of memory in the theatre, examines in carefully historicising close readings those elements that compose Shakespeare's 'historical dramaturgy', such as rhetoric, stage images and tableaux, the sequencing, rhythm and repetitions of 'units of action' that shape the dramatic narrative, verbal and visual echoes within and between plays, as well as the use of props and stage space. Her aim has been to reconstruct a 'theatrical vocabulary' and a 'common spatial code ... that conveyed particular kinds of meaning' on the early modern stage. According to Dillon, the history plays employ a characteristic dramaturgy whose signatures are vivid, often also symbolically charged, 'stage pictures' that function like emblems.[74] This is the point at which I see her stage performance approach intersect with scholarship on the early modern theatre as a site of memory: such stage images are structurally related to the mnemonic images in Willis's and Fludd's memory theatre. In my readings of Shakespeare's histories I therefore adopt Dillon's method and vocabulary but shift the focus to what I will call Shakespeare's 'mnemonic dramaturgy'. This term encompasses the specific configurations of verbal, textual, visual and material signs that each play employs to form and transform historical memory through acts of remembering as well as of forgetting; these mnemonic acts operate in and across the dimensions of historical and topical reference, intertextual and intertheatrical memories, performance and audience. Taken together, the concepts outlined in this introduction allow me to understand and describe the differential interventions of Shakespeare's theatre in the cultural memory of early modern England. Rather than assuming a stable reference point for the plays in a monolithic notion of the past, or a sense of national unity, or a homogenous audience,[75] the following chapters acknowledge the dynamic interplay of past and present in performance and emphasise the plurality of memory values that may emerge from it.

---

[74] Dillon, *Shakespeare and the Staging of English History*, pp. 12, also pp. 4–5, 8.
[75] In the introduction to their volume *Imagining the Audience in Early Modern Drama*, Jennifer A. Low and Nova Myhill note the difference in criticism between 'an audience' as a collective entity to whom players might direct their

Recalling, erasing and rewriting memories, the history plays created a palimpsest of meanings that informed what contemporary audiences 'remembered' as history each time they re-encountered it on the stage. This study is about the theatrical practices through which that palimpsest was created and the forms it took on the stage. Each chapter identifies one form of memory and explores the different ways in which it engages with oblivion or even becomes a form of forgetting itself: oral and written history, ceremony, embodiment, distraction, nostalgia – and, throughout, theatrical performance. These forms are not restricted or specific to any individual play alone; rather, they are characteristic forms that memory and oblivion took on Shakespeare's stage, with different forms converging in one play or stretching across his career. These forms were not Shakespeare's invention alone, of course. As Janet Dillon points out, his dramatic vocabulary was taken from and shared with his collaborators and colleagues working in the theatre profession: 'It was in the context of such shared social and spatial assumptions and shared theatrical practice that Shakespeare's writing, both individual and collaborative, emerged.'[76] Nevertheless, she continues, his history plays show a distinctive and recognisable dramaturgy that develops over the course of his career. I have therefore arranged the chapters roughly in the chronological order of the plays' first performances, a sequencing that will allow us to trace the pattern of intertheatrical references between plays as well as the recurring mnemonic devices of Shakespeare's historical dramaturgy. The first chapter explores the media of historical memory against the background of the increasing spread of print culture and the emergence of the public theatre as a new medium. *Henry VI, Part Two* grafts onto the historical scenes of rebellion the rivalry between literacy and writing and connects it

---

performance and 'audiences' as a heterogeneous population of individuals with a variety of experiences and viewing practices (p. 2). While my close readings of the play-texts, which address their audience implicitly or explicitly as one body, lean toward the first understanding, I do not assume a monolithic audience response (what 'the audience' remembers or forgets) but rather hope to explore the mnemonic dynamics between stage images and spectators.

[76] Dillon, *Shakespeare and the Staging of English History*, pp. 4, 12. Brian Walsh's study examines in particular the 'foundational contributions' to the 'historical and theatrical imagination of Shakespeare' of the Queen's Men's 'set of dramaturgical strategies' (*Shakespeare, The Queen's Men and the Elizabethan Performance of History*, p. 3).

with the question of power, resulting in a tension between the power of writing (which is affirmed) and the power over writing (which is criticised). *Richard III* adds the question of the role of theatrical performance, yet again the affirmation of the superior mnemonic efficacy of performance is qualified by its abuse at the hands of those in power. Show-casing also the kind of gullible audience such manipulative stage-managing of history requires, the play encourages the theatre audience to encounter any mediated image of history knowingly and sceptically. Taken together, these plays stage the different mnemonic properties of oral report, written record and theatrical performance, and in so doing reflect on the potentials and limits of each form of making historical memory.

Chapter two engages with the impact of the Reformation on early modern commemorative culture. It resumes the discussion of *Richard III* but now traces a different form of memory: ceremony. While the constant interruption of ceremonial grief in this play points to a general sense of the precariousness of memory in post-Reformation England, Shakespeare takes the exploration of ceremony one step further in *Richard II*, where ritual lament and ceremonial acts themselves become vehicles for erasing and remaking memories. This is continued in *Henry IV, Part One* when Prince Hal, on the battlefield at Shrewsbury, turns ritual commemoration into rites of oblivion proper, and when Falstaff's mocking performances empty out ritual forms in order to fill them with alternative meaning.

Falstaff is also the focus of the next chapter on embodiment, which covers the two parts of *Henry IV*. It takes as its starting point antitheatrical writings which described the pernicious effects of theatre-going in terms of a sinful forgetfulness whose visible sign was the lethargic body. The stage itself, rather than merely rejecting this charge, took up the image of lethargic embodiment and turned it into a positive asset of performativity. Beginning with King Henry' s and Prince Hal's strategic employments of forgetting, the chapter centres on Falstaff as a positive figure of lethargy and explores the ways in which his altogether more playful forgetfulness becomes a source of self-hood in the play and, due to its performative nature, a property of the theatre itself. In a second step it traces the many transformations of this figure from historical Lollard rebel over proto-Protestant martyr and parody of Puritan hypocrisy to a figure of theatricality, and identifies a pattern of recall, erasure and replacement that makes Falstaff an embodiment of the dynamic of remembering and forgetting underlying the making of history itself.

The next chapter on *Henry V* explores this dynamic through a close reading of scenes that, while themselves highly memorable moments in the play, work toward inducing what I will call 'nationalist oblivion'. This form of memory emerges from a rhetoric of nationalism and a fast-paced sequence of action that is intended to sweep away the audience, both on stage and in the theatre, on a wave of patriotic enthusiasm, fed by memories of military triumph. Seemingly geared towards remembering, this is in fact a strategy of distracting the audience from the ideological implications and ethical problems of nationalism. That the play is not a straightforward piece of nationalist propaganda, however, is ensured by a set of interspersed scenes and figures that, while themselves rather inconspicuous and hence easily forgotten, provide a locus for important counter-memories. From this contrapuntal sequencing and framing emerges a mnemonic pattern that cautions us to question the memory politics of nationalism and in particular the oblivional potential adhering to moments of national commemoration.[77]

The oblivional thrust behind official memory politics is also the topic of the final chapter, which takes us into the Jacobean period. It offers a discussion of the workings of the nationwide nostalgia for Elizabeth as another form of remembering that is premised on forgetting: trading on comfortable and conveniently reassuring images of the past, nostalgia at the same time has to suppress alternative versions that acknowledge the past's negative aspects. Nostalgic memories thus offer only a very selective version of the past, but they authorise and legitimise that version through addressing the emotions. Nostalgia is a 'historical emotion',[78] a passion for the past that results from dissatisfaction with the present. Faced with such strong feelings for his predecessor Elizabeth that, moreover, implied dissatisfaction with his own reign, James mounted a campaign to rewrite the memory of Elizabeth, co-opting nostalgia for his own royal memory politics. While several plays of the early Jacobean era, including Shakespeare and Fletcher's

---

[77] 'Oblivional' is a coinage that signals a deliberate, strategic forgetting, which I will use along with the more active participle 'oblivionating' in contrast to 'oblivious' as a state of unmindful, unconscious ignorance.

[78] Boym, *The Future of Nostalgia*, p. 10.

Henry VIII, or All is True, participated in the nostalgic enthusiasm for Elizabeth, they also provided a critical insight into the memory politics behind nostalgia. Without being subservient either to James's strategies or to the idealised image of Elizabeth, these plays rather examine the affecting spectacle of nostalgia and call for a sceptical audience able to recognise that not all is true that can be seen on stage. Far from dismissing the power of theatrical spectacle, Shakespeare's last history play in particular offers once more a pertinent analysis of the dynamic of remembering and forgetting at work in the theatre's project of making memory.

1 | *Media: oral report, written record and theatrical performance in* 2 Henry VI *and* Richard III

Edward Hall's chronicle history *The Union of the Two Noble Houses of Lancaster and York* (1550) opens, somewhat surprisingly for a work dedicated to remembrance of things past, with the word 'Oblivion', highlighted by a beautifully ornate capital. Taking oblivion as the point of departure for a project devoted to preserving historical memory, the prefatory dedication establishes an opposition between remembering and forgetting that is systematically aligned with the distinction between oral report and written record throughout. This media difference is inscribed into a teleological narrative of progress from 'the first and second age of the worlde' and their societies, whose origins and identity are lost to oblivion because of their incapability to record history, on to modern civilisations whose social hierarchy and moral values are preserved in and by written records. Hall explicitly traces the invention of letters, 'the treasure of memory', to a double origin in Judaeo-Christian and classical antiquity, thus investing it – and his own account as well – with cultural authority.[1]

More important than the origins of writing and of writing history are, however, the social functions attributed to it. In suppressing 'that dedly beast Oblivion', Hall claims, historiography does nothing less than uphold social hierarchies and moral values, even humanity itself: 'For what diversitie is between a noble prince and a poore begger, ye a reasonable man and a brute beast, if after their death there be left of them no remembrance or token.'[2] Remembrance of the dead is presented here as crucial to the society of the living in providing a sense of order and direction. The wealth of funerary rituals and rites of remembrance inherited from the Middle Ages testifies to this importance.[3] When the Reformation abolished many

[1] Hall, *The Union of the Two Noble Houses*, sig. A.ii^r.
[2] *Ibid.*, sig. A.iii^r.
[3] A detailed account of early modern practices of remembering the dead, their social functions and how they were transferred to other cultural arenas after the Reformation can be found in Döring, *Performances of Mourning*, pp. 24–39, and Mazzola, *The Pathology of the Renaissance*, passim.

of these practices of ritual remembrance it left a mnemonic vacuum which was to some extent filled by historiographical practices in various forms, covering a wide range that included chronicle history, chorography and antiquarianism, the hagiography of Foxe's *Actes and Monuments*, or as it is more commonly known, *The Book of Martyrs*, as well as the empirical methodology of Bacon, the poetic histories of Daniel and Drayton as well as the new genre of English history plays. The Reformation may indeed have prompted an increasing sense of history by severing the continuity between England's Catholic past and the Protestant present, thus rendering the past as radically other.[4]

A second important function of historiography, habitually quoted in numerous defences, is its exemplarity.[5] Its ability to provide the living with examples of good and bad behaviour makes it an invaluable guide to right conduct in private life as well as in affairs of the state. This moral authority is connected to an argument about the media best suited to such moral education that is resolved by Hall in favour of written history: 'So that evidently it appeareth that Fame is the triumph of glory, and memory by litterature is the verie dilator and setter forth of Fame.' Hall stresses here the importance of the written and, by extension, of the printed word for promoting heroic conduct as well as social hierarchies and values. His argument winds up triumphantly with a triple row of conclusions initiated by an anaphoric 'thus', with the syntactic parallel suggesting an irresistibly logical argumentation: 'Thus, wryting is the keye to enduce vertue, and represse vice. Thus memorye maketh menne ded many a thousand yere still to live as though thei wer present: Thus fame triumpheth upon death, and

---

[4] Goodland, *Female Mourning*, p. 3. Elizabeth Mazzola even maintains that 'Protestant iconoclasm must also be viewed as an historiographical practice, since rejecting Purgatory inspired new paradigms for human history and new limits for human practice' (*The Pathology of the Renaissance*, p. 10). This suggestion has been recently taken up and richly substantiated by James Simpson in *Under the Hammer: Iconoclasm in the Anglo-American Tradition*, whose impressive study demonstrates how iconoclasm has worked as a category of history and, more specifically, of art history from the Middle Ages to our own post-modern moment.

[5] The didactic power of history was a standard topos of ancient and early modern historiographical thinking, repeated so often that its expressions verge on the formulaic. Brian Walsh points out that while such declarations may be 'mere nods to convention, they also indicate an anxiety in Elizabethan historical culture that the "use value" of history was not self-evident after all' (*Shakespeare, the Queen's Men and the Elizabethan Performance of History*, p. 17).

renoune upon Oblivion, and all by reason of writing and historie.'[6]
This line of argument is as teleological as its rhetoric is circular: in the
beginning there was the written word, and it all comes down again to
writing and history.

   Hall's dedication thus establishes a set of binary oppositions in which
writing is aligned with memory, fame, moral order and civilisation, as
opposed to oral culture, oblivion, death, disorder and wilderness. The
latter part of the equation is summed up in the image of 'that dedly
beast Oblivion', expressing the view that forgetfulness is a wild, destructive force of nature against which civilisation must be defended by the
arts of memory. Hall's historiographical project consciously builds on
this opposition, yet a closer look reveals that his praise of memory
in the dedication actually performs a double act of forgetting itself –
and that it does so by means of writing. First, its insistence on the
written word as the only reliable medium of memory effectively obliterates the rich mnemonic culture of the Middle Ages which was predominantly, if not exclusively, oral in nature. The principles and practices of
the medieval *ars memorativa* have been conclusively reconstructed by
Mary Carruthers in *The Book of Memory* (1990). While the title of her
study would seem to suggest a similar bias toward 'memory by litterature' as exhibited by Hall, the term 'book of memory' is to be understood in its metaphoric function within the memory arts: it refers to the
wax-tablet as one of the traditional images for the cognitive processes
of remembering. Since antiquity, memory had been understood as a
physiological act in which perceptions received through the senses were
impressed in the soft material of the brain. These impressions were likened to engravings left by a stylus in the soft wax on a writing tablet.
Thomas Aquinas, the famous thirteenth-century scholastic philosopher
and divine, made the metaphorical nature of the relation between writing and memory explicit: 'A thing is said metaphorically to be written
on the mind of anyone when it is firmly held in memory'.[7] Yet when
Hall speaks of 'memory by litterature', he is taking this metaphor literally. He reifies the medieval simile that the process of remembering
works *like* the act of writing into the notion that memory *is* writing.
In doing so, he reduces the wealth of medieval mnemotechnics to only
one: memory by the book.

---

[6] Hall, *The Union of the Two Noble Houses*, sig. A.ii[r].
[7] Aquinas qtd. in Carruthers, *The Book of Memory*, p. 10.

Hall's conflation of history and writing into a 'memory by litterature' that increasingly displaced the *artes memorativae* was echoed
widely by sixteenth- and seventeenth-century historiographers.[8]
This reliance on writing and literacy as the props of historical truth
amounts to a 'scriptorial turn' in early modern memory culture.
Historian Daniel Woolf maintains that already by 1500 writing was
considered as an acceptable, even desirable, substitute for a memory based on oral culture.[9] This self-confident view presented early
modern historiography as the rightful heir to the medieval mnemonic
arts and denotes a transfer of cultural authority. It was accompanied, indeed perhaps even prompted, by a shift from the traditional
techniques of memorialisation to the modern technology of print
that facilitated the multiplication and distribution of books and book
knowledge. Contemporaries – at least those directly involved in the
emergent print culture – invariably regarded this as an enhancement
of personal and cultural memory.[10] By the end of the seventeenth century, Daniel Woolf suggests, a clear hierarchy had emerged in which
oral tradition and popular memory had lost their authority as sources
of history.[11]

A somewhat different picture emerges, however, when we take
into account the public theatre as another emergent medium that

[8] Francis Bacon, for instance, whose magisterial *Advancement of Learning*
laid the foundation for historiography as a discipline, categorically
claimed: 'Assistant to Memory is writing; and it must by all means be noted,
that Memory of it selfe, without this support, would be too weake for prolixe
and accurate matters; wherein it could no way recover, or recall it selfe, but by
Scripture' (p. 253).

[9] Woolf, *The Social Circulation of the Past*, p. 262.

[10] William Caxton, for example, who set up the first printing press in England,
described the rationale of his 1482 print edition of a manuscript chronicle
written by the medieval monk Ranulf Higden as follows: the book is to
commemorate 'such thynges as have ben don syth the deth or ende of the
sayd boke of polycronicon [sic] [which] shold be had in remembraunce and
not putte in oblyuyon ne forgetynge' (*Polycronycon*, p. 428). This is the
penultimate sentence of Caxton's massive project of over four hundred-pages,
which thus ends on the very note that would open Hall's *Union* some seventy
years later: oblivion is vanquished by print. Intriguingly, Caxton's choice of
phrasing and tense – 'should have been had in remembrance' – suggest that the
chronicle not only stores historical treasures but indeed can restore what had
already been forgotten, thus keeping oblivion in view as a fundamental point
of departure for the historiographical project.

[11] Woolf, *The Social Circulation of the Past*, p. 298.

increasingly dominated the reconstruction of England's national past from the 1570s on. According to Thomas Nashe's defence of the stage in *Pierce Pennilesse*, its ability to bring the heroes of the past back to life was emphatically superior to the 'moth-eaten records' of the chronicles, which he likened to 'the grave of oblivion'.[12] The theatre as a new and exciting practice of making history is superior because of its ability to make the past present. We should be wary, however, of simply adopting this teleological narrative of a development toward greater mnemonic capacity, mimetic authenticity or moral authority. In championing history plays over prose history, Nashe seems simply to reverse Hall's judgement, which denounced the mnemonic efficacy of the spoken in favour of the written word. A closer look at early modern history plays, however, shows that they did not side readily with either oral or written culture, but rather were situated between them. With its double aspect of text and performance, the theatre participated in both oral and written culture and continually reflected on the gaps and clashes between the two. This in-between status, as we shall see, manifests itself less in polemic statements such as Nashe's and more in nuanced commentary about the media of historical memory available, the stage itself included. Such metahistorical commentary was a staple of prefaces and dedicatory letters of the chronicle histories. As the playwrights' main source of information about England's past, these reflections entered the history plays along with the historical subject matter. 'Shakespeare's history plays', Phyllis Rackin argues, 'show the pressures of the cultural changes that made the representation of historical truth a difficult – and dramatically appealing – enterprise at the time ... Played out in the theatre, the problems of historiographical representation were redefined and intensified.'[13] However, Graham Holderness cautions, these plays were 'not just *reflections* of a cultural debate: they are *interventions* in that debate, *contributions* to the historiographical effort to reconstruct the past and discover the methods and principles of that reconstruction'. Against the background of the increasing spread of print culture and the emergence of the public theatre as a new medium, early modern history plays staged the different mnemonic properties of oral report, written record and theatrical performance.

---

[12] Nashe, *Pierce Pennilesse*, pp. 86–7.
[13] Rackin, *Stages of History*, pp. 21–2.

They explored the formation and transformation of historical memory through the lens of how different media generate different kinds of historical consciousness, and can therefore themselves be read 'as serious attempts to reconstruct and theorise the past'.[14] Moreover, in so doing they also explored the power as well as the limits of the theatre as a medium of memory. The following discussion of *2 Henry VI* and *Richard III* examines the ways in which historical drama reflected on how the public theatre performed memory and, related to this, how it might have functioned not only as a medium of remembering, as Nashe so categorically put it, but also as a medium of forgetting.

Shakespeare's *Second Part of King Henry the Sixt* is a play that insistently stages the early modern debate about literacy and orality. The play's main theme, announced in its convoluted Quarto-title as *The First Part of the Contention between the two Famous Houses of Yorke and Lancaster*, is structurally linked to a contention between the media of making memory: the rivalry between oral and written culture, which erupts in the fourth act with Jack Cade's rebellion. The rebellion is directed against literacy as the prime means of establishing and supporting social hierarchies: written documents appear as the basis of the social and political power of the aristocracy, while the illiteracy of the common people ensures their continuing subjugation. Therefore the rebels justify their violent destruction of the agents, institutions and material documents of written culture as the return to a pre-literate state of grace in which the spoken word guarantees truth and justice: 'Away, burn all the records of the realm, my mouth shall be the parliament of England', their leader Jack Cade famously commands (4.7.11–12). The rebellion fails, however, and order and authority based on written culture are reinstated. This raises the question of whether the play subscribes to Cade's demonisation of writing, or whether the failure of his rebellion echoes the early modern triumph of literacy.[15] Much critical energy has been spent on trying

---

[14] Holderness, *Shakespeare's History*, p. 31; original emphases.

[15] For Shakespeare as a champion of oral and theatrical performance, see the works by Robert Weimann, most recently his *Shakespeare and the Power of Performance*. A different view of the playwright as an eminently literary dramatist who supervised the printing of his play-texts with meticulous care is offered by Lukas Erne's *Shakespeare as Literary Dramatist*. Two recent collections of essays, *A Concise Companion to Shakespeare and the Text* (ed.

to determine whether the play advocates a containment of subversive forces or champions resistance to oppressive authorities.[16] Depending on how we assess the political affiliations of play and playwright, 2 *Henry VI* either affirms the power of writing or rebels against it. Such either/or answers, however, remain unsatisfying to the extent that they disregard the fact that this is a play not only about politics but also about the politics of representation.[17]

I would suggest that the play, rather than blatantly stating its affiliations, offers a complex analysis of early modern memory culture and its media. Despite the strident anti-literacy voiced by Jack Cade, which establishes a strict opposition of written and oral culture, memory and forgetting, authority and rebellion, the play neither just rehearses nor simply reverses these oppositions. Instead, it stages the capacities of each medium to record historical truth; and in doing so, it shows that both written records and oral report can be used to produce historical 'truth' – as well as to appropriate it for one's own interests. In other words, it does not so much express a partiality for one medium over the other but, since both media can be employed to create a partial account, rather casts doubts on the notion of historical truth itself. This raises the urgent question of the role that power plays in the formation of cultural memory, as Geraldo de Sousa reminds us: 'Literacy, in this context, becomes the metaphor for the power of the dominant culture, the power to make history.'[18] Neither rejecting nor embracing literacy in unqualified terms, the play differentiates between the

---

by Andrew Murphy) and *Shakespeare's Book* (ed. by R. Meek, J. Rickard and R. Wilson) explore the material conditions of textual production and reception and their poetic articulation in Shakespeare's plays.

[16] For an overview see Fitter, '"Your captain is brave and vows reformation"', 175–7.

[17] Stephen Greenblatt's essay 'Murdering peasants' (1983), one of the earliest examples of new historicist practice, makes precisely this point. He discusses the commemoration of peasant revolts in early modern monuments and texts above all as a representational problem (and hence a matter of form): how to represent the victory over rebellious peasants without generating pity for the vanquished, or compromising the honour of the noble victors. Stephen Cohen, however, points out that already here an interest in politics begins to override attention to poetics, since Greenblatt does not make a difference between media or genres, but lumps them all together under the label of 'heroic commemoration' ('Between form and culture', p. 26).

[18] Geraldo de Sousa, 'The peasants' revolt and the writing of history in 2 *Henry VI*', p. 180.

power *of* writing, which is acknowledged throughout, and the power *over* writing, which is viewed with considerable distrust. This suspicion centres on the authority that the written word wields over the present as well as the past: access to writing determines one's position and privileges in the social hierarchy, just as it allows one to determine historical memory in one's favour.[19]

Each time the power of writing is evoked in the play, it is shadowed by an anxiety about the power over writing. At the very outset of the play, the peace contract which the Duke of Suffolk has negotiated with France *a propos* the marriage of King Henry VI and the French princess Margaret and which results in the loss of two English territories on the continent already indicates the two dimensions. The written document's performative power is considerable: it establishes peace, transfers territories and memorialises these steps as part of national history. Interestingly, this is presented as an act of remembering as well as of forgetting. Outraged by the terms of the treaty, the Duke of Gloucester intones a patriotic lament:

> O peers of England, shameful is this league;
> Fatal this marriage, cancelling your fame,
> Blotting your names from books of memory,
> Razing the characters of your renown,
> Defacing monuments of conquered France,
> Undoing all, as all had never been!

(1.1.94–99)

The contract blots out the memory of England's glorious victories, won by Henry V just a generation before, and reinscribes shame instead. The result is a realignment of political, national and geographical memory which is explicitly couched in the language of oblivion: cancelling, blotting, razing, defacing and undoing are the operative verbs here, which suggests that forgetting is an active, personalised force. Yet this

---

[19] The political and mnemonic rationale of Cade's blunt order to burn all the records of the realm is spelled out in one of the chronicle sources, the account of the 1381 Peasant Rebellion, which explains that 'all court rolls and old moniments should be burnt so that once the memory of ancient customs had been wiped out their lords would be unable to vindicate their rights over them' (repr. in Dobson, *The Peasant's Revolt of 1381*, p. 133). Both the peasants of 1381 and Shakespeare's rebels realise that texts, whose production and dissemination they cannot control, govern their lives (de Sousa, 'The peasants' revolt and the writing of history in 2 *Henry VI*', p. 186).

forgetting is not, as Eco would have it, an uncontrollable, catastrophic force of nature; on the contrary, it is brought about through the ritualised social practices of a marriage and a peace contract. While the scene thus affirms the power of this piece of writing, it criticises at the same time that Suffolk has shamefully abused his power over its terms. Such an awareness of the potential abuses of the power over writing necessarily affects the alleged truth-value of historical records themselves. Only a few lines after Gloucester's lament, York, who rejects the marriage contract for far more selfish reasons, explicitly references chronicle sources to lend authority to his position: 'I never read but England's kings have had / Large sums of gold and dowries with their wives' (1.1.124–5). In a later scene, where a recitation of genealogical trees is taken directly from Hall, Holinshed and Stow, the phrase 'As I have read' (2.2.40) is supposed to lend credibility to Salisbury's support, *pace* the chronicles, of the Duke of York's claim to the throne. These scenes affirm the belief in the power of written history as a means of legitimating political authority. That York is the arch-villain of the play foregrounds the fact that this authority is not necessarily coupled with morality, justice or truth.

The nobility's abuse of its power is further showcased when several commoners produce petitions in which their grievances and calls for justice are recorded. 'Let's stand close', urges one of the petitioners: 'My lord Protector will come this way by and by, and then we may deliver our supplications in the quill' (1.3.1–3). Instead of the 'good man' (4), the Lord Protector Duke Humphrey, however, it is the Queen and her adulterous paramour Suffolk who appear. Much less inclined to protect the commoners' interests than their own, they are biased judges. The Queen spitefully tears up a supplication because it is directed to the Lord Protector as the most powerful arbiter of the realm instead of to the King or herself (31–44). Suffolk even stands accused himself: one of the petitions is 'Against the Duke of Suffolk, for enclosing the commons of Melford' (23–4), and another promises to disclose a usurper, which prompts a suspiciously nervous reaction from Suffolk as well. Exclaiming 'Who is there?', he '*[Snatches Peter's supplication]*' and orders the petitioner to be arrested (F 1.3.33–6). The scene demonstrates both the power of writing and the power over writing: the fact that the commoners are forced to submit their petitions in written form, 'in the quill', which would have involved the costly services of a clerk, marks that writing as an instrument of discipline and subjection – and the nobles in turn demonstrate their power through the unjust appropriation and wilful destruction of those supplications. I would argue, however, that the scene also shows the power of writing as a potential instrument of resistance in the hands of the commoners: having entered the legal process, their supplications become official documents that have the power to indict members of the nobility. When the petitioners submit them 'in the quill' they do so, according to the *OED*, 'in a body; in concert; together': the term evokes an image of solidarity among the lower classes.[20] That the quill as an instrument of writing can become a weapon of rebellion in the hands of the lower classes is proleptically suggested by the first description we get of Cade. In 3.1, the Machiavellian villain York announces Cade's potential as a tool for his stage-managed rebellion by recalling how, in an earlier uprising, he 'fought so long till that his thighs with darts / Were almost like a sharp-quilled porcupine' (3.1.362–3). Darts become quills, but the bows from which they were shot are actually those of the rebellious Irish soldiers, while Cade in that case fought on the side of the English colonial masters; a subtle hint that his own rebellion in the play is actually spin-doctored by a member of the English nobility, the Duke of York. The politics of writing are therefore presented as highly ambiguous: the word, proverbially mightier than the sword, can be seized by those in power as well as by the underprivileged. It is not clearly associated with either but is presented as an instrument in the struggle for power.

Having learned from painful experience what power can be derived from control over the written word, the rebels also try to make that power work for them. Their efforts, however, fail when their leader reverts to reliance on oral memory. In act 4, scene 4 the rebels themselves send the King a supplication that lists their grievances and claims. As was the case with the earlier scene of petitioning, this can be seen as a forced submission under the discursive rules of those in power. But the previous instance of supplicating 'in the quill' also makes it possible to see the written petition as a medium of political participation, of transposing the lower classes' voice into a written register where it will be 'heard'. The successful communication proves

---

[20] The *OED* cites 2 *Henry VI* as the first recorded example for meaning 2.) 'in the (or a) quill: in a body; in concert; together; to jump in quill: to act simultaneously or in harmony'.

that possibility right. King Henry reacts in kind by sending another written document, an amnesty that grants 'free pardon to all of them who will forsake' Cade (4.7.153–4). The King's amnesty – a word that translates literally as 'not remembering' – constitutes a complex act of forgetting and remembering: it promises to erase the memory of the rebellious division and at the same time rallies the English people to a shared memory, namely 'The name of Henry the Fifth' (4.7.160, 198), uniting them against 'The fearful French, whom you late vanquished' (184). Yet Cade, true to his revolutionary programme that aims at throwing out written culture along with its exploitation by the upper classes, pre-emptively counters by invoking the much older, unwritten memory of the 'ancient freedom' (4.7.26), which the common people allegedly held before the Norman Conquest in 1066. Appealing 'against the internal enemy, the Anglo-Norman, whose yoke of foreign aristocracy bore heavily over an indigenous Saxon yeomanry',[21] this ancient memory fuses with Cade's utopian vision of a future egalitarian society, paradoxically both pre- and post-literate. The King's power over present and past, shored up by his command over the records of the realm, is greater than Cade's, however, and the rebels, accepting the royal vision of Englishness and patriotic obedience along with the royal amnesty, desert their leader.

As these scenes suggest, writing can also become a means of erasing historical memory; the mnemonic effectiveness of either written or oral memory is therefore not an inherent feature of the medium itself but rather a function of the power held by those who employ the medium for their own memory politics. Shakespeare's play thus problematises how historical memory can be constructed and reconstructed through (re)mediation. Moreover, as though to foreground this concern with memory and the media of history, the play itself reconstructs its own historical sources considerably. This reconstruction occurs through additions to and subtractions from the medieval chronicle material, thus actively shaping what is staged as national memory. In other words, *The Contention* is not only about forgetting: it performs itself acts of forgetting that form and transform memory.

The play's performative enactment of forgetting can be demonstrated with regard to the rebel scenes in act 4, which conflate the memory of the 1381 Peasant's Revolt under Jack Straw and Wat Tyler

---

[21] Knowles, 'Introduction', p. 97.

with that of the late medieval figure of Jack Cade in 1450, as well as the more recent apprentice riots of the later sixteenth century.[22] In doing so, Shakespeare effectively strips them of their respective historical specificity, making them readable instead as reflections on the mnemonic anxieties about literacy, history and power around 1600. Take, for example, the historical Jack Cade: in most sources, he is described as a well-educated, agreeable young man who does not display any hostility toward written culture. The concern about literacy and its abuses is imported from the 1381 Peasant Rebellion, which was indeed directed at the institutions and representatives of an oppressive system of written legal documents. Shakespeare adds that concern not only to the material of the 1450 Jack Cade rebellion, but to almost every other historical episode which the play stages.

The conspiracy, exposure and punishment of Duke Humphrey's wife, Eleanor Cobham, is a case in point. The connection between writing, power and historical memory, which the play explores through this figure, is absent from the chronicle source. Hall's *The Union of the Two Noble Houses* merely records that the Duchess 'was accused of treason, for that she, by sorcery and enchauntment, entended to destroy the kyng' and that she had to 'do open penaunce, in iij. open places, within the city of London'.[23] In Shakespeare's play, by contrast, reading and writing are foregrounded as part of the occult ritual through which Lady Eleanor seeks to determine the fate of her enemies and her chances for becoming queen:

> Mother Jourdain, be you prostrate and grovel on the earth; John Southwell, read you; and let us to our work ...
> *Here do the ceremonies belonging, and make the circle; Bolingbroke or Southwell reads,* 'Conjuro te' *etc., It thunders and lightens terribly; then the* Spirit *riseth.*

(F1.4.11–12, 22.1–3)

---

[22] Geraldo de Sousa, 'The peasants' revolt and the writing of history in *2 Henry VI*', sums up the well known argument of the conflation of the historical Jack Cade's rebellion of 1450 with the Peasants' Revolt of 1381 in the play; for a reading of Shakespeare's Cade in the context of the 1591 Hackett rising, see Fitter, '"Your captain is brave and vows reformation"'.

[23] Hall, *The Union of the Two Noble Houses*, p. 101.

Written words, read aloud, have the power to raise a ghost. The questions posed to the devilish spirit as well as the answers given are, according to the stage direction, conspicuously recorded. They are again read out aloud when the Duke of York arrests the conspirators and confiscates the records of their Sabbath as incriminating evidence for the trial (1.4.56–7). When Lady Gloucester is publicly exposed afterwards, she has '*[written verses pinned on her back]*' which intensify her punishment: 'Methinks I should not thus be led along, / Mailed up in shame, with papers on my back, / And followed with a rabble' (2.4.31–4). As in the opening scene, a piece of writing inscribes shame and blots out the memory of her former dignity as wife of the Lord Protector. What is more, her 'shameful yoke' (2.4.38), fixed in writing, will be all that is remembered of her, as Duke Humphrey recognises: even if he could spare his wife this public display, 'yet thy scandal were not wiped away' (2.4.66) from the books of memory.

There are further references to the magical power of written words and how they cast their spell in law. Writing is, unsurprisingly, associated with witchcraft by the illiterate rebels. When they arrest the clerk from Chartham and discover that he carries 'a book in his pocket with red letters in't', Cade concludes without hesitation: 'Nay, then, he is a conjuror' (4.2.80–1). This goes hand in hand with the accusation that the clerk is an agent of the law: 'Nay, he can make obligations and write courthand' (82). The parallel syntax of these charges implies a logical parallelism between conjuring and the ability to draw up legally binding documents. Parchment and sealing-wax, seemingly innocuous objects, are transformed by the evil magic of law – evil, at least, from the perspective of the rebels – into legal documents that can dispossess a man. Thus one of them complains: 'Is it not a lamentable thing, that the skin of an innocent lamb should be made parchment; that parchment, being scribbled o'er, should undo a man? Some say that the bee stings, but I say 'tis the bee's wax: for I did but seal once to a thing and I was never mine own man since' (4.2.69–73). For Cade, the uses to which government and law put a lamb's skin and bees' wax amount, like witchcraft, to a perversion of nature.[24] Imagining writing as a direct, causal link between being spellbound and being bound by the law, the rebels thus unwittingly assert the power of the written word.

---

[24] Chartier, 'Jack Cade, the skin of a dead lamb, and the hatred for writing', 77–9.

Superstitious belief in the power of writing is not restricted to women or the lower classes, but is also embodied by male members of the nobility. When Suffolk is captured by pirates on his way into exile, the Duke angrily challenges one of them whom he recognises as a former bondsman of his: 'This hand of mine hath writ in thy behalf / And therefore shall it charm thy riotous tongue' (4.1.64–5). Again, the syntax suggests a logical concatenation between words cast in writing and casting a spell: they are actions performed by the same 'hand of mine', both working together to 'charm' a 'riotous tongue'. The struggle between outlawed nobleman and lawless pirate is couched in terms of a contest between the powerful charm of literacy and a rebellious oral culture. Suffolk tries to reinstate the feudal relationship in which his power over writing shores up his power over the socially inferior, illiterate bondsman. Yet the scene takes place in a legal vacuum, on board a pirate ship and between two persons who, by this point, exist outside the law. In this context, the power of writing is suspended, and all that remains is the brute force of violent words. A lieutenant responds to Suffolk's arrogant challenge: 'let my words stab him, as he has me', whereupon Suffolk scoffs: 'Base slave, thy words are blunt, and so art thou' (67–8). Against all cultural odds, the spoken word wins over written ones in this scene. This, as well as the fact that the lieutenant acts as eloquent spokesperson for the commoners' grievances (73–103), points forward to the scenes of Cade's rebellion with its radical rejection of both literacy and the law which serves the upper classes.

What this means for our topic of how historical memory is mediated and shaped, and in particular for the role that the early modern theatre played in this process, is, I would like to suggest, that this play about English medieval history speaks not only of the events of that past but also, and perhaps even primarily, of issues and concerns of the present. Such a topical reading was the dominant mode of perceiving history in the Middle Ages and the Early Modern period: history functioned as a mirror for the present. As John Frow comments in a different context, each reconstruction of the past is inevitably shaped by conditions and constraints determined by the present.[25] In Shakespeare's play, such conditions and constraints are figured through the connection of literacy and social power. When Cade, for example, upbraids Lord Saye: 'Thou hast most traitorously corrupted

---

[25] Frow, 'Toute la mémoire', p. 228.

the youth of the realm in erecting a grammar school [and] thou hast caused printing to be used and ... built a paper mill' (4.1.27–31), he directly addresses an issue of the Elizabethan audience's present. Print, paper-mills and grammar schools would have been anachronistic phenomena in 1450, the time of the historical Jack Cade, and even more so in the time of the 1381 Peasant Rising which provides the main source for the rebels' anti-literacy.[26] What Shakespeare's Cade articulates here are late Elizabethan concerns about the pervasive economic, legal and educational impact written culture had on everyday life, and by which the illiterate classes saw themselves increasingly disadvantaged.[27] In the light of the Tudor 'reading revolutions', to borrow the title of Kevin Sharpe's study, during which more than 400 grammar schools sprang up, Cade's anti-literacy, rather than speaking for the common people who probably esteemed and desired the acquisition of literacy as enabling their own social aspirations, may well have articulated aristocratic anxieties about upward social mobility.[28]

Such a topical reading does not extend only to the issues the play ostensibly speaks about, such as rebellion and the abuse of power by a selfish aristocracy. I think we can also profitably employ the perception habit of topicality to contextualise the acts of remembering and forgetting dramatised in the play. The context of the Reformation as one of the most pressing concerns of the Elizabethan present is important here: the repeated confessional change – from Catholicism to Protestantism under Henry VIII and Edward VI, back to the Catholic faith under Mary and again to a more moderate Anglican position under Elizabeth – was accompanied by a concerted, often violent, destruction of monastic houses and their libraries. This scenario would seem to be replayed, in inverse hierarchical order, by Jack Cade's command to destroy all written records. The historical situation was more complex, though, as is its recreation in Shakespeare's play. Jennifer Summit has shown that the dissolution of the monasteries in 1535 did indeed mean a dispersal and wide-scale destruction of the monastic libraries; but it also inspired a generation of bibliophiles to collect and rebuild these stores of national memory: 'For these post-Reformation book collectors, rebuilding the nation's libraries meant repairing the

---

[26] Linton, 'Shakespeare as media critic', 16.
[27] Smith, 'Shakespeare and the representation of the press', p. 69.
[28] Fitter, '"Your captain is brave and vows reformation"', 198–9.

nation's memory'.[29] Restoring the nation's memory was not only an act of reparative remembering, however; it performed its own acts of forgetting as well, because the objects deemed worthy of preservation were dictated by the collectors' religious and political affiliations. As agents of the Protestant state, antiquarians such as John Bale sought versions of the past that supported the Reformation, and hence their methods of preservation tended to be 'selective rather than comprehensive'. Far from effecting a wholesale restoration of national memory, the post-Reformation library-builders actively contributed to its transformation in a process of salvaging and discarding. Thus, ironically, 'the Dissolution's longest-lasting creation was a dialectic of remembering and forgetting',[30] which Summit then goes on to trace in Spenser's *Faerie Queene* and which we can also observe at work in Shakespeare's history plays. Read in this context of post-Reformation concerns about the material media of national memory, *Henry VI, Part 2* is not only a play about medieval or Elizabethan political culture. It is also a play about the very process of making historical memory, a process that is conceived of as a dialectic of remembering and forgetting.

While the play examines literacy and orality as the two media of history engaged in this dialectic process, staging their mnemonic properties and limits, the question of how the theatre itself functions as a medium of making history remains implicit. Jack Cade as a Lord of Misrule and a Vice-figure can of course be seen as an embodiment of the theatre, as James Knowles[31] suggests, yet his histrionic energies are directed at reflecting on literacy and oral culture, less on questions of theatrical performativity. Nevertheless, the play's insistent preoccupation with historical memory and its media also raises the question of the stage's role in forming and performing it. It is necessary to turn to another Shakespeare play for an answer. The third act of *Richard III* offers a series of self-conscious reflections on the media of historical memory, the theatre included. These scenes ostensibly address the question of where truth resides, in written record or oral report, and who its warrantors are, historical documents and monuments or

[29] Summit, 'Reading reformed: Spenser and the problem of the English library', p. 165.
[30] *Ibid.*, pp. 165–6.
[31] Knowles, 'Introduction', pp. 101–2.

present eyewitnesses. They moreover destabilise the very notion of 'truth' and 'authenticity', and thus take the issue of the theatre's mnemonic impact beyond the point of moral authority or historical truth.

At the beginning of the third act of *Richard III* the young Princes are led into the Tower, never to emerge from it alive. Prince Edward wonders about the history of the building and addresses Buckingham: 'Did Julius Caesar build that place, my lord?' (3.1.69) In the ensuing dialogue, the edifice becomes a materialisation of historical memory as well as of the historiographical process: its foundations were laid by Julius Caesar, but his original edifice has been 're-edified' since by 'succeeding ages' (71). The imagery and choice of verb, signalling an ongoing process of edification, are revealing in regard to the conception of history articulated here. In the sense of 'to give instruction', it registers the dominant view of history as offering instructive examples that invite reiteration. In the sense of 'to construct' or 'to build further', it voices an understanding of the past as something artificially created. This suggests that, just like the historical monument, written documents can be 're-edified' from age to age, necessarily changing their shape in the course. This imagery admits, indeed even presupposes, the possibility of knocking down, building over, incorporating or closing off parts of the building, in short, of various acts of reshaping which form and transform the historical monument just as they do cultural memory.[32]

The play itself is an example of this process in that it 're-edifies' the historical account of Richard III as recorded in the chronicles by Holinshed and Hall, which in turn incorporate the one by Sir Thomas More. However, More's *History of King Richard III* (1513) does not provide a final reference point of historical truth either.[33] It draws on oral report as well as on pieces of Tudor propaganda such as the *Vita Henrici VII* by Bernard André, who was Henry's official historiographer,

---

[32] Michael Hattaway further notes that 'edification' was a term also connected with 'the craft of the playwright or the maker of theatrical ceremonies'. Drawing on Philip Sidney's *Apology for Poetry*, he argues that writing plays counted among the 'architectonic arts', providing a stepping-stone to true self-knowledge ('The Shakespearean history play', pp. 20–2).

[33] According to the one surviving statement in the 1557 folio edition, in which the *History* was published for the first time, More wrote it 'about the yeare of our Lorde .1513'. More likely, he worked on the English and Latin version simultaneously over the years 1514–18. See Sylvester's introduction to More's *The Complete Works*, pp. lxiii–lxv.

Polydore Vergil's more detached *Anglica Historia* (written between 1506 and 1513) and John Rous's late fifteenth-century *Historia Regnum Angliae*, which invented the story of Richard's prolonged gestation and the picture of the villainous hunchback.[34] What we can conclude from these textual reincarnations of Richard III, each 're-edified' according to the political interests of 'succeeding ages', is that history is the product of an ongoing transformation through remediation. The distorted figure of Richard himself becomes a figure for the distortions of historiography, Marjorie Garber points out: Richard's deformed shape encodes 'the whole strategy of history as a necessary deforming and unforming – with the object of reforming – the past'.[35] Interpreting Richard as an embodiment of the distortions of history enables us to see both remembering and forgetting as the twin forces at work in the historiographical process, and at the same time prevents us from casting them as mnemonic opposites: historical remembrance is always already a purposeful forming *and* deforming of the past.

The example of More's *History* is particularly instructive because it offers a view of history as an artificial fabrication, to the extent that it performatively undermines its own status as historical truth. It not only speaks about the ways in which the historical record might be orchestrated – an act of exposure that would have made it possible to claim truthfulness for itself – but constantly highlights that it is itself subject to such manipulation simply because it already engages in a representation of historical events. Throughout, metahistorical reflection is coupled with a reflection about the manipulative potential of language.[36] Far from being a transparent, reliable medium for recording factual truth, words can be ambivalent, imprecise and falsifying – they create a 'historicity effect' that is then taken for history.

[34] For a philological account of this textual history, see Sylvester's introduction to More's *Complete Works*, pp. lxv–civ, as well as Pollard's 'The making of Sir Thomas More's *Richard III*' and, from a more critical perspective, Garber, *Shakespeare's Ghost Writers*; Kinney, 'The tyrant being slain: Afterlives of More's *History of King Richard III*'; and Schmidt, '"To set some colour vpon ye matter"'.

[35] Garber, *Shakespeare's Ghost Writers*, p. 36.

[36] Examples of the manipulative power of representation abound in the text. One must suffice here: Dr Shaa's sermon at St Paul's, which is supposed to cast doubt on the legitimacy of Edward's heirs and to present Richard as new king instead. At the moment of this declaration Richard himself is to appear, 'as thoughe y⁰ holye ghoste had put them in the preachers mouth, & should haue moued the people euen ther, to crie king Richard king Richard, y³ it might

The humanist ideal of language as a reliable medium is thus shown to be somewhat naïve: far from being a measure of truth, *eloquentia* becomes the chief technique of manipulation in More's *History*.

In highlighting language as a medium of orchestrating historical knowledge, More's text casts doubt on written historical records – his own included – as sites of 'distortion, displacement and "de-featuring"'.[37] Shakespeare's *Richard III* performs a similarly critical analysis of the media of historical memory, albeit from a playwright's perspective and attuned to the conditions and limits of his own medium, the public theatre. Both texts foreground the principle of 're-edification' by which historical truth becomes an effect of representation – be it in written documents, speech acts, or dramatic performances. These mediated renderings do not mimetically represent the truth but rather produce partial versions of historical events that draw on different strategies to authorise themselves as truth.

The Tower scene with its short dialogue about the building's history is a case in point. The Prince acknowledges the fact that Caesar's foundation is legendary and that no written record of it has survived to the present day. Nevertheless, he does not doubt the truth of this fact, even though it has no stronger base than oral report: 'But say, my lord, it were not registered / Methinks the truth should live from age to age' (3.1.75–6). This conviction echoes the belief in the immortality of 'good and evil fame', as Jonson's introductory poem for Ralegh's *History of The World* put it, a belief which humanist historiography embraced.[38] Again the Prince: 'Death makes no conquest of this conqueror, / For now he lives in fame, though not in life' (87–8). It seems an astute enough assessment of the historical process, as the longevity of

---

haue bene after said, yᵗ he was specially chosen by god & in maner by miracle' (More, *The Complete Works*, p. 67). Richard comes too late, however, and the desperate Dr Shaa sees himself forced to repeat his speech verbatim. The carefully devised miracle, unsurprisingly, suffers from repetition: 'the people were so farre from crying king Richard, yᵗ thei stoode as thei had been turned into stones' (p. 68). The attempt at manipulating eyewitness accounts with the help of a stage-managed speech backfires completely; yet the scene nevertheless asserts ex negativo the power of words.

[37] Kinney, 'The tyrant being slain', p. 37, note 2.

[38] The first stanza of the poem reads: 'From Death and darke Oblivion (neere the same), / The Mistress of Mans life, grave Historie, / Raising the World to good, or Evill fame, / Doth vindicate it to Aeternitie.' (Ralegh, *The Works of Sir Walter Ralegh*, vol II: ll.1–4).

Richard's image as monster, living on in popular memory until today, amply demonstrates.[39] Yet in its unthinking equation of moral and historical truth, the Prince's view is also utterly naïve. For him, neither the circumstance that written records are continually re-edified nor the absence of such documents has any consequences for the reliability of history. Truth will out; it will always, somehow, be 'retailed to all posterity' (77). Thus detaching truth from its media of transmission, the Prince unwittingly hits upon his uncle's own chosen device of manipulation: separating the truth from the record. Richard of Gloucester ironically acknowledges this (as well as his intent to erase the person and the memory of his precocious nephew) in the next aside: 'So wise so young, they say, do never live long' (79). When asked to repeat his comment aloud, he quickly corrects himself: 'I say, "Without characters, fame lives long"' (81). Seemingly submitting to the Prince and his belief that oral fame (or character) will survive independent of written records (characters), Richard at the same time demonstrates his mastery over oral memory as well: he draws on familiar proverbs ('they say', 79) and twists their seemingly stable, conventionalised words to his own meanings ('I say', 81). This exchange raises the issue of literacy and orality as rivalling media of memory, and casts doubt upon the humanist ideal of a historical and moral truth that is unequivocally preserved in these media, or might even exist independently of them. The following scenes, however, inexorably demonstrate that there is no historical truth, only partial representations of historical events that draw on different media to authorise themselves as truth.

The Scrivener scene, a very brief but important one, exposes the mechanisms and extent of Richard's mnemonic machinations. It comes at the end of his intrigue against the Lord Chancellor Hastings, who as the last staunch supporter of the heirs of Edward IV is an obstacle on Richard's way to the throne. Richard has him executed without trial and now seeks to cover this crime with the help of falsified documents. The Scrivener's task is to produce fair copies of certain manuscripts, thus turning them into legally binding documents. His short soliloquy reveals 'how the sequel hangs together' (3.6.4), from informal manuscript to formal indictment to legal trial and, as the last step, execution. In this case, however, the temporal sequence is utterly 'out of joint' (*Hamlet*, 1.5.189). The Scrivener notes that the account

---

[39] See Höfele, 'Making history memorable'.

reporting Hastings' execution, including the reasons justifying it, was penned several hours before the Lord Chancellor was even arrested. 'Eleven hours I spent to write it over', he announces and immediately points out the temporal discrepancy with legal proceedings:

> The precedent was full as long a-doing;
> And yet within these five hours lived Lord Hastings,
> Untainted, unexamined, free, at liberty.

                                                          (3.6.7–9)

The existence of the document thus does not guarantee historical truthfulness, nor that 'the form of law' (3.5.40) has been obeyed. Instead, it has become a mere formality, although one with considerable power. The indictment, which in the normal sequence of law would have authorised Hastings' trial, now serves to legitimise his murder in retrospect. Moreover, as an archival document it claims the status of historical evidence: the very act of recording the treason charge and multiplying the record in copies serves to produce and circulate a cover-memory which effectively and conveniently obliterates what happened. The truth of 'such bad dealing', the Scrivener glumly concludes, can only 'be seen in thought': it survives in what memory and imagination bring before the mind's eye or, indeed, onto the stage. This at least is how John Jowett interprets the Scrivener's lesson: 'The critique of textual record and the vindication of thought and memory are exactly appropriate to a stage work that breaks free from chronicled history, creates the illusion of events re-membered, and depends on the actors' memories as the conduit from script to audience.'[40] As an analysis of the Scrivener scene alone, this is an astute reading of the play's scepticism about written records. It ignores, however, that this critique is framed by two scenes which expose the very fact that performance can likewise be a means of falsifying historical memory. Both these scenes, 3.5 and 3.7, are spin-doctored by Gloucester and Buckingham for chosen spectators on the stage, who serve as eye-witnesses to what Richard would like to have 'retailed to all posterity' (3.1.77) as truth; both are highly metadramatic in that they double the act of playing as well as the act of watching; and both complicate the notion that the truth may indeed 'be seen in thought' (3.6.14).

In the first scene, Hastings is already dead, and Gloucester and Buckingham, apparently justified by Hastings' alleged treason, play the

---

[40] Jowett, 'Introduction', p. 60.

roles of innocent victims turned justified executors. All this is staged for the benefit of the Mayor who is thereby convinced that the killing has happened according to 'the form of law' indeed. The scene is presented as a play within the play: Richard and Buckingham appear in costume (*'in rotten armour, marvellous ill-favoured'*, 3.5.0) and immediately embark on a rehearsal of their histrionic repertoire, including the conventionalised postures, gestures and speech patterns, the 'Ghastly looks' and 'enforced smiles' of 'the deep tragedian' (3.5.1–10). Enter the Mayor who provides the unwitting audience for their farce about Hastings' death, which is presented as the just, if ill-timed, execution of an 'ignoble traitor', doubly dangerous because he 'daubed his vice with show of virtue' (21, 28). Charging Hastings with deceit and dissimulation allows Richard and Buckingham to hide their own: their performance puts up a smoke screen that conceals the truth effectively from the Mayor (whose ocular testimony is, ironically, appealed to twice in the scene). At the same time, however, it allows the audience to see through their schemes more clearly. Even without the Scrivener's following explanation, the metadramatic framing already indicates that what actually happened may be different from what one sees and will remember. By staging this incongruity, the scene warns the audience that appearances may lie, yet it does so, paradoxically, through stressing appearances: the audience observes Gloucester's manipulations and thus has a privileged access to the truth (at least with regard to the play). The challenge therefore is to know what one sees or, to use a phrase from More's *History*, to 'watch kynges games cunningly'.[41]

Scene 3.7 reinforces and at the same time complicates this lesson in media use by presenting different audience reactions to Richard's manipulations of the events. At the beginning of this scene, we hear Buckingham's report of his off-stage performance before the citizens at the Guildhall, followed by Richard's and Buckingham's performance

---

[41] More, *The Collected Works*, p. 80. More's *History* contains several instances of knowing audiences, the most famous of which explicitly acknowledges the theatrical nature of politics. Watching the wooing-scene at Baynard's Castle, More reports, the spectators shrewdly conclude that 'these matters bee Kynges games, as it were stage playes, and for the more part plaied vpon a scafoldes. In which pore men be but yᵉ lokers on. And thei yᵗ wise be, wil medle no farther' (pp. 80–1). Shakespeare's play does not explicitly repeat this trenchant, tongue-in-cheek analysis from below (which he would have found repeated verbatim in his chronicle sources) but rather enacts its lesson. Staging the silence of More's 'pore … lokers on', the play settles for a more implicit critique that also allows for the possibility of an alliance between stage-play and 'kynges games'.

before a group of citizens and nobles at Baynard's Castle, now assembled on the stage. Both performances pretend to persuade a supposedly reluctant Richard to accept the crown; yet both actually aim at persuading their audience in the play-world that this show of reluctance is true. This is not mere disingenuousness on the part of Richard. Rather, the citizens' approval furnishes Richard with scapegoats onto whom he can shift his responsibility and guilt for seizing the crown:

> But if black scandal or foul-faced reproach
> Attend the sequel of your imposition,
> Your mere enforcement shall acquittance me
> From all the impure blots and stains thereof;
> For God doth know, and you may partly see,
> How far I am from the desire of this.

(3.7.221–6)

Knowing full well the power of oral memory in the form of gossip, rumour and scandal, Richard seeks to deflect as well as direct it through manipulating these eyewitness testimonies. The citizens, however, retain an uncomfortable silence, realising that his reluctance is indeed only 'partly', and so the Mayor is conspicuously the only one to satisfy Richard's unvoiced demand when he promises enthusiastically: 'God bless your grace! We see it, and will say it' (227). However, the Mayor's vision, too, is at best partial, both in the sense that he cannot see the entire extent of Richard's scheming and that he does not want to see it.

Critical readings of this scene often stress that the audience in the theatre is implicated in Richard's ocular and mnemonic manipulations as well. Gillian Day, for example, sees the on-stage onlookers at Baynard's Castle as our representatives, and their conspicuous silence as an expression of our own connivance:

The artificiality of the scene is patent, the layering of truth mirroring the rank of the figures. Only those above and we beyond are fully in the picture. The rest form part of it, the play-in-the-play of a would-be king fooling with show his silent audience to confer their token voices on his coup d'état. Perhaps our presence as an extension of the silent crowd condemns our own collaboration in the fiction.[42]

---

[42] Day, '"Determinèd to prove a villain": Theatricality in *Richard III*', 152.

This is a shrewd analysis of the intentions behind Richard's imposture; it falls short, however, as an analysis of its possible reception effects. For one, Day's appraisal of the audience, both in the play-world and in the playhouse, as a foolish, submissive crowd is problematic because it uncritically doubles the nobles' view of the people as 'dumb statues or breathing stones' (3.7.25). Moreover, it is contradicted by the play itself, which suggests that there may be different kinds of silence indicative of different stages of knowledge or, at least, suspicion. Thus the dumb-struck silence with which Richard's political charade at Baynard Castle is received (punctured only by the Mayor's enthusiastic assurance of support) contrasts pointedly with the 'wilful silence' (3.7.28) the citizens preserved at the Guildhall. While the one may indeed register collusion, the other is recognised by both Buckingham and Richard as a refusal to accept their histrionic farce as historical fact. Buckingham's indignant report bears this out: instead of being able to command the citizens' shouts of support, he has to submit to their decision to use silence as a response; involuntarily self-deprecating before them, he is shamed by his own words. Through remaining obstinately silent, the citizens gain the upper hand in this language game.

Such a silence may well have been the common people's only way of expressing resistance, as Paola Pugliatti points out: 'By their silent speech, the citizens have launched a challenge which perturbs the norms established by the ruling power ...; by refusing to speak, they have communicated to Richard, who thought that he possessed their production of discourse, that this is still their prerogative.'[43] The play admittedly does not eventually resolve the tension between these two silences, since Shakespeare gives us this scene only from the point of view of the courtiers trying to impose on their audience. Moreover, because the curtain does not fall, as it were, on Richard's play-within-the play, his charade is allowed to become an accepted historical fact, at least in the play-world. This may indeed be interpreted as Shakespeare's own act of collusion with the powers that be; yet it is impossible to determine which silence is held up here as the good and which as the bad example to the contemporary audience.

Moreover, these scenes harbour uncomfortable implications for the stage: since historical events can be staged and false memories produced, eye-witness testimony becomes dubious. The play's own claims about

---

[43] Pugliatti, *Shakespeare the Historian*, p. 211.

the truthfulness of performance are thus necessarily paradoxical. The theatre seemingly exposes manipulations of the historical truth, but at the same time play-acting emerges as what enables this manipulation. What is more, the history play itself frequently adapts historical records to achieve a more 'dramatically appealing' version of the past.[44] What emerges in performance, both in the play-world and in the playhouse, is not so much a superior kind of truth but rather the superior power of performance. Far from celebrating the theatre's power to make and unmake memory, *Richard III* presents it in an ambivalent way: on the one hand, the play challenges, and thus to a certain extent undoes, the reliability of the theatre as a medium of historical memory; on the other, it highlights the mnemonic efficacy of theatrical performance precisely by offering striking, memorable scenes of past events. The 'purpose of playing' (*Hamlet*, 3.2.18), from this perspective, would lie neither in representing historical truth (as Nashe's defence would have it) nor merely in revealing how it can be manipulated. Rather, its lesson seems to be that there is no historical truth that exists independent of textual or theatrical mediation and beyond the process of reconstruction and reception in which the audience is always implicated.

This lesson emerges from the doubling of the audience *in* the play and *of* the play, a repetition with a crucial difference: perceiving the bad example of the Mayor's ocular gullibility, the theatre audience is encouraged to exert a more critical spectatorship. As Phyllis Rackin points out with regard to history plays in general, by thus becoming 'increasingly self-reflexive, [they] encourag[e] their audiences to meditate on the process of historical representation rather than attempting to beguile them into an uncritical acceptance of the represented action as a true mimesis of past events'.[45] In staging the same 'play' with two different audience reactions, the scene at Baynard Castle moreover alerts the spectators in the theatre to the different qualities of silence. By foregrounding this difference, the audience is invited to recognise that silence, far from being complicit, can also be a means of resistance.

Taken together, the plays discussed in this chapter engage in different ways with the early modern debate on the practices and media of historiography. Participating in both oral and written culture but

---

[44] Rackin, *Stages of History*, p. 21.   [45] *Ibid.*, p. 29.

not fully converging with either, the theatre offers a critical perspective on their role in preserving historical memory. In so doing, it also self-reflexively explores the mnemonic potentials and limits of theatrical performance. These are fundamentally ambivalent. As the example of *Richard III* demonstrates, dramatic spectacle can be a means of manipulating memory and of consigning unwanted historical events to oblivion. In the sense that '[t]he Shakespearean Richard demonstrates the power of theatre as a form to shape the historical imagination',[46] performance itself can be seen as a practice of selecting and erasing, in other words, as a practice of forgetting that gives form to memory. By highlighting this oblivional potential, plays like *Richard III* at the same time encourage an audience to see through such manipulations and remind them, if not of the historical truth, then of the fact that whatever emerges from mediation as 'truth' is always partial and selective, constructed through acts of remembering as well as forgetting. The moral, if perhaps not historical, authority of the stage, I would argue, resides in its ability to employ the whole range of mediation – written record as well as oral report, theatrical performance as well as silence – and to enable the audience to use these media knowingly.

[46] Walsh, *Shakespeare, the Queen's Men and the Elizabethan Performance of History*, p. 169.

2 | Ceremony: rites of oblivion in Richard II *and* 1 Henry IV

At the end of *Richard III*, the eponymous villain has lost the decisive battle against the Earl of Richmond, who as King Henry VII ends the bloody Wars of the Roses and ushers in a time of 'smooth-faced peace' and 'fair, prosperous days' (5.8.33–4). Promising that everything will be different now, the play invokes one of the pieties of the Tudor myth that helped to legitimise the reign of a dynasty whose claim to the throne was as problematic as that of Richard Duke of Gloucester. Significantly, the play marks the difference between Yorkist tyranny and Tudor reign as a different stance toward religious ceremony and in particular toward burial rites: the new king's first command is that all fallen soldiers are to be interred 'as become their births' (5.8.15). In so doing, he reinstates the performance of traditional rites of mourning, which had fallen into neglect under Richard. As many critics have pointed out, interrupting ceremonies of mourning is one of Richard's chief strategies of establishing his power over his subjects' wills as well as their memories. Not allowing the memory of his misdeeds to survive either in the official records (as we saw in the previous chapter) or in individual recollection supposedly exempts him from charges of murder and usurpation. In scene after scene, ritual laments and ritual curses against his crimes are cut short by Gloucester's entrances or interjections.[1] In the post-Reformation context in which the play was performed, the argument continues, Richard would have been perceived as the embodiment of a reformed, anti-ceremonial attitude, while the ritualistic nature of the Queens' laments, enacted through speech, gestures and emotionally charged interjections, recalled

---

[1] As when Richard turns scenes of mourning into a play of courtship with Lady Anne (1.2.) and Queen Elizabeth (4.4.) respectively, when he interrupts with business of royal succession the communal lament for his brothers in 2.2 and for the young princes in 4.1., or when his interjection cuts short Queen Margaret's curse and turns it against her (1.3.); for a detailed analysis of these scenes, see Goodland, *Female Mourning*, pp. 143–53.

patterns of actual mourning practices that were viewed as increasingly problematic after the Reformation.[2] If the ritualistic character of their mourning as well as its memorialising impetus marks them as deeply conservative figures,[3] Richard's strategic forgetfulness is, in John Jowett's reading, nothing short of 'revolutionary, in that his emphasis on the destroying moment of here and now crumples up and eradicates the past ... he attempts to expunge memory as an active force in the present.'[4] While such a reading of Gloucester as carrying the forward-looking, post-Reformation attitude to an extreme holds considerable explanatory power, it is too dichotomous to do full justice to the complexity of the play's explorations of the relationship between ceremony and memory. After all, Richard is not fully opposed to ceremony but, as a Vice-figure, acts himself as 'a highly transgressive master of ceremonies', as Robert Weimann has pointed out.[5] In fact, the performance of ceremony is his strategy of forming and transforming historical memory, as we saw in scenes 3.5 and 3.7, discussed in the previous chapter, where his and Buckingham's charade serves to obscure their part in the murder of Hastings and to make Richard's usurpation of the crown look like a reluctant submission to duty.

We therefore need to reconsider the critical view of Richard of Gloucester as an anti-ceremonial, post-Reformation villain, a view that culminates in the final scene with its seeming affirmation of the opposition between ritual commemoration and its oblivionating disturbance, between rightful rites and unlawful forgetfulness, in the light of previous scenes. By the same token, neither can Henry Earl of Richmond be seen straightforwardly as a hero who returns his traumatised countrymen (and Shakespeare's theatre audience) to a state of peaceful unity which, on the level of the contemporary *platea*, doubles as the return to a pre-Reformation commemorative culture.

---

[2] This is the argument put forth by Patricia Philippy's *Women, Death and Literature*, Katherine Goodland's *Female Mourning in Medieval and Renaissance English Drama* and, in an essay less oriented toward gendered commemoration than the theatricality of history, by Stephen Marche ('Mocking dead bones: Historical memory and the theater of the dead in *Richard III*'). William C. Carroll interprets Richard's interruption of ritual as a representation of another traumatic rupture threatening early modern England, the issue of succession, in '"The form of law": Ritual and succession in *Richard III*'.
[3] Döring, *Performances of Mourning*, p. 56.
[4] Jowett, 'Introduction', pp. 37–8.
[5] Weimann, 'Performance, game, and representation in *Richard III*', p. 48.

Richmond's act of reinstating the proper funeral rites, after all, is not only an act of cultural remembrance but can also be seen as an act of oblivion, which aims at burying the divisions of civil war (as well as obscuring the fact that he is not Richard's rightful successor, but has likewise usurped the throne). That his command is indeed part of a strategic memory policy is made explicit when Richmond decrees an amnesty, an officially commanded forgetting, in the very next line: 'Proclaim a pardon to the soldiers fled' (5.8.16). The penultimate line announces the beneficent result that 'Now civil wounds are stopped, peace lives again' (40), echoing Lady Anne's lament over the open, bleeding wounds of Henry VI in the presence of his murderer Richard of Gloucester at the beginning of the play: 'O gentlemen, see, see! Dead Henry's wounds / Ope their congealed mouths and bleed afresh' (1.2.55–6). The play commences with the maimed rites of burial and the bleeding body of the King, both signalling a disrupted body politic; it ends with the dead properly buried and the 'civil wounds' closed. Peace and national unity are premised just as much on rites of memory as on rites of oblivion.

Moreover, the promise of peace and unity brought about through ceremony is framed ironically, both on the levels of textual and of topical reference. The final scene uncannily echoes another one in which peace and unity had been declared in almost the same terms and with the same ceremonial gestures. In 2.1, the antagonists, who just before had outbid each other with curses and invectives, are now addressed as 'this united league' (2.1.2) by the sickly King Edward IV. Expecting his demise, he wishes to make 'my friends at peace on earth' and enjoins them to 'make me happy in your unity' (2.1.6, 31). This unification of the factious court is performed through ceremonious oaths which are couched in terms of oblivion: 'my soul is purged from grudging hate', Rivers swears, followed by Queen Elizabeth's oath to Hastings that 'I will never more remember / Our former hatred: so thrive I, and mine' (2.1.9, 23–4). To all purposes and intents, this is a scene of communal forgetting, an amnesty, to be sealed with a day of commemoration: 'A holy day shall this be kept hereafter' (2.1.74). Yet even before the play is over, unity has given way to the 'dire division' Richmond seeks to bury anew in the final scene (5.8.28). Remembering this earlier scene, the Elizabethan audience may well have wondered to what extent peace and unity had been achieved in their own time, and at what cost.

When *Richard III* was first performed, the promise of 'smooth-faced peace' to the heirs of Richmond and the Lady Elizabeth, 'the true succeeders of each royal house' (5.8.30) had to all appearances been fulfilled in the reign of Elizabeth I. Richmond's final speech 'is, as it were, remembering the future, resonating with the inflections of Elizabethan polity'.[6] As such it can surely be read as a compliment to Elizabeth's governmental skills; but it is also a pertinent analysis of them. For it was under the very house of Tudor that England experienced another 'dire division' of the country, not dynastic but religious. The confessional conflicts of the Reformation boiled underneath the calm and stable surface: a merely 'smooth-faced peace' indeed. As in the play, it was achieved through a complementary strategy of remembrance and oblivion. 1559, the first year of Elizabeth's reign, for example, saw several official acts that illustrate this. The pageant celebrating her coronation explicitly looked back to the nation's pacification under Henry VII; its theme, 'Unity', referred specifically to a concord aimed at healing the strife between church reformers and Catholics.[7] This was at least temporarily achieved in the Elizabethan *Act of Uniformity* of the same year, a highly tenuous attempt at hybridisation. Its thirty-nine articles abolished doctrinal heresies like purgatory and did away with mass, yet at the same time it managed to accommodate the traditional religion by reinstating some of the liturgical rituals, saints' days and prayers associated with Catholicism. The necessary adjustments of cultural memory could only be achieved through a strategic deployment of forgetting the most contentious issues and their representatives. The 1559 *Injunctions* thus proceeded likewise by regulation as well as erasure, a procedure announced by its double goal 'to plant true religion' as well as to effect 'the suppression of superstition'; in practice, however, the emphasis fell indeed on the latter.[8]

Thus when the opposition between memory and forgetting, between ritual and its disruption in *Richard III* is displaced by a realisation of their complementary dynamics, this is something we can observe in Elizabethan England as well. Richmond's revivification of ceremony, which effects an erasure of unwanted memories, raises the urgent question to what extent ceremony itself might be engaged in processes of forgetting. This question has been taken up by historians

---

[6] Jowett, 'Introduction', p. 70.   [7] *Ibid.*
[8] Duffy, *The Stripping of the Altars*, pp. 567–8.

of the English Reformation only recently. Peter Marshall, for example, argues convincingly that Protestantism in fact developed its own
distinctive rites of commemoration. He accordingly rewrites the history of the Reformation's impact on English religious culture in terms
of 'two intersecting trajectories of erasure and regulation'. The first
trajectory consists of the campaign on the side of bishops, theologians
and ordinary clergy to eradicate all traces of purgatory and intercessory prayer. In other words, their efforts aimed at forgetting traditional Catholic ceremonies of mourning and commemoration. The
second trajectory that Marshall sees also at work in post-Reformation
England consists in attempts at 'regulating the relationship between
the living and the dead through establishing a new framework for
the liturgical and ritual commemoration of the dead'. The forgetting
of ritual is therefore complemented, and at times counteracted, by
new rites of remembering. 'Despite the dissolution of chantries and
fraternities, the proscription of requiem masses and intercessory
prayers, the putting out of obit lamps, and abrogation of bede-rolls',
Marshall points out, 'Elizabethan and early Stuart England possessed
a plethora of methods and occasions for memorializing the dead, and
sanctifying their memory.' Nevertheless, the changes in ritual practice also changed the ontological and epistemological status of ritual
itself. The vast amount of 'social and cultural engineering' that had
gone into the process left its traces on how ritual was perceived: no
longer a religious habit taken for granted, but a potentially precarious practice that carried with it an awareness of the forces at work in
forming and deforming memory. I am interested in how the changed
ritual practice commemorated a knowledge of the very changes it had
undergone and had helped to achieve; and how the performance of
ritual, be it in a religious or a theatrical context, registered a kind of
loss of innocence regarding such ceremonies and their commemorative power. Marshall bids us 'recognize that the English Reformation
was not merely a force acting externally to change rituals, structures,
and meanings of commemoration, but that the lived experience and
inherited awareness of radical change could itself promote, in some
quarters at least, a markedly heightened sensibility about the memory
of the dead'.[9] This awareness of a radical change acting not externally

---

[9] Marshall, *Beliefs and the Dead in Reformation England*, pp. 124, 187, 265,
    306–7.

to but rather through rituals, structures and meanings of commemoration, is what I will trace in my readings in this chapter.

These insights urge us to rethink a range of assumptions that under-
pin scholarly discussions of the relation between the confessions in early
modern England. Instead of aligning Protestantism and Catholicism
with acts of oblivion versus commemorative culture, official doctrine
versus local practice, Reformation versus ritual respectively, we have
to assume a more complex interplay between those terms as well as
across confessional lines.[10] Such an adjustment of our critical perspective necessarily changes our assessment of the Reformation's impact
when we leave the sacred realm of commemorative ritual proper and
enter the secular realm of cultural memory. Up to now, the dominant model to account for this impact operates in dichotomous terms
of demolition and compensation. It has been most thoroughly conceptualised by Elizabeth Mazzola in her classical study of what happened to the 'remains of the sacred', such as discarded ritual practices,
in post-Reformation culture. She starts from the general insight that
'in the course of more important projects, cultures routinely discard
symbols and other imaginative habits'.[11] These abandoned symbols,
habits and practices, however, 'do not simply disappear from the mental landscape; and sometimes, this discarded material takes up far
more space. No longer scrutinized so carefully or clung to as dearly
as official public knowledge, outworn symbols can find their powers
increased by occupying the margins of accepted ideas ...'. This was
clearly the case with the Reformation, and corresponds with the first
trajectory Marshall identifies. Because Reformation theology 'required
a radically different framework to hold in place sacred meanings and
values', ideas that had been held in reverence before were now 'publicly acknowledged to be false or groundless or unpersuasive, like
Catholic conceptions about purgatory and transubstantiation. Simply
put, these ideas – along with the symbols they employ and the practices they encourage – no longer work: they fail to describe reality.'[12]
While in the long run traditional Catholic beliefs and practices were
successfully demolished, neither the emotional need for consolation

[10] Edward Muir's study of *Ritual in Early Modern Europe* (1997) offers a
detailed survey of how the Reformation changed not only Protestant ritual
practices, but those of the Catholic and the Orthodox churches as well.
[11] Mazzola, *The Pathology of the English Renaissance*, p. 1.
[12] *Ibid.*, pp. 4, 9.

they offered nor the imaginative habits they catered to could simply be erased. In Mazzola's words,

sacred symbols and practices still powerfully organized the English moral imagination in the sixteenth and seventeenth centuries, continued to orient behaviors and arrange perceptions, and persisted in specifying to believers and non-believers alike the limits of the known world. These sacred symbols remained the primary guides to and deepest structures for feeling.[13]

Accordingly, Mazzola raises the possibility that the devalued signs and practices were displaced onto other cultural sites where they continued to fulfil important psychic and social functions, and thus compensated for the loss of traditional religion.

This kind of compensation-model has great explanatory power, as a range of important studies of the fate of religious beliefs, signs and practices in the Elizabethan culture demonstrate. In particular the early modern theatre has been identified as the cultural site to which discarded rituals, due to their shared performativity, migrated most easily and pervasively. Historians agree that the 1580s constitute a watershed for the secure establishment of the Reformation because the generation that could tell of the traditional customs gradually died out. It is perhaps no coincidence that these individual reminiscences, in danger of dropping out of the 'communicative memory' (J. Assmann), were salvaged by the newly emergent institution of the public stage which transformed them into collective memories and in turn became one of the most important sites of cultural memory. This at least is the well-substantiated claim made by studies such as Huston Diehl's *Staging Reform, Reforming the Stage* (1997), Michael Neill's *Issues of Death* (1997) and Stephen Greenblatt's *Hamlet in Purgatory* (2001), all of which argue that the theatre compensated for the loss of ritual in the religious sphere.

Huston Diehl examines the interrelations between theological discourse and theatrical practice. She demonstrates 'how the popular London theatre ... rehearses the religious crisis that disrupted, divided, energised, and in many ways revolutionised English society'.[14] The stage did not only mirror that debate but actively intervened in

---

[13] *Ibid.*, p. 3.
[14] Diehl, *Staging Reform, Reforming the Stage*, p. 1.

it. Because of its stakes in representation, spectacle and the imagination, drama was influenced by and responded to Reformation controversies concerning the rituals and images of the medieval Church. Engaging with such issues, it participated in turn in shaping its audience's understanding of religious reform. Elizabethan and Jacobean tragedies, concerned as they are with death and loss, articulated the anxieties created by Protestant assaults on late medieval piety, but they also alleviated them in that they typically stage rituals and spectacles of the traditional Church in order to demystify and contain them.[15] Diehl hints here at a complementary liberating potential that is close to my understanding of the oblivional potential of dramatic performance and which will be explored further below.

The studies by Neill and Greenblatt, by contrast, rather emphasise the compensatory function of the theatre in terms of consolation, preservation and remembrance. Neill argues that English Renaissance tragedy's obsession with death catered to 'a culture that was in the throes of a peculiar crisis in the accommodation of death'. Its equally obsessive concern with memory likewise needs to be understood 'in terms of a wider preoccupation with the importance of remembrance in a culture forced to devise new ways of accommodating itself to the experience of mortality'.[16] The psychological value of tragedy's displays of agony, despair and, he adds at a later point, of maimed funeral rites, restless ghosts and violated sepulchres was that they provided audiences with a way of confronting the implications of their own mortality as well as the impact which the Reformation had had on commemorative culture. In particular the genre of revenge tragedy answered to the oblivional anxieties triggered by the Protestant abolition of purgatory and its attendant rites. Neill's assessment of revenge tragedy as 'a fantasy response'[17] fits well with the compensation model: since the possibility of active intercession on behalf of the deceased was officially forbidden, the revenge plot acts out both the impulse of doing something for the beloved dead and the frustration at being denied to do so by law, which emerges in the transformed shape of the revenger's rage.

Greenblatt's study focuses more narrowly on the cultural meanings of the ghost figures that turn up in late sixteenth-century literature, and

---

[15] *Ibid.*, pp. 2–5.   [16] Neill, *Issues of Death*, pp. 30, 38.
[17] *Ibid.*, p. 246.

especially on the public stage, as a consequence of the official denial of purgatory. 'Staging Ghosts' (the title of the relevant chapter in his study) fulfilled a range of overlapping functions in the Shakespearean theatre. They appear as 'desperate explanatory hypotheses about the world' that cannot be understood any more in traditional frames of reference, as signs of guilt in villains' nightmares, as embodiments of a deep psychic disturbance, and finally also as a figure for the theatre precisely in the sense that, after the Reformation, they emphatically exist only in and as theatre.[18] Stage ghosts can be seen as a theatrical response to the great sixteenth-century rupture in the relations between the living and the dead. At the same time, ghosts, real or imagined, are 'good for thinking about theater's capacity to fashion realities, to call realities into question, to tell compelling stories, to puncture the illusions that these stories generate, and to salvage something on the other side of disillusionment', Greenblatt claims. The ghost thus serves as a metatheatrical trope through which the stage reflects self-consciously on its own role as a medium both of memory and of the imagination. In either case, an important aspect of the theatre's function lies in compensating for what is lost, in 'salvag[ing] something on the other side of disillusionment'.[19]

As these examples show, the model of compensation has been very useful in gauging the impact of the Reformation on early modern commemorative culture and in articulating the psychological, social and cultural functions of the public stage in the context of the formation and transformation of cultural memory. Productive as it has undoubtedly been to see the theatres as agencies of salvaging pre-Reformation memories, I would like to suggest a different perspective that highlights the complementary nature of remembering and forgetting. The early modern stage functions as a medium of memory not only in the sense that it preserves discarded symbols, rituals and practices, but also in the sense that it remembers the acts of oblivion at work in post-Reformation English culture. This is quite different from treating the representation of maimed rites, restless ghosts and destroyed sepulchres merely as the effects of such cultural forgetting, figured as a return of the suppressed ceremonial unconscious. We do so at risk of precluding a consideration of the very process that brings these effects

[18] Greenblatt, *Hamlet in Purgatory*, pp. 158–61, 168–80, 185–8.
[19] *Ibid.*, p. 200.

about in the first place. Mazzola points out perceptively that the textual or literary 'habits and projects of the Renaissance are some of the most self-consciously sophisticated methodologies for the burial and retrieval of cultural knowledge'.[20] Taking the cue from this observation, I would like to propose that early modern plays perform not only acts of memory but also rites of oblivion, and that they do so quite self-consciously. The scenes of remembering and forgetting often double as moments in which the theatre reflects on its own function for the process through which cultural memory is made. We should therefore also pay attention to the ways in which early modern plays preserve the contents of discarded knowledge, but also the knowledge of the cultural techniques of consigning something to oblivion. In what follows, I will put what we may call a model of complementarity to the test by focusing on the enactment of commemorative rites of mourning in two other history plays, *Richard II* and *1 Henry IV*. Due to the programmatic double focus of history plays on *locus* and *platea*, their scenes of mourning stage memories of the traditional rites which, after the religious settlement, could not be practised any more.[21] Epitaphs and elegies, deathbed and funerary speeches, scenes of grief and lamenting both perform and comment on the ways of commemorating the dead which were no longer permissible in Elizabethan England. The historical scenes of grief, in other words, thus lend themselves to a topical reading of contemporary grievances. In this sense they might indeed also be seen as examples of the compensation-model. But I would suggest that this model unduly restricts our view. For within its framework, the relation between Reformation and ritual typically appears in terms of a strict opposition between oblivion and memory. From such a perspective, the stage only ever registers the traumatic impact of the Reformation on ritual commemoration in terms of loss, erasure and absence. My discussion of *Richard III* at the beginning of this chapter has already suggested that such a view shows only half the picture: when we pitch memory and oblivion, ritual and its interruption against each other, we are at risk of overlooking the ways in which ritual performances of ceremony – be it in a ritual context or on the stage – can themselves work toward the erasure of memories. I would therefore like to reconceptualise the relation of ceremony and memory,

---

[20] Mazzola, *The Pathology of the English Renaissance*, p. 2.
[21] Döring, *Performances of Mourning*, p. 48.

and so arrive at a more complex description of the mnemonic and theatrical culture of Elizabethan England. In order to do so, a 'model of complementarity' is needed which takes into account the interplay of remembrance and forgetting rather than seeing them as opposites; which recognises oblivion as a force that can be constitutive, rather than destructive, of cultural memory; and which makes visible the cultural devices available for consigning things to oblivion. As my following reading of *Richard II* will show, funerary ritual and in particular ceremonial lament functioned as one such device. John Kerrigan has observed that 'complaint is problematic, because stagey before it is staged'.[22] Due to its spectacular nature or, in Kerrigan's words, the 'stageworthiness of grief', ritual lament also functions as a vehicle of metatheatrical reflection. The object of those reflections is the role of the theatre itself in the processes that shape cultural memory.

Let us enter the play at a pivotal moment: after coming back from Ireland, King Richard learns that Bolingbroke has returned from exile to lead a rebellion against him. One catastrophic message after another arrives, and Richard momentarily succumbs to despair. Instead of charging into action, he laments his losses, ultimately anticipating even the loss of his crown. His speech rehearses the traditional poetics of lament, its topoi and gestures, signalling that it is quoting a well-established tradition: 'Let's talk of graves, of worms and epitaphs, / ... let us sit upon the ground / And tell sad stories of the death of kings' (3.2.141, 151–2). These ritual accounts of 'the death of kings' also evoke the political uses of lament, the authorisation of the mourner's particular story of the past as well as his or her alliance with the dead: remembering the sad stories of kings who have preceded him, Richard inscribes himself into a royal lineage, thereby affirming his status as an anointed king while anticipating his violent end as a crime against a legitimate ruler.

So far, this scene of lament functions quite conventionally, down to the appropriate gestures of sitting on the ground and the shedding of tears: 'Make dust our paper and with rainy eyes / Write sorrow on the bosom of the earth' (3.2.142–3). These gestures of mourning implicitly perform another staple of lament, the *sic transit gloria mundi* topos. Writing with tears in the dust serves as a powerful image for the vanity of the world, 'for within the hollow crown / That rounds the mortal

---

[22] Kerrigan, *Motives of Woe*, p. 56.

temples of a king / Keeps Death his court' (156–8). Death conquers all, and the state and pomp of kings are no more than theatrical trappings, 'a little scene / To monarchize' (160–1). Realising this, Richard rejects the very ceremonies that make him a king: 'Cover your heads and mock not flesh and blood / With solemn reverence. Throw away respect, tradition, form and ceremonious duty, / For you have mistook me all this while' (170–2). This sounds like an outright renunciation of ceremony along with tradition. The abdication scene will show, however, that while Richard does indeed divest himself of his royal prerogatives, he does so through a ritual performance that in effect reinvests his person and his story with new authority. Ritual lament allows him to do so by naming what is lost and then discarding it; by dissociating his person from 'the name of king' (3.3.145) in order to attach another name and meaning to his life; and finally by substituting the popular 'lamentable tale of me' for the 'grievous crimes' that are on historical record.

The ritual discarding of one set of symbolic props and substituting it for another, is enacted in scene 3.3, in which Richard rehearses his abdication speech in the circle of his supporters. He laments his predicament and anticipates his forced submission to the rebel Bolingbroke. Interestingly, he prays not for strength or dignity but for oblivion:

> Oh that I were as great
> as is my grief, or lesser than my name,
> Or that I could forget what I have been,
> or not remember what I must be now!

> (3.3.135–8)

Here, the separation of Richard as a person from his 'name', of the body natural from the body politic, begins. This separation is explicitly linked with the desire to forget what he had been – a king in name and person – and what he is now – a king in danger of becoming a subject. The aim of this ritual divestiture, however, is not to leave Richard as a mere person of 'flesh and blood' (167), but rather to transform him into another state where he is secure from subjection. His speech performs an inverse coronation ceremony, which at the same time doubles as a ritual of saintly investiture:

> I'll give my jewels for a set of beads,
> My gorgeous palace for a hermitage,

My gay apparel for an almsman's gown,
My figured goblets for a dish of wood,
My sceptre for a palmer's walking staff,
My subjects for a pair of carved saints,
And my kingdom for a little grave
A little, little grave, an obscure grave.

(3.3.146–53)

The ritualistic character of this speech is highlighted by its formulaic language, its anaphoric repetitions and syntactic parallelisms. It enumerates the signs and rites of kingship about to be discarded, from the royal insignia to the subjects whose 'ceremonious duty' ritually affirms his kingship. These signs of royal authority are not merely rejected (as in the previous scene), but replaced with signs of a different sacred authority: the beads and hermitage, poor gown and wooden dish, walking staff and carved saints of a hermit. He even envisages for himself an 'obscure grave' without an epitaph; all he will have is a lamentable tale written with tears into dust. Yet as we will see, Richard's lament brings about his erasure from official history only to reinstate his memory on a mythical scale. For this speech sets into motion the process of Richard's 'self-iconisation as a Christ-like figure', a process in which 'Christological metaphors and allusions to sacrifice and martyrdom are painfully embodied in the act of performance itself'.[23] Richard's initial desire to renounce the ceremonies of kingship and be only 'flesh and blood' (3.3.167) takes on a different meaning in retrospect: he transforms himself into the sacrificial flesh and blood of Christ through the very use of ceremony and its performative powers, which are captured in the speech act of the Eucharist alluded to here: 'this is my flesh and blood'. With lament providing the ritual frame, his abdication speech performs the complementary acts of obliterating his memory as a subjected worldly king and of remembering him as a heavenly king, subject to no one.

This dynamic of forgetting and remembering also undergirds Richard's public abdication in 4.1. The whole scene has a highly ceremonial setting: as the stage direction indicates, the lords and commons *Enter as to Parliament*, carrying the royal regalia before them

---

[23] Joughin, 'Shakespeare's memorial aesthetics', p. 54; for Richard as saint-like figure, and specifically the parallels to Thomas Beckett, see Harmon, 'Shakespeare's carved saints'.

that Richard has already renounced and will officially forswear in the second half of the scene. The first half mirrors the play's opening scene with its examination of 'noble Gloucester's death' (4.1.3) and the ritual challenge between several nobles, though this time it is Bolingbroke who presides over the ceremonies of chivalry. This ceremonial framework does not change when Richard, about to be officially excluded from the 'pomp and majesty' of kingship, is brought before Parliament. On the contrary, the speech through which Richard himself enacts the ritual of decoronation intensifies the ceremonial character of the scene. It echoes the one rehearsed in 3.3, with its anaphoric lines and syntactic parallelisms as well as its insistence on the first personal and possessive pronouns:

> With mine own tears I wash away my balm,
> With mine own hands I give away my crown,
> With my own tongue deny my sacred state,
> With mine own breath release all duteous oaths.
> All pomp and majesty I do forswear.
> My manor, rents, revenues I forgo.
> My acts, decrees, and statutes I deny.

(4.1.197–203)

With this speech, Richard imaginatively erases the material and symbolic signs of kingship from his own person: the anointment balm, his crown and his sacred state that commands absolute loyalty. It is also an obliteration of his person from history: the palpable effects of his reign, grounded in 'acts, decrees and statutes', are effaced. While this ceremonial obliteration of Richard as king spells an absolute loss of political authority, the performance of this ceremony itself invests him with power, as he points out to his audience both on and off the stage: 'Now mark me how I will undo myself' (4.1.193). Richard becomes the beginning and end of himself, not in terms of interiorised subjectivity but rather in terms of a self-perpetuating power of ritual performance.

The inverted coronation ceremony might seem to suggest Richard's unfitness as a ruler, since it supposedly demonstrates his disregard for ritual and tradition. Naomi Liebler reads it more accurately as evidence of his care for the proper formalities of his civilisation's rites, and points out Richard's capability of turning them into rites of oblivion: 'The speech is both pitiable and dangerous. Richard undoes

himself, as well as his kingship. In denying his acts, decrees and statutes he erases all records of his existence and occupation of the throne.
This is more than the passage of control; it widens the hole in the historical record, the breach in the "fair sequence and succession" of the
Plantagenet dynasty.'[24] The power inherent in ritual spectacle is, then,
not only the ability of shaping the perception of the present moment,
but also how it will be perceived in historical memory, as the following
contest between Richard and the Earl of Northumberland indicates.
Northumberland tries to force Richard to perform yet another ritual,
that of public confession and penitence. By reading out the official
accusations against him, Richard is to submit himself to a specific version of the history of his reign, to be recorded in legal documents.
Richard refuses to conform, knowing full well the power of such a
performance. So does his opponent, who expects 'That by confessing
them [his crimes] the souls of men / May deem that thou are worthily
deposed' (4.1.216–17). Against this attempt at erecting the monumental image of Richard as criminal and thus as a 'worthily deposed' king
in the empty place of renounced kingship, Richard sets the performance of himself as a Christ-like martyr:

> Nay, all of you that stand and look upon ...
> Though some of you, with Pilate, wash your hands,
> Showing an outward pity, yet you Pilates
> Have here delivered me to my sour cross,
> And water cannot wash away your sin.

(4.1.227, 229–32)

His counter-performance evokes elements of traditional lament, as
when Richard pleads that he cannot read the incriminating articles
because his 'eyes are full of tears; I cannot see' (234) and, despite his
own consent to 'undeck the pompous body of a king' (240), keeps
harping on the erasure of his title and name, leaving him only as a
'mockery king' (250). This expression recalls the cruel jokes played
with Christ at the crucifixion, when he was mocked as the King of
Judea, and establishes an alternative image of Richard as martyr
against that on record in the official indictment.

---

[24] Liebler, 'The mockery king of snow: *Richard II* and the sacrifice of ritual',
      p. 231, original emphasis.

Part of this struggle over the validity of images is, perhaps unsurprisingly, an act of iconoclasm. Pressed by Northumberland to read out his 'grievous crimes' (214), Richard calls for a mirror and substitutes his own face as the truthful record of his sins:

> I'll read enough
> When I do see the very book indeed
> Where all my sins are writ, and that's my self.
> *Enter one with a glass.*
> Give me that glass and therein will I read.

(4.1.263–5)

Richard interprets his mirror image not as a guilty countenance but as the 'flattering' (268) portrait of a youthful prince beguiled by the 'brittle glory' (277) of splendour, of admiration and prosperity. This image, while more favourable than the one Northumberland holds up, is not how Richard wishes to be remembered either, and he goes on to demolish it, rhetorically as well as materially. Similar to Richard's previous separation of his person from 'the name of king' (3.3.145), he calls into question whether this mirror image really represents him. A series of rhetorical questions beginning with 'Was this the face ...?' (4.1.271, 273, 275) culminates in a word-play on the meanings of 'face' that obliterates any clear reference between image, person and word:

> Is this the face which faced so many follies,
> That was at last outfaced by Bolingbroke?
> A brittle glory shineth in this face,
> As brittle as the glory is the face.

(4.1.275–8)

The verb formation 'to face' opens up a dizzying plurality of meanings. One points to Richard's habitual countenancing of all kinds of follies during his reign, and in the particular sense of 'to put a new face on sth (as in a cloth facing)', it recalls York's harangue on novel fashions that distract Richard from his duties (2.1.284).[25] This behaviour is now 'outfaced' by Bolingbroke, in the sense of 'silenced or defeated' or 'defied, confronted fearlessly' – or, with an ironic twist,

---

[25] See note to line 2.1.284 in *Richard II*, ed. by Andrew Gurr. The New Cambridge Shakespeare, p. 158.

in the sense of 'outdone, brazened out', implying that Bolingbroke's 'follies' will prove as costly for the realm as his own.[26] Finally, the meaning of 'face' oscillates between the visage, metonymically standing for the person; the representation of the person in the mirror; and the surface, or outward appearance, which is all to which glory, and a 'brittle glory' at that, can amount. The erasure of stable reference is enhanced by the close syntactic parallelism amounting to almost identical repetition. The overall effect is to rhetorically efface the face, or image, of Richard that his enemies would like to monumentalise in legal documents.

Richard completes this rhetorical obliteration with the material destruction of the mirror. This act of iconoclasm, I would argue, is not so much directed against images per se as against an unfavourable one that represents him as a criminal or foolish king. When he symbolically destroys this image and sets up another one in its place, that of 'a rightful king' (5.1.50) deposed and a Christ-like martyr, iconoclasm does not function to stop image-making and ceremony. On the contrary, it is an important part of the ritualised process of remaking them with a political difference, thereby shaping the semiotic and hence also the mnemonic economy of Elizabethan culture. In this respect, iconoclasm does indeed function as a rite of oblivion, but not in the destructive, anti-ceremonial sense Eamon Duffy seems to have had in mind when he called iconoclasm the 'central sacrament of the reform'.[27]

Images, just like coins, gain currency only through circulation. Richard's vehicle for circulating his image as martyr-saint is again ritual lament. In the very next scene, which enacts Richard's tearful parting from his wife, he enjoins his Queen to take his story back with her to France and to spread it there according to the traditional poetics of lament:

> In winter's tedious nights, sit by the fire
> With good old folks, and let them tell thee tales
> Of woeful ages long ago betid,

---

[26] The OED cites 'to outface' as = 1. a. To disconcert, silence, or defeat (a person) by face-to-face confrontation or a display of confidence, arrogance, etc.; to stare down; 2. To face boldly or defiantly, to confront fearlessly or shamelessly; to brave, defy, stand up to; 3. a. To maintain (something false or shameful) with boldness or effrontery; to brazen out.

[27] Duffy, *The Stripping of the Altars*, p. 480.

And ere thou bid good night, to quit their griefs,
Tell thou the lamentable tale of me
And send the hearers weeping to their beds ...
For the deposing of a rightful king.

(5.1.40–50)

The ritual of mourning creates a community of grievers who sit together, relating their losses, weeping and sympathising with each other. Interestingly, this community is emphatically different from Richard's audience in the previous scene. Where before the members of Parliament, led by Northumberland and Bolingbroke, sought to implement an official, negative memory of his reign, Richard now imagines a non-elite group of sympathetic listeners for his lamentable tale. Anticipating his being mourned and remembered as a martyr by 'good old folks', he turns his story into folklore, his history into myth. The way he achieves this transformation is through ritual lament as a tool of deleting one image and creating another.

While geographic and temporal distance can support the myth-making politics of lament, they also work at home, as the final scene of the play suggests. Bolingbroke – now King Henry IV – has just received the news of Richard's murder, condoned if not explicitly commanded by the new ruler. Henry rejects responsibility for the heinous act of regicide, along with the interpretation of Richard as a criminal king, which he had so staunchly supported before. Instead, he adopts the image of Richard as a Christ-like figure as well as Richard's chosen conduit of ritual lament:

Come mourn with me for what I do lament,
And put on sullen black incontinent.
I'll make a voyage to the Holy Land,
To wash this blood off from my guilty hand.

(5.6.47–50)

In accepting Richard's mythical self-image, Henry accordingly views himself as a treacherous Pilate. Despite his factual lack of authority since the deposition, Richard has succeeded in effacing the official memory of his reign, recorded in legal documents. Graham Holderness aptly comments that in this play at least, 'history is not written by the victors, but unforgettably formulated by the dispossessed, in a poignant poetry of defeat and inconsolable loss [so that] the myth of the deposed king will live far longer than the practical achievements of his enemies'.[28] As Manfred Pfister has observed about the history plays in general, each staging becomes a ritual commemoration of the historical characters which increasingly sacralises them as mythical figures.[29] This process of mythologising history is staged by Richard's transformation from historical king into mythical saint. The erasure of unwanted memories necessary for this is enacted not though disrupting commemorative complaint but, on the contrary, through employing it.

These scenes engage with the post-Reformation conflict about ceremony and spectacle in an ambivalent way. On the one hand, Richard's reliance on ritual lament in order to create a memorable image of himself suggests not only that ritual remained an actively powerful force in post-Reformation England, but also that the Reformation itself, instead of abolishing ceremony and images, appropriated them for its own purposes. Gordon McMullan cautions that '[w]e tend to think of early modern reformers as iconoclasts *par excellence*, yet the protagonists of reform knew an effective ideological weapon when they saw one, and despite their reputation as enemies of the visual image, they often preferred to reform, rather than eradicate, Catholic iconography.'[30] *Richard II*, I would argue, stages the appropriative politics behind ceremonial commemoration as well as the reforming properties pertaining to it that were at work in Elizabethan culture.

More specifically, the figure of Richard could be read as a comment on Elizabeth's use of ritual to fashion and circulate her own image. The topical link between Richard and Elizabeth, unforgettably forged by herself in a remark to the royal antiquary William Lambarde, has often been explored in the political context of rebellion and usurpation.[31] It is seldom if ever examined in regard to their use of ceremony and their shared skill in image-making: just as Richard turns himself into a Christ-like figure, mythologising himself in the process, Elizabeth turned herself into the Virgin Queen by appropriating the Catholic cult of the Virgin Mary

---

[28] Holderness, *Shakespeare: The Histories*, p. 196.

[29] Pfister, 'Shakespeare's memory', p. 235.

[30] McMullan, 'Introduction', pp. 67–8.

[31] For a detailed account of the analogies that contemporaries drew between Elizabeth and Richard II in the context of the Essex rebellion, see Fitter, 'Historicising Shakespeare's *Richard II*'; and Hammer, 'Shakespeare's *Richard II*, the play of 7 February 1601, and the Essex Rising'.

and effectively turning the forms of ritual to her own advantage.[32] From this perspective, the usual valences of iconoclasm are altered: iconoclasm is not necessarily opposed to image-making and its circulation through ceremony, but rather becomes part of this process itself.

On the other hand, the act of iconoclasm also gestures toward a certain antitheatrical scepticism that is voiced most prominently in the play by Bolingbroke. Commenting on Richard's spectacular iconoclastic gesture, he points out that Richard's complaint exaggerates his actual cause for grief: 'The shadow of your sorrow hath destroyed / The shadow of your face' (4.1.282–3), he remarks, thereby dismissing Richard's lament as precisely what it is, a performance. Richard sarcastically thanks him for not only giving him 'cause to wail but teach[ing him] the way / How to lament the cause' (290–1). This struggle over the right manner of lament reveals that it is precisely the *manner*, the performance of grief that determines how its cause will be remembered. Likewise, the Abbot of Westminster highlights the histrionic character of the pivotal scene and thereby introduces, albeit unwittingly, an ironic distance to the sacred spectacle: 'A woeful pageant have we here beheld' (311).

This irony, which could be more or less pronounced in performance, also inflects how we read the final words of the play. While we could take Henry's evocation of traditional mourning rites to indicate that his acts as king are subjected to the rule of Richard's poetics of lament, we should be alert to the possibility that he might also employ it to his own political ends. 'Bolingbroke's general invitation to participate in the official rites of collective mourning', noted by John Joughin,[33] goes hand in hand with an attempt at erasing the memory of his own guilt in Richard's murder: he imaginatively washes Richard's blood off his hands and projects a pilgrimage to the Holy Land as a rite of atonement that is to wash his sin from the heavenly book as well (5.6.49–50). That this pilgrimage also serves to distract his nobles' heads from the possibility of rebellion and thereby

---

[32] An example of this is a verse register that commemorates the English Protestant martyrs who had died under her sister's reign; the last line of each stanza invokes Queen Elizabeth's name in the vein of a patron saint. This register of martyrs aims at conditioning and constructing social memory in Protestant England, yet in doing so, it appropriates old Catholic rituals (Döring, *Performances of Mourning*, pp. 58–9).

[33] Joughin, 'Shakespeare's memorial aesthetics', p. 60.

to secure his rule highlights Henry's political use of lament in retrospect. From this perspective the ritual commemoration and rhetoric of lament Bolingbroke invokes become suspect. While the King commands his nobles to display immediately all the 'external manners of lament' (4.1.286) that Richard had dismissed as outward show, such as dressing in 'sullen black' mourning garb and marching 'weeping after this untimely bier', and twice emphasises the sincerity of his sorrow ('I protest my soul is full of woe ... / Come mourn with me for what I do lament', 5.6.45–7), the attentive audience, alerted by now to the theatricality of ceremony, may well have called his sincerity into doubt: the lord protests too much. The 'monumental overkill'[34] of Henry's final lament is thus informed by a dynamic of remembering and forgetting, as it erects a rhetorical monument to the memory of King Richard in the obscure shadow of which he can more securely carry out his own political plans. Viewed, moreover, as an ironic quotation of Richard's ritual lament this moment serves to demystify the workings of image-making and commemorative ceremony even while it proclaims the continuing power of spectacle, in the theatre as well as in religion and politics.

If indeed 'complaint is problematic because stagey before it is staged', as John Kerrigan maintains,[35] the lamentations of this final scene serve to problematise the status of religious ritual after the Reformation by drawing attention to its political uses as well as its theatrical character. In this sense, the end of the play stages the changed ontological and epistemological status of reformed ritual under the Elizabethan settlement. It depicts a symbolic world whose signs and practices, while dismantled and displaced onto other cultural sites, continue to exert their mnemonic power. At the same time, it displays a heightened awareness of the cultural forces at work in forming and deforming memory. Add to this the spectacular nature of grief and its ritualised expressions, and the scenes of commemoration become a vehicle of metadramatic reflection about the theatre's role in the process of making cultural memory.

Whereas in *Richard II* traditional lament mainly serves as a vehicle for the erasure of Richard's kingship, in the following play the rites of

---

[34] *Ibid.*, p. 60. [35] Kerrigan, *Motives of Woe*, p. 56.

commemoration become rites of oblivion proper. I will concentrate on key scenes toward the end of *Henry IV, Part One* which explore the memory politics of ritual lament most explicitly. We see Prince Hal on the battlefield of Shrewsbury, standing over the dead body of the rebel Harry Hotspur and delivering the following speech in remembrance of his rival and namesake:

> Fare thee well, great heart.
> ... This earth that bears thee dead
> Bears not alive so stout a gentleman.
> If thou wert sensible of courtesy,
> I should not make so dear a show of zeal;
> But let my favours hide thy mangled face,
>   [*He covers Hotspur's face*]
> And even in thy behalf I'll thank myself
> For doing these fair rites of tenderness.
> Adieu, and take thy praise with thee to heaven.
> Thy ignominy sleep with thee in the grave,
> But not remember'd in thy epitaph.

(5.4.86–100)

This speech functions as a ritual act of remembrance for the dead: Prince Hal calls on the ghost of Hotspur, acknowledges his enemy's heroic status and leaves his own heraldic insignia, the 'favours' on his gloves or helmet, as a token of his respect. By calling his obsequies 'so dear a *show* of zeal', however, Hal's speech also alerts us to the fact that internal grief and its ritual expressions may well diverge. It moreover raises the possibility that this act of memory might perform quite a different mnemonic gesture: covering Hotspur's face with the Lancastrian colours serves to commemorate the victor's identity rather than that of the deceased. Rather than speaking on behalf of Hotspur's memory, Hal's speech manipulates that memory in his own favour, for what Hotspur might have found memorable about his life and death is explicitly 'not remembered in [his] epitaph': his rebellion against a usurping king, carried out in the name of honour. But if Hal's aim is to erase the rebellion that Hotspur stands for, why does he not simply leave the dead body unidentified, allowing it to sink into the grave of oblivion among the anonymous mass of bodies on the battlefield? A possible answer, one that would be entirely in keeping with the historical Lancastrians' policy of actively re-scripting the past,[36] is that leaving Hotspur's corpse behind would open up the possibility of an alternative construal of this figure and his life which might harm the ruling dynasty: Harry Hotspur as martyr. Remembering Hotspur as a noble hero who loyally served his king, by contrast, supports the Lancastrian claim to the throne. Instead of leaving behind a semiotic vacuum, the Prince, through performing the commemorative rite of the funeral speech, claims for himself the interpretative authority over history. Just as Prince Hal's glove conceals his opponent's mangled face, his speech covers the story rebellious Hotspur could have told.[37]

In the play-world, then, a rite of remembrance has become a powerful rite of oblivion working in favour of the Prince's memory politics. In the playhouse, this appropriation of ritual commemoration by politics would have spoken forcefully to an audience who lived during the aftermath of the profound transformation of commemorative culture in post-Reformation England. Harry's obsequies on Shrewsbury field do more, however, than simply remind the audience of rites now lost to them. By employing a ritualised form of commemoration in order to effect an erasure and reinscription of memory, this speech also recalls the practices of the reformers concerning ritual: the Protestant Reformation, rather than oppressing ritual categorically, aimed at transforming its structures and meanings.[38] In fact, the Reformation itself can be understood in terms of ritual procedure, as Edward Muir points out: 'Even as it promoted scriptural reading, lucid preaching, and spiritual understanding, the Protestant Reformation was itself a ritual movement that employed traditional ceremonies in new ways and introduced new ceremonies to demarcate differences among

---

[36] Paul Strohm's brilliant study discusses the textual and mnemonic politics of Lancastrian historical records. These were informed by a strategic forgetfulness to such an extent, he argues, that they are 'amnesiac texts'. Based on his analysis of these texts, he concludes that 'Henry and his sons were committed from the outset to a program of official forgetfulness: a forgetfulness embracing their own dynastic origins, their predecessor's fate, the promises and opportunistic alliances which had gained them a throne.' (*England's Empty Throne*, p. 196).

[37] Christopher Ivic discusses this speech, too, but reads it in the secular context of the Wars of Roses as national trauma ('Reassuring fratricide in *1 Henry IV*', p. 106).

[38] Marshall, *Beliefs and the Dead in Reformation England*, p. 306.

various religious groups.' The reformation of ritual was conducted not so much through doctrinal theory, which indeed did insist on eradicating all traces of purgatory and intercessory prayer, but in the field of popular practice, and it often took a ritualised form:

> ... there were protests that occurred within the frame of the liturgical calendar, such as the singing of 'scurrilous songs' during mass on a solemn feast day; disruptions of Catholic rites by an apparently anti-ritual action, such as throwing the baptismal font from the roof of the church to prevent infant baptism; there were parodies of Catholic rites that created a carnivalesque counter-liturgy, such as the mock administration of last rites to a man who play-acted sickness; and there were iconoclastic acts that took place within a ritual context, such as the damaging of an image of a saint on his or her feast day.[39]

In each case, the systematic evacuation of ritual practices is not merely destructive; rather, new rites are employed as a means of undoing previous ones by filling the old ceremonial structures with new meaning or by developing alternative ones. Prince Harry's epitaph for Hotspur provides one example of how a commemorative rite can be used to discard a specific memory and install a new counter-memory in its stead.

The scene does not end here, however, and neither does its interrogation of the oblivional uses of commemorative ritual on the post-Reformation stage. Prince Harry finds another body nearby, that of his old friend Sir John Falstaff. He devotes a spoken obituary to him as well, but again the effect of this ritual act is undercut in an interesting way.

> What, old acquaintance! Could not all this flesh
> Keep in a little life? Poor Jack, farewell.
> I could have better spared a better man.
> O, I should have a heavy miss of thee,
> If I were much in love with vanity.
> Death hath not struck so fat a deer today,
> Though many a dearer in this bloody fray.
> Embowelled will I see thee by and by.
> Till then, in blood by noble Percy lie.

> (5.4.101–9)

---

[39] Muir, *Ritual in Early Modern Europe*, pp. 181, 186–7.

This farewell speech, too, follows the conventions of ritual mourning, though in a notably lighter register. Again we hear an apostrophe to the deceased through which the mourner identifies both the dead man and his own relation to him. Again we hear the merits of the deceased, which cause his loss to be mourned: 'I could have better spared a better man. / O, I should have a heavy miss of thee'. We even hear echoes of the first epitaph when Hal laments the contrast between the men in life and death: Hotspur's 'body did contain a spirit' which was larger than life but now is confined in 'two paces of the vilest earth', while 'all this flesh' of the fat knight cannot 'keep in a little life'. The exchange of pathos for bathos is the central difference between the two speeches: Hotspur is remembered for his 'great heart'; Falstaff for his great stomach. Hotspur's courage is evoked in the phrase 'stout gentleman'; Falstaff, too, is stout, but rather as a 'fat ... deer' is. And while Hotspur's face and story are hidden under the victor's 'favours', Falstaff's body is to be 'embowelled' like a hunted prey and a trophy for Henry's victory over his own 'vanity'. The epitaph for Falstaff is clearly a parody of that for Hotspur, and in this sense the scene illustrates one of the cultural techniques of transforming ritual through ritual identified by Muir as available in post-Reformation England.

In another sense, however, the epitaph for Falstaff is much more appropriate in that it not only recalls the fat knight's love of food, but also re-enacts his equally characteristic love of jesting through the use of puns and quibbles. In this second sense, Hal's rather ironic address is well suited to confer the power of speech on the deceased man, to raise his disrespectful spirit. In a markedly different way than in the farewell speech for Hotspur, the epitaph for Falstaff thus testifies to the continuing mnemonic power of ritual performance. Moreover, it demonstrates the powers of theatrical performance, strategically employed by Hal but embodied most fully by Falstaff. For when the Prince leaves the stage after his obsequies, Falstaff 'rises up as if responding to the language of prosopopoeia with a literal force that gives him back his face and voice', Tobias Döring points out.[40] Indignantly rejecting the planned embowelling, Falstaff launches into praise of an act of counterfeiting that saved his life, indeed that comes to stand for life, for 'to counterfeit dying, when a man thereby liveth, is to be no counterfeit, but the true and perfect image of life indeed' (5.4.115–16). As a 'true

---

[40] Döring, 'Shadows to the unseen grief?', p. 8.

and perfect image of life', Falstaff emphatically functions as a figure for the theatre. His resurrection from a pretended state of death provides a metatheatrical comment by staging the contemporary view of the theatre's mnemonic role. And it is precisely in this sense that the theatre's central trope is indeed that of prosopopoeia, of conferring a face and voice onto dead ancestors who could not otherwise be reached after the Protestant abolition of intercessory prayer. Such a view of the stage as a site for salvaging the memory of pre-Reformation rites, however, reduces the theatre to a medium of memory only. The mnemonic manipulations Prince Harry effects through the very use of ritual and rhetoric, as well as Falstaff's own counterfeiting, suggest an additional function, however: severed from the sacred realm that stabilised their mnemonic efficacy and meaningfulness, the performance of commemorative rites on the stage explores in addition their oblivional potential, and through parody divests ritual of its sacred authority.

In particular Falstaff's famous catechism on honour demonstrates the use of ritual in order to discard traditional meanings. When Falstaff is challenged by Prince Hal in the battle of Shrewsbury that he owes God a death and should therefore be less concerned about his personal welfare than his honour in the upcoming fight, Falstaff wittily interrogates the status of honour as a value in itself and dismisses it as useless in the real world:

'Tis not due yet – I would be loath to pay him before his day. What need I be so forward with him that calls not on me? Well, 'tis no matter, honour pricks me on. Yea, but how if honour prick me off when I come on, how then? Can honour set to a leg? No. Or an arm? No. Or take away the grief of a wound? No. Or an arm? Honour hath no skill in surgery then? No. What is honour? A word. What is in that word honour? What is that honour? Air. A trim reckoning! Who hath it? He that died o' Wednesday. Doth he feel it? No. Doth he hear it? No. 'Tis insensible, then? Yea, to the dead. But will it not live with the living? No. Why? Detraction will not suffer it. Therefore I'll have none of it. Honour is a mere scutcheon – and so ends my catechism. (5.1.127–38)

The rhetorical form of this speech parodies not a Catholic, but a Protestant ritual form, the catechism, a set of questions and answers learned by heart as a method of religious-moral instruction as well as a mnemonic device. The mnemonic ritual is appropriated here and turned to quite a different use: it serves not to remember and validate the aspects of honour, but rather to void the concept of 'honour' of all meaning. For Falstaff, words like honour are mere 'air' and 'trim reckonings', as his catechism makes abundantly clear. The quasi-ritual repetition effects a semantic evacuation of this category that allows him to set up 'life' as an alternative value. What is discarded in the process is the memory of a chivalric code of honour and courage that structured the relationship between the individual and the sovereign and affirmed their identities in terms of a social hierarchy.

Declaring these traditional concepts and their rites null and void does not, however, amount to discarding them altogether. Rather, parody allows Falstaff to put them to his own use. After Hal has left the stage, having delivered his two epitaphs to foe and friend respectively, Falstaff rises from the dead and, seeing the body of Hotspur on the ground, seizes on it with the intention of presenting it as false evidence of his own courage:

> There is Percy!
> [*He lays the body on the ground.*]
> If your father will do me any honour, so.
> If not, let him kill the next Percy himself.
>
> (5.4.134–6)

His reinterpretation of the immediate past and his willingness to appropriate a corpse for his manipulation of memory mimics Prince Hal's previous act of manipulative commemoration. In so doing, he asserts the efficacy of Lancastrian memory politics and simultaneously repudiates it through parody. In the play-world, the disruptive energy of this ironic dismantling is contained by the fact that Prince Hal himself later validates this new version as the truth (5.4.150–1), thus asserting his royal control over memory. To the attentive observer in the playhouse, Falstaff's parody might, however, self-reflexively expose the history play's own dramatic re-scripting of the past. For what we see on stage in Falstaff's performances of ritual is not a faithful representation of history but a much more complex 'image of past life' resulting from the interplay of remembering and forgetting. (The next chapter will examine in greater detail the mnemonic pattern of erasure, recall and substitution that produced and is produced by the figure of Falstaff.) Moreover, just as Falstaff's resurrection provides a comic relief after the scenes of violent death and loss, the resurrection of traditional modes of grieving in a transformed and theatricalised shape may well have provided a similar relief in that they are publicly acknowledged and, at the same time, publicly abandoned on stage. Instead of affirming the ongoing mnemonic relevance of signs, practices and rituals after the Reformation, scenes like the one discussed here would seem to evacuate and eliminate them. In this sense, Prince Hal and, to a greater extent, Falstaff, as a metatheatrical figure, can be seen to stand for the ways in which the early modern theatre performed not only rites of memory, but also rites of oblivion.

3 | *Embodiment: Falstaff's 'shameless transformations' in* Henry IV

For early modern antitheatrical writers, the public theatre's 'wooden O' seems to have stood, above all, for oblivion. Many sermons and tracts forcefully expressed the view that play-going was a sinful activity that induced forgetfulness of one's duties toward God and, by extension, toward one's sovereign and one's family. The Puritan preacher William Rankins, for example, wrote a tract against the evil of theatre, in which he claims that 'Playes make them forgette GOD'. This explicit warning, set off as a marginal gloss, spells out the simple message of an elaborate imagery employed in the main text that likens the sinful state of stage-induced oblivion to the effects of gluttony and inebriation: going to the theatre is like 'drinking of the wyne of forget-fulness'. The effects of this 'wyne of forgetfulness' are in turn couched in the language of play-acting: it 'tempered theyr tongues, and out-ward gesture with such talke, that theyr action might be uniforme to the rareness of theyr banquette', consisting of a 'diuersitie of [daintie] dyshes'. It remains unclear whether the personal pronoun refers to the players or the guests of this 'banquet in the Hall of misery', who watch the play as they glut themselves. This referential ambivalence also blurs the distinction between play-acting and eating: both are equally sinful in that they induce bodily and spiritual lethargy. Drinking the wine of forgetfulness here coincides with the actors' own practice of giving feigned speeches (in Rankins's view, speeches that make one for-get the truth) which are supported by trained 'outward gesture[s]' so that they render 'theyr action' as pleasurable and diverting as the ban-quet to which their play is likened. Shifting the imagery slightly from human-made wine and entertainment to their devilish origin, Rankins goes on to assert that play-going is a form of idleness invented by Satan himself, '[who] called forth Idlenes, from his boyling Caldron of insatiate liquor'. What is so dangerous about this liquor is that it tastes 'more sweete then *Nectar*, and farre more pleasant then *Manna* from Heaven', so that the addiction to this infernal beverage is immediate.

Moreover, it spreads like a contagious disease: 'But the infection of this vice [Idleness] is so contagious, that as the River Laethes maketh hym that drynketh thereof presentlie to forget his own condition & former deedes, so this damnable vice of idlenes, so besotteth the sences, and bewitcheth the myndes of menne, as they remembred not the profitable fruites of virtuous labour.'[1]. Idleness is figured as an illness here, a simile which indicates that forgetting was understood as a somatic rather than a purely cognitive process in the early modern period. This is underlined by Rankins's invocation of Lethe, the mythical river of forgetfulness in the underworld, which was habitually cited as the etymological root of lethargy, a pathological state of oblivion. '*Litargi* ... is a postume bread in the hinder cell of the head', a contemporary physiological treatise explains, adding that it 'hath that name *Litargia* of *Lethos*, that is forgetting, for it induceth forgetting'.[2]

As Garrett A. Sullivan Jr. has shown, lethargy as a disordered state of the body as well as of the soul was habitually linked to immoderate eating and drinking in early modern medical discourse. From there, the physiological vocabulary found its way into moral-religious attacks like Rankins's that regarded theatre-going as a sin next to gluttony and inebriation.[3] In a wide range of antitheatrical writings, food metaphors served to denounce the practices and effects of the early modern stage in terms of a dangerous, pathological, sinful forgetfulness. The use of this imagery is seldom rhetorically foregrounded or commented upon: antitheatrical writers routinely draw on it almost automatically as an obvious way of thinking about their topic.[4] It can be traced back as far as the early fifteenth-century Lollard piece *A Treatise of Miraclis Pleyinge*, and gained currency in the late sixteenth century when the public theatres opened and antitheatrical sentiment sprang up, especially among Puritans but also among other writers of the time. Stephen Gosson, for example, denounced poetry in general and the popular stage in particular by comparing them to the base pleasures of eating: 'I may well liken *Homer* to *Mithecus*, & Poets to Cookes the pleasures of the one winnes the body from labor, & conquereth the sense; the allurement or the other drawes

---

[1] Rankins, *Mirrour of Monsters*, pp. 7, 8, 24.
[2] Batman, *Batman Uppon Bartholome*, sig. 89r.
[3] See Sullivan, *Memory and Forgetting in English Renaissance Drama*, ch. 1.
[4] Lopez, *Theatrical Convention*, p. 27.

the minde from vertue, and confoundeth wit.'[5] The parallel structure
of this statement renders the evil effects of food and theatrical entertainment almost identical: they distract both body and mind from
their duties and subject them to a state of lethargic stupor. If in the
end play-going is more pernicious because it endangers the immortal
soul, even this admonition is couched in physiological terms of inges-
tion: 'those wanton spectacles ... will hurt them more, then if at the
Epicures table, they had nigh burst their guts with ouer feeding. For if
the bodie bee ouercharged, it may be holpe; but the surfite of the soule
is hardly cured.'[6] The *Refutation of the Apologie for Actors*, a response
to Thomas Heywood's earlier defence of the theatre, sees not human
pots and pens but the Devil himself as the source of such pernicious
food: '[Whether plays] be divine or prophane, they are quite contrary
to the word of grace, and sucked out of the Diuil's teates to nourish vs
in Idolatry, heathenry, and sinne.'[7] Here the idleness of play-watching
results not only in an illness of body and mind but amounts to an
act of idolatry, a charge that was based in Puritanical iconophobia.
Explicitly placing the theatre's business of idolatrous image-making
in opposition to the true word of God, the *Refutation* also affords
us a glimpse of the intense rivalry between theatre and pulpit for the
attention of the London audience, which might well account for the
vehemence of the Puritans' attacks.[8]

   Making one forget one's familial and professional duties as well as
one's duties toward God, play-going was seen as a threat to the individual's physical and spiritual health. In medical discourse, the lethargic body rendered visible an inward humoral disposition, thrown out
of balance by overmuch eating and drinking. In a similar vein did the
image of the forgetful body provide the antitheatrical discourse with
a vehicle for articulating the evil effects of stage plays on the cognitive
and moral disposition of theatre-goers. Taken as the external, visible
sign of an inward, hidden self, the language of forgetfulness provided a
vocabulary which helped to probe and to produce that self in the first
place. While lethargy usually was described as a loss of control over

[5] Gosson, *School of Abuse*, p. 79.
[6] *Ibid.*, p. 87.
[7] I. G., *Refutation*, p. 55.
[8] On the material interests of the competition between pulpit and stage
   underpinning these moral invectives see Bruster, *Drama and the Market in the
   Age of Shakespeare*, pp. 2–3.

body and mind and thus in terms of an absence of subjectivity and
agency, much of the invective it attracted, especially in moral-religious
tracts, seems to stem from the fact that lethargy rather enabled a different subjectivity, as Sullivan points out. If self-forgetfulness was
regarded, above all, as a mode of resistance to normative models of
selfhood, it also opened up a space in which alternative, non-normative
practices and modes of being could be imagined: forgetting the self as
a means of forging a self.[9]

   This imaginative space coincided with the material space of the
theatre. One reason for this is the cultural position of the public stage
in early modern society. I agree with Anthony B. Dawson and Paul
Yachnin, who reject the influential new historicist view of the theatre's
marginality and its exclusively oppositional stance to Elizabethan
society's dominant discourses as reductive.[10] They argue that the
polarised model of the theatre as a carnivalesque 'anti-structure'
that disrupts 'official' or 'ceremonial' culture obscures its relation to
central social institutions and cultural issues. Instead, they see 'the
theater as a kind of way-station, a place where different cultural ave-
nues cross'.[11] A kind of discursive marketplace, this location at the
intersections of various elements of culture accounts for the range
of issues negotiated on stage as well as for the cultural relevance
of these negotiations for quite heterogeneous audiences.[12] Dawson
and Yachnin suggest that we should understand the theatre's position
'not in terms of a relatively static margin–center model, but rather
in terms of a process that encourages the participation of actor and
spectator for diverse and contradictory purposes'.[13] This does not
mean that the stage cannot speak to or from liminal positions as well

---

[9] Sullivan, *Memory and Forgetting*, pp. 12–13, 20–1.
[10] Such a view is put forward, for example, in Steven Mullaney's study *The Place of the Stage: License, Power and Play in Renaissance England* (1988).
[11] Dawson and Yachnin, *The Culture of Playgoing*, p. 5.
[12] In a similar attempt at resituating the public theatres, Douglas Bruster goes a step further when he claims that they were actual marketplaces, 'both responsive and responsible to the desires of their playgoing publics, and were potentially no more marginal a part of London than their publics demanded. Places of business, they regularized and normalized carnival ... – and, as a business, [they were] part of a complex of centralizing institutions. This need not imply that the playhouses were without a social vision. Their market function, however, necessarily mediated, even directed that vision.' (*Drama and the Market in the Age of Shakespeare*, p. 10).
[13] Dawson and Yachnin, *The Culture of Playgoing*, p. 6.

as from the centre; it means foregrounding the interplay between margin and centre that undoes the very binarism on which the polarity is based.

This 'ambiguous centrality' entails that the oppositional stance ascribed to the stage in antitheatrical tracts (and, for that matter, new historicist accounts) needs to be questioned. Instead, the image of bodily or spiritual lethargy, which opponents of the stage seized on to demonise and marginalise the theatre, should itself be explored as a nodal point at which various discourses and concerns about individual and collective selfhood intersect. What is at stake in the attacks on stage-induced forgetfulness in antitheatrical discourse is the proper relation of the subject to its place in a divinely ordered society. Both the detractors and, to a lesser extent, the defenders of the theatre use images of the human body to articulate the impact which play-going has on these relations, and both connect this imagery with the language of forgetting and remembering. For the one side, the forgetful body in the theatre materialises the disruption of those bonds of duty, obedience and discipline that hold together the social network. For the other, it functions as a mnemonic device that binds together the collective body of the nation.[14] In the debate about the role of the theatre, material as well as metaphorical bodies – those of actors and spectators, the individual and the social body – loom large. This raises the question of how the stage itself intervened in this debate. Interestingly, early modern plays only rarely took up the arguments, vocabulary and imagery of their defenders (which, in any case, are few and far between). They rather tended to stage the topoi of antitheatrical outrage, and in so doing upstaged them. Stephen Orgel comments: 'One of the most striking characteristics of the Elizabethan and Stuart stage is the degree to which its playwrights seem to share, and even to make

---

[14] Interestingly, defenders of the stage such as Thomas Nashe and, a generation later, Thomas Heywood carefully avoided taking up the image of the lethargic body; instead, they employ a rhetoric of spiritual and bodily renewal through commemoration in the theatre. For Nashe, theatrical performance offers a moment of quasi-religious communion when the audience drinks up the blood of a Christ-like Talbot with their eyes and in turn embalms his wounds with their compassionate tears in commemoration of his heroic deeds (*Pierce Pennilesse*, pp. 86–7). Heywood likewise claims that 'so bewitching a thing is lively and well spirited action, that it hath power to new mold the hearts of the spectators and fashion them to the shape of any noble and notable attempt' (*Apology for Actors*, p. 487).

dramatic capital out of, the prejudicial assumptions of their most hostile critics.'[15] Generally speaking, ideal figures make for poor dramatic characters, and the action on stage rarely focuses on emblems of perfection. Accordingly, it is the forgetful body and the deviant lethargic subject, rather than the obediently remembering subject, which mainly appear on the stage, and forgetfulness, I would argue, becomes a sign which puts various modes of being into play, on the stage as well as between stage and audience.

Moreover, the issues of subjectivity, memory and forgetfulness were central to the project and practice of the early modern theatre as such. Elizabethan and Jacobean drama circles around questions of identity: dramatic plots are driven by challenges posed to a stable sense of the self, they explore the limits of identity and produce alternative modes of being. In Linda Charnes's helpful definition of dramatic subjectivity, plays are about 'the subject's *experience* of his or her relationship to his or her "identity"'.[16] Drama offers insights into subjectivity by staging a person's experience of his or her socially prescribed identity. This relationship becomes matter for the stage when it is fraught, under pressure, problematic – in short, when there is an 'identity crisis' to be staged. This crisis may take the form of a tension between interiority and exteriority, between inwardness and the body, or indeed between remembering and forgetting.[17] What should be noted here is that crisis does not simply mark the imminent end of whatever is deemed to be in crisis. Crisis is in fact a productive mode in that it opens up a space for reimagining and reconceptualising notions of the self. Accordingly, forgetting the self does not so much spell a loss of identity, but rather provides an opportunity for experimenting with alternative forms of selfhood outside of the parameters and dictates of socially acceptable behaviour which are habitually seen as being upheld by acts of remembering.

Jean-Christophe Agnew has described the theatre's function in similar terms of experimentation and novelty. He sees the stage as 'a laboratory of and for the new social relations of agricultural and commercial capitalism'.[18] In this perspective, the marketplace provided

---

[15] Orgel, 'The play of conscience', pp. 148–9.

[16] Charnes, *Notorious Identity*, p. 8.

[17] For these constellations, see Maus, *Inwardness and Theater in the English Renaissance*; Schoenfeldt, *Bodies and Selves in Early Modern England*; and Sullivan, *Memory and Forgetting in English Renaissance Drama* respectively.

[18] Agnew, *Worlds Apart: The Market and the Theater*, p. 11.

the theatre with a pattern of metaphors 'that equates human relations with economic transactions, and at its base is an experimentation with new ways of finding identity and defining human value in the context of a quickly developing social-exchange mentality'.[19] Exploring the impact that the marketplace had on social relationships, the theatre in turn offers that knowledge along with new models of subjectivity and intersubjectivity as a commodity. Thus, it can itself be seen as a marketplace in which new forms of relationships and modes of being were produced and sold as commodities. This is evident already in early modern attacks on as well as defences of the theatre, which frequently characterised the playhouses also in terms of commerce. Against the Puritan contempt for the profane nature of market and theatre alike, Thomas Dekker for example sympathetically describes the latter in terms of the former in *The Gull's Horn-Book* (1609): 'The theatre is your poets' Royal Exchange, upon which their Muses – that are now turned merchants – meeting, barter away that light commodity of words for a lighter ware than words', namely the applause and, by implication, the money of the audience.[20] The stage's 'commodity of words' would have entailed such insubstantial things as the essentially language-centred performance of dramatic action, or the witty dialogues and elaborate soliloquies of characters, which drew a paying audience to the public playhouses. The public theatres were a veritable marketplace for such commodity and had a 'financial stake in exploring and selling novel (as well as familiar) models of selfhood to its audience', some of which were produced through acts of self-forgetting.[21]

The language of commerce thus offered an additional set of tropes through which subjectivity as a theatrical commodity was produced and represented. Rather than being a limiting case of dramatic representation, the forgetful or lethargic subject lies at the heart of this theatrical enterprise: forgetting is the precondition for producing new modes of being which then become theatrical commodities. Because forgetting is bound up with the theatre's conditions and practices, scenes of forgetfulness also lend themselves to metatheatrical reflections about the stage's role in figuring and reconfiguring the relations

---

[19] Fischer, '"He means to pay": Value and metaphor in the Lancastrian tetralogy', 152.

[20] Qtd. in Bruster, *Drama and the Market in the Age of Shakespeare*, p. 7.

[21] Sullivan, *Memory and Forgetting*, p. 20.

of the individual to itself, to social authorities and to the divine order. Turning antitheatrical prejudice into dramatic capital, the theatre deals in forgetfulness in that it exploits and circulates its symbolic, social and commercial value. As we shall see in my discussion of *Henry IV*, the lethargic body figures on the stage as the signifier of a resistant subjectivity, which emerges as a distinctly theatrical property: a product of as well as a model for the theatre.

Shakespeare's two-part *Henry IV* insistently ponders the relation between memory, forgetfulness and the self, a relation that is seen as productive of a sense of selfhood in different ways. Interestingly, memory, as the sole prop for identity, is explicitly devalued in the figure of Hotspur, who appears as a stubbornly remembering subject that clings to outmoded social roles.[22] By contrast, the pleasures of self-forgetfulness as well as the shrewd appraisal of its strategic uses are imbued with vitality and success in the figures of Falstaff and Prince Hal respectively. Both figures are insistently connected with the image of the lethargic body, if in different ways.

In the prodigality scene between King Henry and Hal, the language of self-forgetfulness is employed to expose the prodigal prince's unruly

---

[22] Jonathan Baldo sees Hotspur as a figure of forgetfulness, a reading with which I do not quite agree. While it is indeed true that on at least three occasions he rather conspicuously forgets the point of what he is about to say, this does not mean that 'distraction is indeed the blustery Hotspur's characteristic mental state' (*Memory in Shakespeare's Histories*, p. 63). When Percy forgets the name of the place 'where I first bowed my knee / Unto this king of smiles, this Bullingbrook' (1.3.239–44), for example, he rather seeks to repress a shameful action in the past that is at odds with his exalted notion of honour. And when he forgets the map on which the rebels want to divide the kingdom as their spoil ('A plague upon it! / I have forgot the map', 3.1.4–5), this slip of mind is again directly related to his sense of honour: he believes his prospective share of the kingdom not big enough, a suspicion which is confirmed on consulting the map. Hotspur insists on redirecting an entire river in order to get his fair share, but is obviously embarrassed at his own narrow-mindedness, which does not sit well with his self-image of magnanimity: 'I do not care, I'll give thrice so much land / To any well-deserving friend. / But in the way of bargain, mark ye me, / I'll cavil on the ninth part of a hair' (3.1.131–4). Hotspur finds it difficult here to reconcile his heroic identity, based on the patterns of a feudal, chivalric past, with the demands of an emergent commercial society in which one's value must be continually bargained for. It is of course ironic that his own insistence on honour, which is explicitly couched in terms of remembrance (1.3.128–35, 168–70, 175–9), forces him to commit such momentary, strategic lapses of memory, which in turn link him to King Henry's wilful forgetfulness of the gratitude owed to the Percys for having helped him onto the throne.

behaviour, which is at odds with his identity as heir apparent. What King Henry deplores about his son is aptly expressed by the German word *Pflichtvergessenheit*: a shameful negligence of his duties, which amounts to a denial of that identity and results in the loss of his place in the royal Council (3.2.32). Recalling the bad example of Richard II, the King links Hal's loss of his royal self with a loss of control over his subjects. The Prince's 'vile participation' (88) in the habits and lives of the common people, Henry argues, will diminish their respect for and obedience to him as the future sovereign. Interestingly, this lesson in statecraft is consistently couched in metaphors of theatricality, consumption and lethargy. This is King Henry's analysis of the blunders in self-representation Richard made as a king:

> [He] Enfeoffed himself to popularity,
> That, being daily swallowed by men's eyes,
> They surfeited with honey, and began
> To loathe the taste of sweetness ...
> So, when he had occasion to be seen,
> He was but as the cuckoo is in June,
> Heard, not regarded; seen, but with such eyes
> As, sick and blunted with community,
> Afford no extraordinary gaze,
> Such as is bent on sun-like majesty
> When it shines seldom in admiring eyes,
> But rather drowsed and hung their eyelids down,
> Slept in his face, and rendered such aspect
> As cloudy men use to their adversaries,
> Being with his presence glutted, gorged, and full.

(3.2.69–84)

Henry's argument here is figured metaphorically in terms of theatrical spectacle: Richard had turned himself into a popular sight for the common people, cheapening his dignity through over-exposure and glibness.[23] This violates the economy of royal self-representation in which the value of the king's appearance is heightened by its scarcity. Calculated staging of one's public appearance, by contrast, is one of Henry's chief strategies of maintaining power: 'Thus did I keep my person fresh and new', he explains to his son, 'Ne'er seen but wondered

---

[23] Bevington, 'Introduction', p. 50.

at, and so my state, / Seldom, but sumptuous, showed like a feast, / And won by rareness such solemnity' (3.2.55, 57–9). As a 'show' that is likened to a 'feast', Henry links the images of theatrical spectacle and holiday feasting that inform such conspicuous consumption. The problem is not that the royal person be consumed; it is more a question of controlling this consumption. This introduces another metaphorical level, that of economic consumption with its dynamics of scarcity and demand through which the value of a commodity is controlled. In Henry's view, like Richard II before him, Hal <u>has</u> lost control over the consumption of their image: instead of 'afford[ing] an extraordinary gaze', both princes have suffered from 'being daily swallowed by men's eyes'. The dangerous consequence is that the subjects are 'surfeited with honey, and beg[i]n / To loathe the taste of sweetness'. This recalls the rhetoric of antitheatrical tracts like Rankins's, in which theatrical spectacle is condemned as a 'surfite of the soule' and 'more sweete then *Nectar*, and farre more pleasant then *Manna* from Heaven'.[24] The effect is a state of lethargy which poses a threat to a social order that is based on the subjects' obedient remembrance of their subordinate position, as the sermon 'An Exhortation Concerning Good Order and Obedience' (1559) made clear right at the beginning of Elizabeth's reign. Henry's speech echoes this anxiety as well as the imagery of the subjects' forgetful, disrespectful bodies. Being 'glutted, gorged and full' with Richard's presence, they exhibit all the symptoms of post-prandial lethargy: their eyes are 'sick and blunted with community', they 'drowsed and hung their eyelids down' and even 'slept in his face'. In Henry's view, Hal's own idleness turns him not so much into a lethargic subject (despite his *Pflichtvergessenheit*) but rather into an object of their subjects' lethargy. When Henry charges him with being a 'common sight' (3.2.89), he expresses concern at his son being commodified and consumed by the common people, rather than being a royal subject endowed with agency and own will. In outlining this 'lethargy effect', the King draws here on the language of both physiological and antitheatrical discourse, coupled with a Machiavellian awareness of how to maximise one's personal value by controlling the consumption of one's image.

However, Hal does in fact understand the dynamics of commercial transactions as well as his father does. He signals this by bringing

[24] Rankins, *Mirrour of Monsters*, p. 6.

the language of economy, still somewhat submerged in his father's harangue under the imagery of theatricality and festivity, to the foreground in his own reply. Thus he answers King Henry's charge that the valiant Hotspur 'hath more worthy interest to the state / Than thou the shadow of succession' with the promise to 'redeem all this on Percy's head' (3.2.98–9, 132). Hotspur, moreover, is only his 'factor', that is, in the capacity of an agent in a commercial transaction whom he has ordered to 'engross [i.e. buy up] glorious deeds on my behalf'. He vows to take his rival to 'account' and to settle the 'reckoning' with him by exchanging 'His glorious deeds for my indignities' (3.2.145–52). This overtly economic language appropriates Hotspur's own discourse of chivalry and 'exchanges' it for a more modern, commercial discourse more suitable to the 'business' of statecraft at hand (3.2.177, 179). Royal legitimacy emerges here 'as a node of advantageous purposeful exchanges in an economy of credit and negotiation', Lars Engle comments, rather than as a secure inheritance and identity.[25]

Hal not only understands the mechanisms of commercial exchange, he also understands his own self-performance in terms of debt and payment. Nowhere is this more pronounced than in his first soliloquy (1.2.155–77), where the symbolic and pragmatic connections between self, self-representation, and the rules of scarcity and demand are spelled out. Hal's speech foreshadows the King's rebuke through the use of similar metaphors such as that of the royal sun/son hiding behind 'the base contagious clouds' (in act 3, 'sun-like majesty' is insulted by 'cloudy men', 3.2.79, 83) or of the 'playing holidays' which are more welcome 'when they seldom come' (echoed later by King Henry's simile of the 'sumptuous show' that is like a 'feast', 3.2.58), thus demonstrating in hindsight that his way of thinking is much closer to Henry's than the King suspects. These metaphors likewise articulate an economy of the gaze that obeys the economic dynamic of supply and demand. Rarity increases an object's value, and this is the principle on which his 'reformation ... shall show more goodly, and attract more eyes / Than that which hath no foil to set it off' (1.2.173–5). Moreover, the language of debt and payment ('pay the debt I never promisèd', 1.2.169) and of obligation and redemption ('Redeeming time when men think least I will', 1.2.177) endows Hal's speech with a sense of agency and control. Paradoxically, then, what from King

---

[25] Engle, 'Who pays in the Henriad?', p. 108.

Henry's perspective spells a lethargic loss of control over one's self and one's subjects, emerges from Hal's perspective as the very means to gain control over himself and his future subjects. His outward show of idleness is an admittedly roundabout but nonetheless effective way of controlling the economy of supply and demand: he conveys upon his 'true' royal self – courageous, prudent, manly – a status of rarity which guarantees that it will be perceived as 'fresh and new' (3.2.55), thus enacting his father's economy of royal self-presentation by very different means.

While Hal's strategic self-forgetfulness might entail a temporary loss of his socially prescribed role and place in the Council, as King Henry states in 3.2, it does not at all mean a loss of subjectivity. In fact, forgetting his prescribed identity as heir apparent is what enables him to articulate a sense of self in the first place. Hal begins his soliloquy by describing his present life in terms of the 'humour of ... idleness' (1.2.156) which both antitheatrical tracts and his own father identify as leading to the oblivious state of 'spiritual lethargie'.[26] Confessing to (and no doubt also enjoying) his life of idleness, Hal goes on to declare that this idle life is not really who he is. The metaphor of the sun hiding himself behind 'base contagious clouds' before he 'please again to be himself' (1.2.158, 160) suggests that the Prince's true self is momentarily and, moreover, deliberately obscured. He is wearing a mantle of 'loose behaviour' (168) under which his own princely self waits to be revealed. The imagery he uses thus expresses a claim to interiority, to a true, inner self that is independent of external behaviour or social role. Yet at the same time it also suggests that this inner self will be just another role to perform: he proposes, after all to 'imitate the sun' and imagines his reformation as a 'show' that will 'glitt[er] o'er' his present faults' (173). His speech thus does not uncover an authentic inwardness but rather generates an 'inwardness effect'.[27]

This effect is, of course, what the stage and in particular the dramatic device of the self-reflexive soliloquy produce, as Katharine Eisaman Maus has observed: they put on display the relation between outward appearance and inward disposition. Typically, this relation between interiority and exteriority was viewed with

---

[26] Downame, *The Second Part of the Christian Warfare*, sig. V4ʳ.
[27] Döring, *Performances of Mourning*, p. 123.

scepticism and anxiety. Since the hidden interior is inaccessible and invisible, it can only be approached from the outside, by induction from external signs. This entails the possibility of error, mistake and deception: signs may indeed be only an outward show or they may be misread. Thus when a play stages the fraught relation between inward being and outer show, this has ramifications not only for the question of subjectivity but also for the question of theatricality. Inwardness on stage is always inwardness displayed, and as such has already ceased to exist as inwardness proper.[28] While Maus focuses on the limits of what can be presented on stage, namely an authentic interiority, I would like to suggest a more modest but perhaps equally productive emphasis: in staging a discrepancy between outer appearance and inner self, scenes like Hal's soliloquy enable the notion of inwardness in the first place. Hal's self-forgetfulness is thus productive of a sense, or at least of a semblance of an inward self. He needs to forget about his prescribed identity as heir apparent in order to make room for a subjectivity that affords him a sense of agency and control located in an interiority, however ephemeral. This inward self will, from the end of the first part onwards, conform increasingly to the social scripts of honour, courage and filial duty, but with an important difference: in the end, Hal will not simply have internalised a prescribed social role, but he will enact that role on his own terms. Hugh Grady has argued that Hal dramatically investigates alternative versions of identity even while working on a self that he wants to become, a legendary, glittering marvel to be admired. His protean subjectivity of the first part, which is enabled by a wilful self-forgetfulness, is the vehicle for a fixed identity of 'his own legendary self' in *Henry V*.[29]

This achievement of a fixed identity is one of the main differences between Hal and Falstaff. While both employ self-forgetfulness strategically in order to produce alternative selves, Falstaff never strives for a stable identity. Instead, he promotes a proliferation of alternative selves that are emphatically not based on the idea of interiority but of performativity. His subjectivity consists in enacting ever new versions of himself – youthful riot, ageing penitent, wise fool, zealous Puritan, carnivalesque Lord of Misrule. These incarnations and their

---

[28] Maus, *Inwardness and Theater*, pp. 5, 31–2.
[29] Grady 'Falstaff: Subjectivity between the carnival and the aesthetic', 612.

cultural or ideological contexts have already received a great deal of critical attention.[30] In particular Falstaff's grotesque corporeality has given rise to a by now dominant critical reading of this figure in terms of the festive culture of carnival.[31] However, one problem with this interpretive tradition, as David Ruiter points out, is that it operates within a closed dialectic of festivity versus order, tavern versus court, carnival versus Lent, thus replicating the argumentative stance of early modern attackers and defenders of the stage. Even if one takes into account, as especially new historicist critics in the wake of Foucault and Greenblatt have done, that carnival is complicit in upholding the social order by acting as a kind of safety-valve, the dichotomy itself has remained surprisingly stable.[32] I would therefore like to argue with Christopher Ivic that a shift of focus from power to the interplay of remembering and forgetting shows that the relations between festivity and order in these plays are in fact much more ambivalent, as are Falstaff's performances of possible selves.[33]

---

[30] C. L. Barber reads him as a figure of popular festivity (without drawing on Bakthin's concept of carnival) in *Shakespeare's Festive Comedy*. François Laroque discusses him as a figure of carnival in the Bakhtinian sense ('Shakepeare's "Battle of Carnival and Lent"'), as do Hugh Grady (in 'Subjectivity between the carnival and the aesthetic' and *Shakespeare, Machiavelli and Montaigne*) and David Ruiter (*Shakespeare's Festive History*). For Falstaff as an embodiment of the comic Vice of medieval morality plays, see Robert Weimann, *Shakespeare und die Tradition des Volkstheaters*, pp. 253, 262. Kristen Poole analyses Falstaff as a parody of Puritan hypocrisy in 'Saints Alive! Falstaff, Martin Marprelate, and the staging of Puritanism'. David Womersley offers an important complementary account: in spite of its title, 'Why is Falstaff fat?', his essay focuses on historical and dramatic representations of Henry V in changing confessional contexts and concludes that Shakespeare's aim in taking up Foxe's mocking image of a 'grandpanch Epicure' was to use him as a foil to offset Henry as a figure of 'reformed spirituality' and thus as the perfect Protestant prince (3, 21).

[31] The two poles of festivity and order have usually been discussed either in terms of space (the contrastive worlds of tavern and court) or festive versus historical time. For examples of the first, see Pugliatti, *Shakespeare the Historian*; Jean Howard and Phyllis Rackin's *Engendering a Nation*; Alexander Leggatt's 'Killing the hero: Tamburlaine and Falstaff'; and François Laroque, 'Shakespeare's "Battle of Carnival and Lent": The Falstaff Scenes Reconsidered' (1998). The temporal distinction prevails in Shigeki Takada's 'The first and second parts of *Henry IV*' and Peter Womack's '*Henry IV* and epic theatre'.

[32] See Ruiter, *Shakespeare's Festive History*, pp. 5–16.

[33] Ivic, 'Reassuring fratricide', p. 107.

Falstaff is the lethargic subject *par excellence*. Already with his first appearance on stage he shows all the physiological and temperamental symptoms of lethargy. Having obviously just woken up from a peaceful afternoon slumber, Falstaff asks Prince Hal about the time of the day. The Prince retorts with this playful invective: 'Thou art so fat-witted with drinking of old sack, and unbuttoning thee after supper, and sleeping upon benches after noon, that thou hast forgotten to demand that which thou wouldst truly know' (*1H4*, 1.2.2–5). The Prince's teasing but, in the light of later events, quite accurate portrait of his roguish companion reads like a diagnosis out of contemporary medical tracts. Falstaff habitually and excessively indulges in eating meat, drinking strong wine, sleeping during the day and fornicating with whores, habits which in Hal's account explicitly result in forgetfulness: 'thou has forgotten to demand that which thou wouldst truly know'. Early modern audiences would have been familiar with this line of argument from the numerous medical treatises advocating a healthy and morally sound life-style. Compare, for example, Guilielmus Gratarolus' caution that 'gluttonie and dronkennesse, lyke as they do dull the wyt, so do they also utterly overthrowe and destroy the Memorye'.[34] Falstaff commits sinful acts which come under the purview of a moral forgetfulness. According to the medical part of John Willis's tract on memory, 'Filthy desires, as ... lust, love of harlots and the ardent Passion, *Love*' all induce oblivion.[35] Likewise, Falstaff's habit of 'sleeping upon benches after noon' flies in the face of medical advice like Willis's, who adamantly rules that '*Sleep* offendeth *Memory*. If it be First, overmuch. Secondly, if taken ... under *Lunar raies*. Thirdly, in the day, most of all with shoes on'. That Falstaff takes diurnal naps, no doubt with his shoes on, is even presented on stage when Falstaff is discovered sleeping behind the arras in act 2, scene 4. Moreover, the proscription against sleeping under the light of a full moon recalls one of his self-descriptions as 'squires of the night's body ... Diana's foresters, gentlemen of the shade, minions of the moon' (1.2.21–3). While he is not exactly sleeping under 'Lunar raies', he commits sinful acts which come under the purview of a moral forgetfulness.

---

[34] Gratarolus, *The Castel of Memorie*, sig. G.iiii^v.
[35] Willis, *Mnemonica*, p. 141.

Because of his dietary excesses, Falstaff has not only a fat body, he is also 'fat-witted' (1.2.2). The expression is glossed as 'thick-witted' in the standard editions, which the OED references as 'of slow wit, dull'. This meaning is rendered somewhat unlikely by Falstaff's later demonstrations of an extraordinary imagination and ready wit, however. The comparison with another Shakespeare play suggests an alternative meaning that is more in keeping with Falstaff's character. When the ghost commands Hamlet to revenge his murder, he admonishes the young prince not to delay its execution: 'And duller shouldst thou be than the fat weed / That roots itself in ease on Lethe wharf / Wouldst thou not stir in this' (*Hamlet*, 1.5.33–4). But of course Hamlet does delay and hesitate throughout the play. In this, as well as later scenes, the ghost seeks to interpellate Hamlet into acting on his identity as the murdered king's son and revenger. This is an identity that the play problematises as oppressively prescriptive, in the double sense of the word: as action demanded by filial duty and as dramatic action that follows a literary script, that of the revenge play. In both senses, vengeance and remembrance are intimately linked in that the act of retribution is driven by, indeed even constitutes, an act of commemoration and that the action on stage recalls the ancient pattern of the Senecan revenge tragedy which saw its heyday in the 1580s.[36] In Shakespeare's play, resistance to this pattern is proleptically figured by the ghost as an act of forgetting: in so doing, young Hamlet will be like a 'fat weed … on Lethe wharf' indeed. The effect of such lethargic delaying and pondering is to open up an imaginative space for an alternative sense of self, both for the character and the play. Only through delaying, hesitating and to all appearances forgetting his prescribed duty of revenge does Hamlet emerge as a subject.[37] In a similar sense, the 'fat-witted' Falstaff is a lethargic figure unwilling to act out prescribed patterns of behaviour or modes of being.

His physiological and temperamental propensity toward lethargy having thus been established from the start, Falstaff's character sustains it throughout the play. Forgetful of social rank and the behaviour appropriate to it, he calls the Prince familiarly by his first name

---

[36] John Kerrigan discusses in *Revenge Tragedy* its origins in ancient Greek culture and provides insightful readings of its Elizabethan forms, in particular Thomas Kyd's *The Spanish Tragedy* (late 1580s) and Shakespeare's *Hamlet* (ca. 1601), which both remember and also disremember the classical pattern by reworking it.

[37] Sullivan, *Memory and Forgetting*, p. 43.

and accosts him as 'lad', 'sweet wag' and 'mad wag' (1.2.35, 13, 39). Trading bawdy jokes and insults with the Prince, or masquerading as king and heir apparent in the 'play extempore' (2.5.257), are all 'forms of altering and testing identity' in which Falstaff engages with gusto.[38] Throughout, he claims for himself a freedom of speech which ignores their respective positions in the court hierarchy. Not only the content but also the colloquial form of Falstaff's prose speech is a sign of his freedom, highlighting the subversion his lines enact against the dignified blank verse speech of the historical figures.[39] This disregard for hierarchies would probably come under the purview of Willis's indicator of lethargy number XI: 'Rash answers'.[40]

Falstaff's forgetting and forgiving disposition is commented on by a servant in the second part who reports how Prince Hal once played a prank on Falstaff that 'angered him to the heart', only to add in the same breath: 'But he hath forgot that' (*2H4*, 2.4.6–7). While this comment certainly serves to characterise him as good-natured, it also implies that Sir John actually has not quite forgotten about the respect he owes his social superiors: after all, it would be most unwise to hold a grudge against the future king. In fact, Falstaff is not unmindful either of his unruly past or of his future prospects, but keeps reminding Prince Harry of the forgiveness as well as privileges he hopes for 'when thou art king' (*1H4*, 2.1.13–15, 20–6, 51–2, 54). If Falstaff is always ready to forget injuries done to him, he is even more willing to forget his own shameful and dishonourable actions. When Hal discovers his cowardly behaviour in the robbery at Gad's Hill (2.5) or when he is caught claiming that the Prince owes him a large sum in order to prolong his credit at the tavern (3.3), Falstaff simply refuses to be ashamed and wittily offers the most favourable interpretation of his behaviour instead. As was the case with his famous catechism on honour, examined in the previous chapter, such acts of semantic evacuation enable Falstaff to avoid the demands of chivalric behaviour or of honourable dealings, and to carve out an imaginative space in which he recasts the memory of past events in terms of his alternative set of values.

Sir John's self-forgetfulness should thus not be understood in terms of a loss of identity but rather as productive of subjectivity, since it frees

---

[38] Bevington, 'Introduction', p. 51.
[39] Rackin, *Stages of History*, p. 235.
[40] Willis, *Mnemonica*, p. 141.

him to adopt social roles or poses at will. Hugh Grady has suggested
that we see Falstaff's refusal to be tied down to any single identity
and his continually reinventing himself through a series of dramatic
improvisations as a strategy of resistance to Althusserian interpellation: 'This playfulness, this ability to subvert ideological interpellation through theatricality is Falstaff's crucial characteristic'.[41] I would
like to argue that his deliberate forgetting of his former deeds can be
interpreted as a similar act of resistance. This is nowhere more obvious
than in Falstaff's encounter with the Lord Chief Justice in the second
part of *Henry IV*. In a scene that resembles Althusser's prime example
of interpellation,[42] the Lord Chief Justice, as principal representative
of state authority, attempts to call Falstaff to account for the Gad's
Hill robbery he committed in the first part. Falstaff pretends to be
literally deaf to these acts of interpellation. Only reluctantly does Sir
John enter into a conversation, which, however, effectively remains a
monologue on each side. The Lord Chief Justice tries in vain to bring
up the issue of the robbery, while Falstaff seeks to distract from it by
harping on his health and that of the King. Wilfully drifting into medical detail, Falstaff is cut short by the Justice's pointed remark that his
deafness seems to be a symptom of the very disease he is just describing: the disease of 'lethargy' (*2H4*, 1.2.101). Lethargy, as pointed out
before, derives from Lethe, the river of forgetfulness, and Falstaff's
'lethargy' here is nothing but an attempt to forget his former deeds
and to eschew being interpellated and punished as a criminal. Falstaff
himself marks this forgetting as a deliberate act rather than an acci-
dental disease or innate disposition, when he confesses tongue-in-
cheek that his deafness is '[r]ather ... the disease of not listening, the
malady of not marking, that I am troubled withal' (110–11). In an
intertheatrical echo, this mocking self-description recalls King Henry's
anxious warning of the dangers to royal authority of being consumed
by one's subjects' eyes and in retrospect marks this ocular surfeit as
lethargy: 'He was but a the cuckoo is in June, / Heard, not regarded'
(*1H4*, 3.2.75–6).

[41] Grady, 'Subjectivity between the carnival and the aesthetic', 613.
[42] Althusser likens the act of interpellation, by which individuals become subjects
as they subject themselves to ideology, to that moment when somebody is
hailed by a police officer on the street 'Hey, you there!', and turns around
because he or she identifies himself or herself as the person hailed ('Ideology
and ideological state apparatuses', p. 301).

Forgetfulness can be found not only on the side of subversive resistance, however, but also on the side of order and authority. This emerges from the second encounter between Falstaff and the Lord Chief Justice, in which the latter simply turns Falstaff's own strategy against himself. When he asks the Lord Chief Justice eagerly 'What's the news, my lord?', he is deliberately and repeatedly being ignored by him (*2H4*, 2.1.131–41). The implication is that the Lord Chief Justice pretends to the same 'kind of lethargy' or 'deafness' in order to put Falstaff into his place. The very moment he attends to the old knight's insistent calls of 'My lord!', however, Falstaff turns the tables once again and ignores the Lord Chief Justice. Upbraided by him – 'What foolish master taught you these manners, Sir John?' (149) – Falstaff manages to insinuate that the Justice was the fool who taught him this habit. Falstaff seems or pretends to have forgotten here that it was in fact he himself who started this game. What he has not forgotten is the name of the game: to get even with his social superior. 'This is the right fencing grace, my lord', he triumphantly calls quits as he leaves the stage, '– tap for tap, and so part fair' (151–2).

Sir John's lethargy in these scenes clearly is a tactical behaviour with the aim to withdraw his person from the grasp of government authority and discipline. The fact that this strategy can be appropriated by authority figures as well only shows the extent to which this is not indicative of identity, but rather a performative practice of forgetfulness that can be adopted at will. Another aim, I would suggest, is to playfully generate alternative selves. These function as a kind of commodity, which Falstaff exchanges for Hal's good will in the form of limitless credit and protection. This economic dynamic behind lethargic subjectivity is highlighted at the end of the scene that saw the first encounter between Sir John and the Lord Chief Justice. Taking stock of his finances, Falstaff complains that he 'can get no remedy against this consumption of the purse: borrowing only lingers and lingers it out, but the disease is uncurable' (*2H4*, 1.2.186–7). The medical vocabulary is here shifted from the realm of personal accountability to the realm of debt and credit, linking the two in a highly suggestive way, for Falstaff does find a remedy for both in his own resourceful self: 'A good wit will make use of anything: I will turn diseases to commodity.' (194–5) This is in fact what he has done throughout. The disease of lethargy has enabled him to reinvent himself anew in scene after scene, discursively producing an endless chain of selves for consumption by spectators on and off the stage. All the characters in the Lancastrian tetralogy, as Sandra Fischer observes, 'reveal a startling link between word and value, discovering in language a flexible and variable medium of exchange that creates their world and identities anew', and among these 'Falstaff most notably and joyfully exploits language, stretching its lexical and moral possibilities not only for money or advancement but also to betoken his personal value.'[43] The same could be said of the way he exploits memory, stretching its moral possibilities as far as possible. Falstaff's linguistic and lethargic mastery constantly re-negotiates his individual value, as is demonstrated by the following exchange of words with Hal:

Prince: Why, what a pox have I to do with my Hostess of the tavern?
Falstaff: Well, thou hast called her to a reckoning many a time and oft.
Prince: Did I ever call for thee to pay thy part?
Falstaff: No, I'll give thee thy due, thou hast paid all there.
Prince: Yea, and elsewhere, so far as my coin would stretch, and where it would not, I have used my credit.
Falstaff: Yea, and so used it that were it not here apparent that thou art heir apparent –

(*1H4*, 1.2.38–46)

With that 'masterly paronomasia',[44] Falstaff discharges his monetary debt to Hal while at the same time avoiding precisely 'to pay his part'. Coining his 'fat wit' into an exchange value of discursive self-performances, Falstaff is indeed able to turn 'disease to commodity'.

Yet his preferred currency is subject to a debasement of value. Prince Harry loses nothing by counterfeiting, that is, by playing parts, as he possesses an intrinsic value of nobility, legitimacy and authority. This is acknowledged by Sir John when he says: 'Never call a true piece of gold a counterfeit. Thou art essentially made, without seeming so' (*1H4*, 2.4.409–10). Because of this, Hal's currency remains good, and he is able to pay his debts. Thus he eventually removes himself from debasing circulation, functioning as the 'true piece of gold' that

---

[43] Fischer, '"He means to pay": Value and metaphor in the Lancastrian tetralogy', 149, 150.
[44] *Ibid.*, 160.

guarantees the stability of his country's values. Falstaff, by contrast, encourages the outflow of his many 'counterfeits' that serve him as a kind of currency by which he defers all final payment of debts through a chain of substitutions and redescriptions.[45] In so doing, he provides himself with seemingly unlimited means of exchange for favours but, at the same time, he triggers an inflation that diminishes the rate of his currency until, in the end, his self-performances have no value in Hal's reckonings any more. In his case, self-forgetfulness is still a valid practice of producing subjectivity, yet when taken to excess the lethargic subject itself is threatened by oblivion. Having indulged too freely in the pleasures of self-forgetfulness, he is himself being deliberately forgotten in the end. Too late to be present at the coronation, the old knight stands in the crowd, trying to catch the young king's attention. Calling him 'King Hal, my royal Hal!', 'my sweet boy' and 'My king, my Jove, I speak to thee, my heart!' (*2H4*, 5.5.39, 41, 44), on a scale of mounting anguish at being ignored by Hal, the scene recalls that earlier one in which he was pointedly snubbed by the Lord Chief Justice. Here, too, the Lord Chief Justice is present to remind him of the gap in rank that separates Falstaff from the King: 'Have you your wits? Know you what 'tis you speak?' (42–3). When Hal, now King Henry V, finally attends to the fat knight, it is to dismiss him with the words: 'I know thee not, old man' (45). Falstaff's commodity of discursively performed selves cannot purchase Hal's protection any more; indeed, his former foster-son rejects it explicitly: 'Reply not to me with a fool-born jest' (53). Having carried out his own reformation, which is imagined as a return to his true royal self, Hal offers his old companion a return of his protection only on the basis of a similar reform (56–9). Sir John, being the lethargic subject that he is, simply cannot understand or accept the concept of a fixed identity however. After the King has left, he assures himself that Hal's severity is only another show: 'Look you, he must seem thus to the world ... This that you heard was but a colour [i.e. pretence]. I shall be sent for soon at night' (74–5, 81, 84). Instead, he is arrested and taken to the Fleet prison. His stage appearance ends on a disheartening note of lethargic deafness when the Lord Chief Justice cuts off Falstaff's protest of 'My lord, my lord!' with the words: 'I cannot now speak. I will hear you soon –' (87–8). Banished from the presence of the King

---

[45] Engle, 'Who pays in the Henriad?', pp. 118, 127.

and thus barred from access to power and privilege, Falstaff sinks into oblivion.[46]

Falstaff thus embodies both the pleasures and the dangers of lethargic subjectivity. On the one hand, his fluid subjectivity – in the double sense of being both unfixed and solvent – allows him to resist being interpellated into a stable identity and thus to eschew the moral as well as monetary debts that come with that identity. On the other, it amounts to an extreme form of 'rampant individualism', in Grady's expression, that is shown as harbouring not only possibilities but also dangers, since in many scenes Falstaff's self-forgetfulness also emerges as solipsistic escapism, egoistic self-indulgence and immoral exploitation of others. Grady concludes: 'Thus the exploitative side of Falstaff can be seen as enacting one of the dangerous aspects of unfixed subjectivity in the service of unchecked appetite.'[47] Joan Fitzpatrick has suggested that the ambivalent nature of this figure can be seen as a result of the glutton's unchecked appetite itself: Sir John's 'casual lack of regard for the welfare of his fellow-man' might well have been recognised as 'an effect of gluttony [as] mentioned in the Elizabethan *Homily Against Gluttonie and Dronkenness*', which advised men of authority to refrain from excessive eating and drinking since this renders them unfit for governing other men.[48] This reading is supported by the metaphor Falstaff uses to express his disdain for the poor men he has pressed into military service: they are merely 'food for powder' (*1H4*, 4.2.23–31, 65).

More generally, this ambivalence seems to result from the co-existence of different discourses on consumption. The different perspectives on the body as a site of pleasurable resistance on the one hand and as a commodified object of exploitation on the other, argues Hugh Grady, coincided with a shift from medieval communal

---

[46] It is one of the ironies of stage history that Falstaff does not sink into oblivion, of course: he holds centre stage again in *The Merry Wives of Windsor* and is at least present in other figures' memories in *Henry V*. Moreover, he remains one of the most memorable and most popular Shakespearean characters along with Hamlet. As Sullivan has argued, Hamlet, too, can be regarded as a lethargic subject, since his sense of self and agency are produced out of forgetting the prescribed identity of revenger pushed on him (*Memory and Forgetting*, pp. 32, 43). Thus the two figures whose subjectivity is predominantly enabled by forgetfulness have themselves become unforgettable in Western cultural memory.

[47] Grady, 'Subjectivity between the carnival and the aesthetic', 619.

[48] Fitzpatrick, *Food in Shakespeare*, pp. 16–17, 22–3.

society to modern commercial society.[49] At the same time, historians of the body have observed that the 'changing attitudes to the notion of embodiment' in early modern physiological, political, religious and social discourses resulted in a 'more closed ideal of the body'. This 'process of bodily enclosure' engendered anxieties and ambivalences about the status of the body.[50] This may explain why Falstaff is not a straightforwardly positive figure of medieval carnivalesque subversion. Seen exclusively in the old context of carnival festivity, Falstaff embodies indeed a 'sense of freedom from the burden of ruling ideologies and concepts of honor, [duty], ambition, and revenge'. However, Grady continues, this liberating spirit of carnival, which belonged with medieval communal society and pre-Reformation holiday structures, was already anachronistic in Elizabethan London society. In the Elizabethan context, carnival was not a lived practice any more. While the figure of Falstaff thus still recalls the carnival tradition, this tradition has lost its meaning as a social practice. Falstaff's grotesque corporeality becomes in a sense an empty figure, a chiffre of carnival that can be filled with new meaning in a new urban commercial context. Or perhaps more accurately, the old meaning is only partially evacuated from and a new meaning is only partially invested in this figure, rendering it ambivalent. Hugh Grady concludes that whereas the structures of carnival would have contained Falstaff's plebeian cunning and amoral self-preservation, and asserted his exuberance as a crucial value, in the real-life absence of such structures, he embodies a new, value-free individualism that will become the hallmark of a modern capitalist society.[51] Through Falstaff, I would add, the theatre negotiates that 'shameless transformation' (*1H4*, 1.1.44) and provides a model for life in a world newly open to the pleasures and dangers of modernity. In this brave new world, forgetting is a main generative force in the formation of selfhood, but Falstaff's fate also reflects on the possible costs of forgetting social and ethical imperatives. The 'disease' that Falstaff embodies and turns into a 'commodity' is also a symptom of the early modern society.

---

[49] Grady, 'Subjectivity between the carnival and the aesthetic', 619.
[50] Hillman, '*Homo clausus* at the theatre', p. 161.
[51] Grady, 'Subjectivity between the carnival and the aesthetic', 618–19.

Falstaff stands not only as a figure for society but also for the theatre: his character can also be seen as a model for how the early modern stage dealt with its own theatrical tradition in order to find a new, modern sense of itself. Recalling a wide range of theatrical, folk and literary types, the figure of Falstaff fuses them into a protean subjectivity whose core principle is theatricality itself.[52] The comic Vice-figure of the medieval morality plays is a good example of how such a shameless transformation proceeds: while Falstaff playfully acknowledges this tradition when he alludes to the 'dagger of lath' (2.4.116), the Vice's signature stage-prop, his own figure is emptied of the clear moral values which once imbued the medieval morality plays. Although he self-consciously fashions himself after literary and cultural traditions, Falstaff's sense of self is nevertheless not established through acts of faithful reminiscence. On the contrary, Falstaff exhibits at every turn an awareness that he deals in imaginary commodities – in jokes, speeches, performances erasing and replacing the ones that went before – just as the early modern theatre did. In the figure of Falstaff, the contemporary stage reflects on its own practice of emptying out traditional structures of meaning in order to make room for new forms of subjectivity and, indeed, of theatricality. In this sense, we can take Falstaff's claim that he is able to 'turn diseases to commodity' as a self-consciously metatheatrical comment. He provides a model for the stage which, like him, turns the disease of lethargy into a commodity of new subjectivities. Falstaff's self-forgetfulness can thus be seen as a cultural trope through which the early modern theatre arrives at a sense of itself. This self-awareness is balanced by a perceptive premonition that oblivious self-performances, taken to solipsistic extremes, might come detached from the world of interpersonal relations which, after all, give the theatre's insubstantial commodities social validity and commercial value. In the figure of Falstaff, the Shakespearian stage examines the possibilities as well as the limits of its own imaginative, economic and mnemonic practices.

---

[52] For an overview over these literary types and historical figures see Bevington, 'Introduction', pp. 23–34. On protean or chameleon-like changeability as a characteristic feature of the stage in antitheatrical literature, see Barish, *The Antitheatrical Prejudice*, pp. 99–114.

'One word more, I beseech you', the Epilogue to 2 *Henry IV* once more brings Falstaff to our attention, after he has just been officially banished into oblivion by the King: 'if you be not too much cloyed with fat meat, our humble author will continue the story with Sir John in it, and make you merry with fair Katherine of France, where, for anything I know, Falstaff shall die of a sweat, unless already a be killed with your hard opinions; for Oldcastle died martyr, and this is not the man' (20–5). The Epilogue here advertises the sequel to the play we have just seen. That play will be called *Henry V*, yet the chief commodity announced is the gluttonous, cowardly and immensely entertaining figure of Falstaff. At the same time, the Epilogue announces the structural interplay of remembering and forgetting that has produced this very figure: 'for Oldcastle died martyr, and this is not the man'. Falstaff, as is well known, was called Oldcastle in an earlier version. Shakespeare had been compelled to change the name because it had given offence, presumably to Sir John Oldcastle's descendant, Sir William Brooke, Lord Cobham, who as the Lord Chamberlain occupied a high office in the state and had the Master of the Revels report to him. With the offended in such a position of power, the censorship was a foregone conclusion. It is perhaps an irony of history that in seeking to protect the good name of Cobham through suppressing the name Oldcastle, the Cobham family managed to put itself into the grave of oblivion, at least as far as popular memory is concerned. The historical fact of censorship and the figures involved have long been appreciated by Shakespeare criticism.[53] The name that is still remembered widely, however, is that of Falstaff.

That final paragraph of the Epilogue is often treated as a last-minute addition, due to the external pressure of censorship; yet there are ample intertextual as well as intratextual traces in the play-text itself to suggest that the change in name, and the acts of forgetting to which it draws attention, are more than an afterthought forced upon the play. When Gary Taylor and Stanley Wells made the decision to restore the name Oldcastle in the Oxford Shakespeare *Complete Works*, they were guided by the assumption that this was no more than a perfunctory revision that needed to be revoked. Taylor listed external and internal evidence to substantiate this decision in an article, 'The Fortunes of Oldcastle'

---

[53] Taylor, 'The Fortunes of Oldcastle', 87.

(1985). I will not go through the complete list here, nor through the well-founded criticism this decision met with.[54] Since my argument does not concern issues of editing and textual memory specifically but rather the question of theatrical memory, I will focus on those examples that help to substantiate my own point, namely that the substitution of names may be seen as symptomatic of the interplay between remembering and forgetting that is constitutive of the figure of Falstaff.

For the Epilogue does more than evoke a simple exchange of one name for another. In recalling Oldcastle, it also alludes to the process of historiographical changes that produced the memory of Oldcastle in the Elizabethan period. The name of Oldcastle thus does not provide a stable point of reference for an 'original' figure, but only refers us to a series of erasures and replacements. The historical Oldcastle, born in the late 1370s, was a member of the landed gentry but rose to privilege through two advantageous marriages and as a friend of Prince Henry, the later Henry V. He was also a prominent critic of Catholic forms of worship and abuses of church privileges. Such religious dissent was coupled in the public view with rebellion against state authority: contemporary upheavals among the lower orders of society became quickly, if falsely, associated with the heretical movement of Lollardry. Oldcastle himself was examined for heresy in 1413, accused of a rebellion he may or may not have led in 1414, and eventually executed as heretic and traitor near St. Giles's Fields, London, in December 1417.[55] It was thus as a rebel that Oldcastle was

[54] This criticism occurs mostly in form of the editorial decisions made and discussion of these in the introductory material or in reviews. 'Falstaff' has remained the standard naming since the First Folio, but the lines of argument have differed. Thus R. A. Foakes dismisses the change in names as editorial pedantry in his 'Review' (439); David Bevington insists on retaining 'Falstaff' in his edition of *1 Henry IV* in the Oxford single-volume series on the grounds that the stage figure had become a fictional entity requiring a single name already in 1623 ('Introduction, pp. 108–9); Giorgio Melchiori's edition of *Part Two* for the New Cambridge series puts forth the theory that there was an original, one-play 'Oldcastle'-version of *Henry IV* and that the extensive revisions which produced the two-part versions in which Falstaff features were so substantial that the reinstatement of the name Oldcastle would be not just pointless, but counterproductive ('Introduction', pp. 14–16); Pendleton in '"This is not the man": On calling Falstaff Falstaff' and Goldberg in 'The commodity of names: "Falstaff" and "Oldcastle" in *1 Henry IV*' likewise engage critically with the evidence Taylor marshalled in 1985. They provide key arguments for my discussion of the internal evidence and will be cited in the text.

[55] See Corbin and Sedge (eds.), *The Oldcastle Controversy*, pp. 2–8.

remembered in the official trial records, which subsequently became the basis of historiographical texts.

The juridical proceedings already constitute a first step of erasure and deformation of historical memory, as Paul Strohm has pointed out. Since all oppositional writings by or in the possession of Oldcastle had been destroyed, the official account that cast him exclusively in terms of rebellion and treason was the only contemporary source. This 'skewed textual situation' enabled a Lancastrian propaganda that re-inscribed the Lollards as menace in order to legitimise its own authority.[56] In the absence of another perspective, the vilification of Oldcastle as seditious heretic, outlaw and traitor continued in the writings of fifteenth-century Catholic historians. Annabel Patterson gives us a daunting list of the highly partial authors of that image:

Walsingham, a monk who was an inveterate enemy of the Lollards; Titus Livius de Fulovisiis, whose *Vita Henrici Quinti* was written in the context of his patronage by Humphrey, duke of Gloucester, Henry's younger brother; and the anonymous cleric who wrote the *Gesta Henrici Quinti* as explicit propaganda for use at home and abroad; ... In the next generation of historians the Oldcastle story passed to Polydore Vergil, to Fabian, and to the anonymous translator of Titus Livius, who produced what is known as the First English Life of Henry V.

'For all of these writers', she concludes, 'Oldcastle is a demon whose appearance at the beginning of the reign has to be exorcised before the miracle of Agincourt can take place.'[57] With the coming of the Reformation to England, however, this image had in turn to be exorcised. Now the religious dissent of the Lollards, which manifested itself in a rejection of over-elaborate ritual and the destruction of false images, turned them into admired examples for the Reformation's own project. Specifically Oldcastle became a proto-Protestant martyr. The historians of the Tudor era thus faced the problem of legitimising him as such a model against the overwhelming odds of existing historiography.[58] In other words, they had to forget the rebel in order to remember the martyr.

---

[56] Strohm, *England's Empty Throne*, p. 34.
[57] Patterson, 'Sir John Oldcastle as symbol of Reformation historiography', pp. 8–9.
[58] Corbin and Sedge (eds.), *The Oldcastle Controversy*, p. 6.

Many Protestant historians addressed this need to erase the, in their eyes erroneous, memory of Oldcastle as heretic and traitor explicitly. John Foxe's *Acts and Monuments*, for example, not only numbered Oldcastle among the prominent Protestant martyrs, but also preserved the very acts of erasure and reinscription through which this image change came about. Foxe reports how Edward Hall, when compiling his monumental chronicle history, hastened to change his account of Oldcastle's life (first derived from Polydore Vergil who had vilified the Lollard's 'demoniacal sting') upon reading a copy of Bale's *Brefe Chronycle* that downplayed his threat to official authority and highlighted the pacifism of the Lollards instead: 'the said Hall with his pen, at the sight of John Bale's book, did utterly extinguish and abolish ... all that he had written before against John Oldcastle and his fellows ... adding in the place thereof the words of Master Bale's book'.[59] Hall's own description of Oldcastle is determinedly non-committal and non-evaluative; when Holinshed compiled his *Chronicles* on the basis of his account, he shifted the emphasis further toward the revised image, offering Oldcastle explicitly as an example to be followed. In highlighting Oldcastle's virtues as a proto-Protestant reformer, Holinshed even managed to get away with a covert recommendation of his anti-authorial stance, and thus to preserve a faint memory of Oldcastle as rebel.[60]

Toward the end of the sixteenth century, the figure of Oldcastle underwent yet another change, from a model for Protestantism to a grotesque parody of Puritanism. This 'shameless transformation' occurred in the context of the Marprelate controversy, a veritable pamphlet war that raged between a group of young radical Puritans, who published their invectives against a degenerate clergy under the pseudonym 'Martin Marprelate', and another group of anti-Puritan writers, who turned their weapons against them by depicting 'Marprelate' as a grotesque Puritan given to gluttony, fornication and sin. Out of their texts, the figure of the hypocritical Puritan was born.[61] Its most famous incarnation on the early modern stage was Shakespeare's Falstaff, and it was this image that the Cobham family objected to. Their intervention

---

[59] Patterson, 'Sir John Oldcastle as symbol of Reformation historiography', p. 14.
[60] *Ibid.*, pp. 13, 19.
[61] On the stage history of this figure, see Poole, 'Saints Alive! Falstaff, Martin Marprelate, and the staging of Puritanism'.

resulted in censorship and suppression which, however, did not achieve much to erase these associations.[62] This is substantiated by the fact that Shakespeare was not the only playwright to revive Oldcastle on the stage. Other plays, such as *The First Part of Sir John Oldcastle*, were however clearly 'committed to the hagiographical tradition initiated by Bale and mediated through Foxe and Holinshed', thus giving no offence.[63] When the Epilogue to *2 Henry IV* claims that 'Oldcastle died martyr, and this [Falstaff] is not the man', his words at the same time foreground the difference between the historical and the theatrical figure, as well as the long process of erasure and reinscription in cultural memory that marks this distance.

Let us now turn to the internal evidence. A key argument for Gary Taylor's claim that nothing more than the names were changed under censorship was that the play-text shows the traces of this intervention in the form of metrical and semantic inconsistencies. One line he cites in evidence occurs toward the end of the robbery at Gad's Hill, when the Prince dismisses his fellow robbers with the words: 'Away, good Ned – Falstaff sweats to death / And lards the lean earth as he walks along' (2.3.16–17). Taylor opines that the first line should read: 'Away good Ned – Oldcastle sweats to death', arguing that only a three-syllable name would make the line, which in the Falstaff-version is one syllable short, metrical. He infers from this that nothing but the name had been changed, which would be in keeping with the hypothesis of last-minute changes due to the pressures of external censorship.

Yet critics have disagreed with this argument on a number of points. First, the line had originally not been in verse, but in prose.[64] It was Alexander Pope who at the beginning of the eighteenth century

---

[62] Nor does the story end here: there seems to have been an ongoing protest against the portrayal of the Protestant hero as a rebel, a heretic or a coward on the contemporary stage and page. Pendleton notes references to travesties of Oldcastle (under this name), mostly in the form of complaints against such slander, as late as 1682. The broad and popular protest against such a mistreatment of a hero of Protestant England makes it more likely that the change in names was not only due to the 'autocratic and individual decision' of the Lord Chamberlain, but also 'because it proved offensive to a considerable segment of Shakespeare's countrymen' assembled in the audience ('On calling Falstaff Falstaff', 66–7). For a detailed account of the 'Versions of Sir John' on the contemporary stage and popular responses to them, see Whitney, *Early Responses to Renaissance Drama*, pp. 73–122.

[63] Patterson, 'Sir John Oldcastle as symbol of Reformation historiography', p. 22.

[64] Goldberg, 'The commodity of names', pp. 78–9.

arranged these lines into blank verse, an emendation which became itself canonised as uncovering Hal's true character – with versification signalling nobility and moral purity in the prosaic company of scoundrels – as well as the true intention of the playwright. Since the scene appears in prose in the early Quarto and Folio editions, however, the argument by metrical scanning falls flat.[65] However, even if we put the line in blank verse, Jonathan Goldberg argues, the Falstaff version would scan as well. With the caesura before his name functioning as a weak beat, 'the accent of Falstaff's name occurs where one would expect it in a line of iambic pentameter'; Oldcastle or Falstaff, 'the line is metrical either way'.[66] Especially in performance, where the question of verse or prose is a moot one anyway, the emphasis shifts from metrical scanning on the page to rhythm in delivery on the stage. In dramatic speech, moreover, the caesura before the name highlights the pause in that line.[67] This brief moment of hesitation opens up a space in which Oldcastle's censored name may be recalled.[68] When the actor commences with the name 'Falstaff', this name in turn becomes a sign, I would add, of the acts of erasure and replacement that produced it.

Moreover, the rest of the speech following the fat knight's name, as Giorgio Melchiori claims persuasively, 'is generally acknowledged as three lines of verse surviving from an earlier version of the play in which Falstaff bore the name of Oldcastle', and which the audience might have recalled from previous performances: 'Away, good Ned; Oldcastle sweats to death / And lards the lean earth as he walks along. / Were't not for laughing I should pity him.'[69] Even if the name Oldcastle had not appeared in this scene in performance any more, the Epilogue to 2 Henry IV echoes that line, and in so doing both points out and rectifies the substitution: predicting that in the sequel, Henry V, Falstaff 'shall die of a sweat' while the virtuous 'Oldcastle died

---

[65] Moreover, Thomas Pendleton points out, to draw a clear line between prose and verse is a futile act in a play that is notorious for crossing this boundary: in 1 Henry IV, there are often rough or hypermetrical lines, and verse rhythms are frequent in prose; characters' speeches shift between verse and prose depending on the semantic context of the scene. In this light, the absence of one unstressed syllable becomes quite a weak nail to hang an argument on ('On calling Falstaff Falstaff', 62–3).

[66] Goldberg 'The commodity of names', pp. 78, 79.

[67] Pendleton, 'On calling Falstaff Falstaff', 62.

[68] Goldberg, 'The commodity of names', p. 80.

[69] Melchiori, 'Dying of a sweat: Falstaff and Oldcastle', p. 211.

martyr, and this is not the man' (Epilogue, 29–30), the pattern of recall and replacement, of forgetting and substitution becomes explicit.

This pattern consistently recurs across the several plays in which Sir John figures, activating the dimension of intertheatrical memory. The audience's attention is repeatedly drawn to the absence of the name 'Oldcastle' through conspicuous moments of forgetting accruing to the name of Falstaff. As we have seen, the Epilogue to 2 *Henry IV* insists that Falstaff is not Oldcastle; Fluellen in *Henry V* has to be prompted to supply the name of 'the fat knight with the great belly doublet' (4.7.50); in *The Merry Wives of Windsor*, Mistress Page asks: 'What do you call your knight's name, sirrah?', and asserts: 'I can never hit on's name' (3.2.17, 21). In Jonathan Goldberg's words: 'Each time, as memory lapses, a pause occurs – and then the name "Sir John Falstaff"; each time ... the audience is reminded of a name that cannot be recalled, made to recall what the play cannot.'[70] T. W. Craik even speculates that such scenes might have prompted someone in the audience to call out 'Oldcastle' in a kind of 'covert joke between actors and audience', a speculation rendered probable if we take into account 'the latter's familiarity not only with the history plays themselves but with their recent theatrical history'.[71] I would argue that Shakespeare's insistent playing with the names of Falstaff and Oldcastle indicates that at least the existence of an intertheatrical memory shared by audience and actors is beyond speculation: else the joke would have fallen flat.[72]

There is one moment, in fact, in which the pattern is reversed and Falstaff's name is replaced by that of Oldcastle. In *1 Henry IV*, the Prince jestingly names his companion 'my old lad of the castle' (1.2.40). This pun certainly plays on the suppressed name. In the light of Taylor's argument, it is a sly allusion to the fact that Falstaff is 'really' Oldcastle and a reference to the act of censorship. 'But there is no joke, no sly allusion in calling Oldcastle "my old lad of the castle"', Thomas

---

[70] Goldberg, 'The commodity of names', p. 80.
[71] Craik, 'Introduction', p. 60, note 1.
[72] R. S. Fraser adds another dimension of intertheatrical memory when he explores the 'iterative process' through which the play might have prompted memories of Falstaff's first actor, Will Kemp. The idea that Kemp played Falstaff, indeed that the role had been written with this actor-clown in mind, is suggested by a similar conjunction of external and internal evidence as in the case Falstaff/Oldcastle, most notably Falstaff's/Kemp's conspicuous absence from Shakespeare's stage in *Henry V*, after he had left the company in 1599 (Wiles, *Shakespeare's Clown*, pp. 118–19).

A. Pendleton insists: 'there is no point to be made unless the fat knight is named something other than Oldcastle'. In this view, the pun is not a residue of an older, original name, as Taylor would have it, but makes more sense as an addition highlighting the very fact of removal: 'There seems to be good reason to suspect that the "old lad of the castle" entered the play only after "Oldcastle" had left.'[73] From yet another perspective, put forth by Goldberg, this pun does not refer, or not only refers, to a proper name but also to a 'cant term for roisterer', which appeared in a range of early modern comedies not connected at all to the historical Oldcastle. Instead of having one stable referent in history, the term 'old lad of the castle' was a widely used popular expression referring to London's contemporary subculture that included taverns, brothels and theatres. Hence, Goldberg concludes, 'Oldcastle is not named in the term – the pun depends upon the dispersal of his proper name'.[74] The line enacts rhetorically the gesture of censorship, and in so doing recalls that which the play was not allowed to name. By staging the effect of censorship, the pun effectively upstages it.

The pattern of displacement and dispersal is facilitated by the fact that the figure of Falstaff and his name are curiously detached. While in *Richard II* the separation of the individual person from 'the name of king' (*R2*, 3.3.145) is a painful, long-winded process enacted through elaborate rites of forgetting, as we have seen in the previous chapter, here the body and name of Falstaff are only loosely connected to begin with. Falstaff has many names: 'Sir John Sack and Sugar' (*1H4*, 1.2.110), 'Sir John Paunch' (2.2.63), 'Ribs' and 'Tallow' (2.4.109). Indeed he has so many that in the end he does not seem to have a proper name, a state of affairs quite fitting for a figure which keeps rejecting a fixed identity and insists instead on performatively producing and inhabiting a series of subjectivities.

In Falstaff's view, names and identities are nothing that one is born with, but rather a 'commodity' in the sense I have been discussing it throughout this chapter. Already with his first appearance on stage, Falstaff wishes that he and the Prince 'knew where a commodity of good names were to be bought' (1.2.81). Names are not signs of an identity; they are a commodity that can be purchased and sold, and they accrue (or can lose, for that matter) value through circulation

[73] Pendleton, 'On calling Falstaff Falstaff', 64.
[74] Goldberg, 'The commodity of names', p. 80.

and exchange. In turning the 'historical' figure of the Lollard martyr into an 'old white-bearded Satan' (2.4.384), the play had devalued the good name Oldcastle, or so the Cobham family claimed. At the same time, the play turns this new figure firmly into a property of the early modern stage. One answer to Falstaff's rhetorical question, then, is that names – in the sense of a commodity produced in and through performance – can be bought at the theatre. Falstaff himself provides a model for how this performative property is produced: through an ongoing process of self-forgetfulness and self-fashioning that plays with the memory of the other figures as well as of the audience. In this sense, Falstaff as the lethargic subject embodies the oblivion that is an integral part of the mnemonic economy in the Shakespearean theatre and in early modern culture.

4 | *Distraction: nationalist oblivion and contrapuntal sequencing in* Henry V

Hamlet's famous vow to recall his father's murder 'while memory holds a seat / In this distracted globe' (1.5.96–7), perhaps among the best-remembered lines from the play, implicitly casts the early modern stage as a medium of memory. Referring to the Globe,[1] the Lord Chamberlain's Men's new theatre building in which *Hamlet* was performed, the round playhouse is invoked as a material and cultural site where memorable images can be seen on stage. The playhouse functions as a place where memories, for example of the nation's past, can be recollected in performance. Hamlet's seat of memory is, however, a 'distracted globe', implying a simultaneous state of attentive recall and distracted oblivion that, while paradoxical, is a structural feature of the early modern stage. This is not to say that theatrical distraction was perceived as unproblematic. Unsurprisingly, contemporary denunciations of the stage vehemently objected to the ways in which it distracted theatre-goers from their duties in worship and work, an effect which was frequently couched in terms of forgetfulness, as we saw in the preceding chapter. If plays were regarded as offering sinful diversions in themselves, there was also plenty that could distract an audience from what happened on the stage. Actors in the 'unruly theatre', to use Anthony Dawson's apt phrase, had to compete with 'noise, self-display, cutpurses, and bawdy assignations … the selling of food and drink, cracking of nuts and even throwing of pippins'; such interruptions, he concludes, 'together with the evenness of light that blurred the distinctions between auditorium and stage … suggests a strong temptation to direct one's eyes and ears away from the stage'.[2] The pit was not the only source of disturbance, however; actors and

---

[1] The line can of course also be read as a reference to the 'memory theatre' of the traditional *ars memoria*, with the 'seat' alluding to the *sedes* or places where memory images are deposited for later retrieval, and the 'globe' as the skull, the physical seat of memory.

[2] Dawson, 'The distracted globe', pp. 104, 91–2.

their performance styles could prove a distraction from the play itself. Hamlet raises this problem of distracting performance in a later scene that gives us a glimpse of an annoyed playwright demanding more attention to the fruits of his labour. At the beginning of 3.2, Hamlet offers detailed instructions to the troupe of players who have come to Elsinore. His chief concern is that the players 'Suit the action to the word, the word to the action' (3.2.16–17). By no means must they through exaggerated gestures, inadequate enunciation or improper jesting divert the audience from the image represented on stage. That image, after all, is 'the purpose of playing, whose end, both at the first and now, is to hold, as 'twere, the mirror up to nature ... and the very age and body of the time his form and pressure' (18–22). Hamlet describes here the theatre's function in terms of its mnemonic and mimetic appeal: it should show an image that is an accurate as well as captivating representation, an impressive image of the time, whose form is stamped in the minds of the audience as though in wax. This is to be achieved through a performance that adequately represents 'the question of the play' (38). But performance is, crucially, also what can distract from the 'the purpose of playing' as envisaged by Hamlet. Actors who 'mouth' their words, 'saw the air too much with [their] hands', or 'tear a passion to tatters' with too much 'dumb show and noise' (2, 4, 8–11) may entirely disrupt the theatrical illusion. Even worse are the clowns, who unduly improvise and speak 'more than is set down for them' or who 'will laugh themselves to set on some quantity of barren spectators to laugh too, though in the meantime some necessary question of the play be then to be considered' (35–8). Theatrical performance itself can be a distraction, then: the spectacle of the actors' body language, the improvisation of the clowns, the laughter shared between actors and audience – all these can go against the grain of the play's alleged purpose of representing 'the very age and body of the time' in memorable stage pictures. To be sure, performance conventions were usually geared toward focusing and directing the audience's attention. As Evelyn Tribble has shown in her recent study *Cognition in the Globe* (2011), this could be achieved for example through the employment of theatrical space, in particular entries and exits through doors, through the positioning of bodies and objects in that space, and through the use of words and gestures to direct the audience's gaze. Interestingly, she also acknowledges that such practices inevitably had the effect of distracting the audience's attention *from* something else: they could be used 'as a crucial tool for audience direction – and, perhaps even more importantly, indirection'.[3] Distraction is not something that happens merely by accident; it is an effect of theatrical attention management.

Distraction is also an important key to exploring the theatre's purpose for politics in early modern England. Hamlet's 'distracted globe' can be understood in the same terms as Thomas Nashe's statement about the 'Pollicie of playes' that lies in keeping the idle, pleasure-seeking 'Gentlemen of the Court, the Innes of the Courte, and the number of Captaines and Souldiers about London' off the streets, where they might cause riot and disorder. This, Nashe asserts, is one of the 'secrects of gouernment'.[4] Stagecraft appears here as another form of statecraft: offering distractions to the populace will 'busy giddy minds' (*2H4*, 4.3.341) and keep them out of trouble. Transposing this policy from the local to the national level, this is sound advice for ensuring peace and unity. Moreover, by focusing attention onto the right kind of spectacle, for instance history plays, the theatre becomes a medium for forging an 'imagined community' (B. Anderson, 1991). As new historicist readings have persuasively demonstrated, theatricality is one of power's essential modes – but serving the powers that be, I would add, is not the entire purpose of playing. I would like to argue here that by attending carefully to the formal features of plays, their rhetoric, sequencing, rhythm and stage pictures, we can arrive at a more nuanced understanding of the relationship between statecraft and stagecraft. Taking the cue from *Hamlet*, I will try to insert the question of mnemonic dramaturgy into the equation of theatricality and power. My reading of *Henry V* acknowledges this instrumentalisation of theatricality in the service of ideology: distraction is indeed a prominent political strategy *in* the play as well as, curtailed to a certain extent by its dramaturgy, *of* the play. Couched in a rhetoric of national memory and monumental history, this strategy of distraction aims at what I will call 'nationalist oblivion'. Curiously, however, such nationalist oblivion emerges mostly from moments in the play that are ostensibly about remembrance or that insistently present themselves to the audience as memorable stage pictures. Although they answer to Hamlet's idea of impressive, captivating scenes – and we should

---

[3] Tribble, *Cognition in the Globe*, p. 36.
[4] Nashe, *Pierce Pennilesse*, p. 86.

bear in mind here that Shakespeare was already engaged in compos-
ing *Hamlet* at the time he completed *Henry V* – they actually perform
the kind of bad-faith distractions, erasures and elisions that form the
deep-structure of ideology. In turn, there are also moments that we
might not remember too well because they seem irrelevant to the plot
(and are often cut in productions today), but which slow down the
action, give pause for thought and thus offer an opportunity for taking a step back and for recollecting 'how the sequel hangs together',
in the Scrivener's memorable lines from *Richard III* (3.6.4). Again
proceeding in seemingly counter-intuitive fashion, Shakespeare makes
some of these scenes explicitly about forgetting, while their structural
function is one of recollection and recall. By viewing both types of
scenes together as integral components of the overall dramatic narrative, we can see at work in *Henry V* a mnemonic dramaturgy that is
aptly described by Hamlet's line 'while memory holds a seat in this distracted globe': a pattern of sequencing, rhythm, rhetoric and intertheatrical echoes that enacts both recollection and distraction, sometimes
setting content and form at odds, sometimes fusing them. That *Henry
V* is characterised by a paradoxical simultaneity of ideology and its
critique, or of subversion and containment, is admittedly not a new
idea.[5] But my focus on mnemonic dramaturgy helps us to forestall a
'flattening out' of the distinctions between the theatre and society typical of new historicist readings,[6] and to acknowledge the specifically
dramatic forms of remembering and forgetting at work in the early
modern theatre.

On the level of the *locus*, the historical events of the play-world,
distraction is clearly the preferred policy of domination in the plays
known as the *Henriad*. It might even serve as the motto of the house
of Lancaster, dictating the very first order that Henry Bolingbroke gives
when he is crowned king at the end of *Richard II*: realising full well that
the regicide which was to secure his own reign has set a precedence that
will become a perpetual danger to his crown, King Henry announces 'a
voyage to the Holy Land / To wash this blood off from my guilty hand'
(5.6.49–50). This pilgrimage is supposed to perform a double act of
erasure: on the individual level, it will cleanse his person from the stain

---

[5] See the classic account by Norman Rabkin in his study *Shakespeare and the
Problem of Meaning* for one of its clearest articulations.
[6] Joughin, 'Shakespeare's memorial aesthetics', p. 44.

of Richard's blood; on the national level, it is designed to distract his nobles from the possibility of a renewed struggle for the crown, either by claiming the sacred loyalty due to a sovereign on pilgrimage or by taking them with him as a royal entourage. This is not piety but policy, and the difference becomes clear in hindsight when, in the first scene of the next history play in sequence, he seeks to quell the rebellion that the Percys will mount in the course of the play by just such an enterprise. In the opening scene of *1 Henry IV*, the King and his closest councillors ponder the precarious peace after the civil war that won him the crown. Now England is engaged in costly border wars against Wales and Scotland, with 'uneven and unwelcome news' (1.1.50) of severe losses coming in incessantly. Lamenting the costs of civil war and vowing that the country shall suffer no more, the King declares:

> Therefore, friends,
> As far as to the sepulchre of Christ –
> Whose soldier now, under whose blessed cross
> We are impressèd and engaged to fight –
> Forthwith a power of English shall we levy.

> (*1H4*, 1.1.18–19, 22)

The causality between civil war and foreign enterprise could not be clearer, and its logic is underlined by grammar: the sentence opens with the conjunctive adverb 'therefore' and begins in mid-line, following directly on his vow that civil war shall be ended. It continues with a vision of 'a power of English', the first mention of nationality in the play; without a noun to qualify or dilute, the adjective 'English' has become the object of undivided attention in this sentence. Of course Henry has to admit immediately that this scheme for national unification has already fallen victim to the rebellion, instead of preventing it. But the vision is there, to be recalled by an attentive audience at the end of the next sequel, *2 Henry IV*. There, King Henry gives his son and heir 'the very latest counsel / That ever I shall breathe': to ward off the ambitions and animosities of his powerful lords by leading them 'to the Holy Land, / Lest rest and lying still might make them look / Too near unto my state.' The same must be his son's policy, whose claim to the throne, while stronger than his own, is still not safe: 'Therefore, my Harry, / Be it thy course to busy giddy minds / With foreign quarrels, that action hence borne out / May waste the memory of the former days' (*2H4*, 4.3.312–13, 340–3). This advice spells out the fact that distraction is a form of erasing dangerous memories, and that it is a political strategy for ensuring peace and national unity.[7]

This insight is brought home to the audience already during the first part of *Henry IV* by the rebels' repeated complaint of King Henry's ingratitude for their support in putting him on the throne. The Percys see this ingratitude as an act of wilful forgetting, calling Henry disrespectfully 'this forgetful man' (1.3.159) and even accusing him openly that he has 'forgot your oath to us at Doncaster' (5.1.58). By the same token, remembrance becomes the constant theme of the rebels. It is in particular Hotspur who acts as champion of memory in his first appearance on stage. More precisely, he champions the memory of Edmund Mortimer, who is Richard's legitimate heir and thus Henry's rival to the throne. The King, unsurprisingly, refuses to redeem Mortimer from his Welsh captivity, arguing that his recent marriage to Glendower's daughter reveals him as a traitor (1.3.79–91). Disagreeing with the royal verdict, Hotspur turns himself metonymically into 'one tongue [speaking] for all those wounds' which he deems proof of Mortimer's honour and loyalty (95). Yet King Henry stubbornly proceeds to shame opposition into silence: 'Art thou not ashamed? But sirrah, henceforth / Let me not hear you speak of Mortimer' (116–17). After the King has left, Hotspur sets himself up as the champion of Mortimer's claims – 'Zounds, I will speak of him, and let my soul / Want mercy if I do not join with him' (129–30) – yet it becomes quickly clear that Henry's treatment of Mortimer only serves as a superficial legitimation for rebellion: the deeper cause is the Percys' disappointment about his ingratitude for their role in putting him on the throne. Nevertheless, by rhetorically wedding memory and honour he manages to legitimate the uprising as a rebellion against the 'shameless transformation' (1.1.44) of truth into lies:

> Shall it for shame be spoken in these days,
> Or fill up the chronicles in times to come,
> That men of your nobility and power,
> Did gage them both in an unjust behalf –
> As both of you, God pardon it, have done –

> (*1H4*, 1.3.168–70)

---

[7] Nashe indicates that this is indeed a longstanding piece of politic wisdom when he gives it to us in the form of a Latin proverb: '*Nam si foras hostem non habent, domie invenient*. If they have no service abroad, they will make mutinies at home' (*Pierce Pennilesse*, p. 85).

Exhorting the other nobles to bear in mind how they will be remembered in oral memory as well as in written chronicles, Hotspur links these false memories to everlasting shame. To redeem Mortimer, although an act of open rebellion against the king, would at the same time 'redeem / [their] banished honours' (1.3.178–9). While the speech presents rebellion as a means to re-establish the truth, this high moral ground is undermined by Hotspur's parenthesis – 'As both of you, God pardon it, have done' – which clearly states that this honourable rebellion is also a means to hide another truth: his father's and uncle's guilt in Richard's downfall. The language of economy further undermines the heroic stance: if honour is 'redeemed', this is not only because honour is a value in itself, but also out of sheer self-preservation, since the King 'studies day and night / To answer all the debt he owes to you, / Even with the bloody payment of your deaths' (1.3.182–4).

Thus the beginning of *1 Henry IV* introduces the political implications of both forgetting and remembering out of which the dramatic events unfold in the play-world; *Henry V* will extend this theme into a dramaturgy that involves the audience in the playhouse into the drama of memory this play stages. The audience reception of *Henry V*, as I will argue, is governed by a paradoxical pattern in which claims of remembrance often serve to erase memories, while scenes that are ostensibly about forgetting are meant to trigger them. The point is not to decide whether the play distracts or directs the audience's attention, and what ideological stance is thereby invited, but to recognise that it does both through a skilful deployment of dramatic devices, thus effectively furnishing the audience with the 'imaginary puissance' (*H5*, 1.0.25) needed to dismantle the workings of nationalist oblivion.

In spite of its failure to prevent rebellion, Henry V accepts his father's advice as the 'secrete of gouernment' but will more successfully turn it to advantage. Already at the end of *2 Henry IV*, we learn that 'ere this year expire, / We bear our civil swords and native fire / As far as France' (5.5.103–4), and the next in the sequence of histories (interrupted, to be sure, by the amusing distractions of the irrepressible Falstaff in the *Merry Wives of Windsor*) opens with an invocation of 'a muse of fire' and 'warlike Harry' as the war-god Mars (*H5*, 1.0.5–6). Harry has made good his promise to the dying King Henry IV and taken an army to France, there to enlarge his kingdom and to keep his nobles busy. The first scenes of the play, however, do not take us to the battlefield; instead, the play opens at the English court, where an official legitimation for the invasion of France is forged out of the written chronicles of history. The opening scene slows down the feverish pace set by the incendiary rhetoric of the prologue: we see two bishops who debate how best to protect the Church's possessions from a crippling tax bill. They set their hopes on the young king as 'a true lover of the holy Church' (1.1.24). The following lengthy praise of King Henry's miraculous reformation from wild youth to wise sovereign is, in terms of dramaturgy, clearly motivated by the playwright's expectation that at least parts of the audience have seen the earlier *Henry*-plays and recall him, above all, as the madcap prince. While they would have gotten only a brief glimpse of the beginning of his reformation at the end of *2 Henry IV*, they are here presented with a narrated memory picture of Henry V that prospectively prepares for his new image as 'mirror of all Christian kings' (2.0.6). However, the bishops themselves interrupt this wonderful vision when they declare that 'miracles are ceas'd / And therefore must we needs admit the means / How things are perfected' (1.2.68–70). They believe that King Henry will save them, not because they regard him as a pious defender of the Church but because they know that he needs money for his French campaign, money they have and that will buy them off the bill. Again, this is a scene not about piety but about politics. Moreover, it is a first moment of recollection, which invites the audience to set the prologue's vision of heroism and patriotism into perspective. This happens not only on the level of content, through the discrepancy between praise and realpolitik. It is also achieved through the tension between historical *locus* and contemporary *platea*. As Graham Holderness points out, 'the bishops, in their conspirational world of financial planning and mercenary calculation, in one sense occupy a modern materialistic and sceptical consciousness remote from their own historical realm of medieval Christianity. They view the church not as the community of Christ's faithful, or as a means of bringing men closer to God, but as an administrative and political apparatus.'[8] While I do not entirely agree with this somewhat nostalgic view

[8] Holderness, *Shakespeare: The Histories*, p. 145.

of the naïve faith and integrity of the medieval princes of the Church, the interesting point is here that the scene activates not only theatrical memories of Prince Harry's earlier stage appearances but also of the historical memory of the Reformation under Henry VIII, a context that at the same time legitimises the bishops' scepticism and casts doubt on the ulterior motivations of all Christian kings. Thus when the Archbishop of Canterbury complains that 'all the temporal lands which men devout / By testament have given to the Church / Would they strip form us' (1.1.9–11), this may have recalled to a post-Reformation audience the systematic diversions of ecclesiastical income into royal coffers under the aegis of Thomas Cromwell from 1534 onwards, conducted in order to finance the military (as well as other) expenditures of King Henry VIII. In this way the memories of two heroic kings are called up precisely in order to question their image as true Christian monarchs.

This double act of recollection occurs in a scene that 'has almost invariably been omitted or abridged in the theatre', as Gary Taylor notes in his editorial gloss, because it fails to engage modern audiences.[9] In terms of Shakespeare's mnemonic dramaturgy, however, it is indispensable as it alerts his contemporary audience to the fact that memorable images such as the prologue or the bishops' praise of the heroic king must be taken with a pinch of salt, at least, since to believe implicitly in the veracity of such memory images is to fall into the trap of ideology. The lesson – which we already encountered in plays like *Richard III* – that memories can be stage-managed and thus pressed into the service of politics, is also borne out by the very next scene. It opens with a long, tedious recital of the juridical and genealogical justification for King Henry's invasion into France, the so-called Salic Law speech. As Jonathan Baldo remarks, the bishops operate here as skilful masters of 'the art of distraction', their objective being 'to divert [Henry] from advancing the bill to appropriate church money and lands' by giving him 'a justification for invading France'.[10] Assuming that King Henry V is the shrewd, subtle stage-manager of his nation's historical memory that the play reveals him to be, however, he might not be the intended victim of the bishop's distraction tactics here: the bishops, I propose, rather act as the agents of Henry's mnemonic policy. In the play-world, the function

[9] Taylor (ed.), *Henry V*, p. 94.
[10] Baldo, 'Shakespeare's art of distraction', 8.

of that lengthy excursion into law and genealogy is to make the legitimacy of his claim to the throne incontestable. At the same time, however, this seems to be a gratuitous exercise since all present during that
recital already believe in its legitimacy after all. This makes it probable
that the speech is actually addressed to the audience in the playhouse –
but to what effect? It is a critical commonplace, Gary Taylor notes
in the introduction to the Oxford edition, that the Salic Law speech
is 'unrivalled for tediousness' in the entire Shakespeare canon. In this
view, the scene's dullness might serve to distract the audience from realising that Henry's claim to the throne is actually not that self-evident.
However, Taylor criticises this as an unhistorical view which projects
modern reception habits back onto an early modern audience that,
Taylor believes, was 'much more interested in the Salic Law ... and
accustomed to listening to long and intellectually complex sermons'.[11]
This view is likewise somewhat one-sided, though, in that it assumes an
attentive, quiet audience like at church; Hamlet's exasperated comment
by contrast suggests that at least some audience members – distracted
by nut-cracking, apple-crunching and generally noisy neighbours –
might have found it difficult to recall just how this genealogical sequel
hangs together. Nevertheless Taylor has a point when he claims that
this speech, even '[i]f an audience begins to grow impatient during this
demonstration', 'is dramatically useful, indeed dramatically necessary'.
For one, he argues, it brings the audience's emotions, excited by the
high-strung rhetoric of the prologue, down a step or two, thus liberating
the playwright from having to provide such excitement in every single
scene. More important, however, is that it instils a necessary measure
of suspicion about the succession of historical events in the audience.
Such a sceptical dramaturgy allows the audience not only to discern
the Archbishop's personal motives behind supporting Henry's claim,
it likewise casts a first doubt on the King himself who at this point
'has already laid claim to some French dukedoms, a claim to which
the French will reply in the embassy we know to be waiting just off-
stage'.[12] For the scene to work in this sceptical way, the audience does
not have to rely on historical memory gained from reading Holinshed
(from whose Chronicles the Salic Law speech is taken almost verbatim). It may as well rely on its theatrical memory of the previous scene

[11] Taylor, 'Introduction', pp. 34–5.
[12] *Ibid.*, pp. 37–8.

as well as of earlier plays in order to realise that what looks like an act
of remembering can serve to distract from or even erase rivalling memories. I will come back later to this device of dramatic sequencing in
order to upstage royal memory politics.

In many ways the opposite of the Salic Law speech is Henry's
St Crispin's Day speech, arguably the best-remembered and most
anthologised speech from the play, perhaps even the entire Shakespeare
canon. Its function in the play-world and the playhouse is similar,
though, in that it constitutes again a conspicuous moment of remembrance that actually performs a complex act of nationalist oblivion.
Well-known as it is, it is worth quoting here the entire speech:

> This day is called the Feast of Crispian.
> He that outlives this day and comes safe home
> Will stand a-tiptoe when this day is named
> And rouse him at the name of Crispian.
> He that shall see this day and live t'old age
> Will yearly on the vigil feast his neighbours
> And say 'Tomorrow is Saint Crispian'.
> Then will he strip his sleeve and show his scars
> And say, 'These wounds I had on Crispin's day'.
> Old men forget; yet all shall be forgot,
> But he'll remember, with advantages,
> What feats he did that day. Then shall our names,
> Familiar in his mouth as household words –
> Harry the King, Bedford and Exeter,
> Warwick and Talbot, Salisbury and Gloucester –
> Be in their flowing cups freshly remembered.
> This story shall the good man teach his son.
> And Crispin Crispian shall ne'er go by
> From this day to the ending of the world
> But we in it shall be rememberèd.
> We few, we happy few, we band of brothers.
> For he today that sheds his blood with me
> Shall be my brother; be he ne'er so vile,
> This day shall gentle his condition.

> (4.3.40–63)

At the level of content, Henry's speech, delivered to his decimated
army just before the decisive battle against the French, is about how
they will be commemorated as heroes. It sets in with a promise of

survival and future remembrance: the events of the upcoming battle are projected into a time when they will be remembered as part of a glorious past. The speech also lists the specific practices of ceremonial remembrance this entails: the institutionalisation of memory in a national holiday; its ritual announcement repeated on the eve of its return; communal feasting and drinking; the showing of physical marks, bodily souvenirs of the battle; a roll-call of names; and turning the past event into a story, a legend of heroism and brotherhood. Ceremony in the form of ritual, bodily and narrative practices is 'how societies remember', as Paul Connerton argued in his classic study of the same title. Its social function is to provide 'significantly recurrent' moments in which 'individuals might celebrate their role and realise their value exclusively in the knowledge that it is a fresh incarnation of the tradition'.[13] Ceremony assures people that they and their individual memories are, in other words, part of a larger entity. Experienced by each man individually, personal remembrance is turned into a communal event through ceremony. In the playhouse, the speech is part of the theatrical spectacle, with the enactment of ceremony on stage as a means of engaging audiences past and present, forging a national community across time. The events at Agincourt will be memorialised in a narrative, retold 'with advantages' and 'in flowing cups'. It is precisely this future retelling of the story, embellished into a spectacle of national valour for the delectation of the spectators that the audience at the Globe may witness and pleasurably identify with.[14] The play can thus be seen as another ceremonial ritual that serves to extend the sense of community from the medieval past into the Elizabethan present.

However, the speech also illustrates the necessary interrelation of remembering and forgetting in the imaginative production of a national community. Forging a nation through remembrance necessitates at the same time forgetting parts of that community's past. In his 1882 lecture 'What is a nation?' the French historian Ernest Renan famously argued that nations emerge, above all, from an interplay of remembering and forgetting. Trying to come to terms with the question of what constitutes a nation, Renan examined and dismissed various definitions of national identity on the basis of dynastic

---

[13] Connerton, *How Societies Remember*, p. 63.
[14] Dawson, 'The arithmetic of memory', p. 55.

lines and race, language and religion, shared interest and territory.[15] Instead he privileged memory as the integrative force that brings about a 'fusion of component populations'. In so doing, he did not focus on commemorative practices formalised in national holidays, memorial monuments or myths of origin that aim at generating solidarity in the present through remembering a shared past, but rather highlighted *forgetting* as the operative principle of that fusion:

Forgetting, I would even go so far as to say historical error, is a crucial factor in the creation of a nation, which is why progress in historical studies often constitutes a danger for [the principle of] nationality. Indeed, historical enquiry brings to light deeds of violence which took place at the origin of all political formations, even of those whose consequences have been altogether beneficial. Unity is always effected by means of brutality … The essence of a nation is that all individuals have many things in common, and also that they have forgotten many things.[16]

The erasure of the past, and in particular of past atrocities that would impede a peaceful co-existence as one people, is a precondition for nation formation. However, this passage from Renan's essay is itself caught in a performative paradox – not unlike the one we observe in *Henry V* – for how can Renan remember that which by his own account should have been forgotten long ago? Moreover, in merely alluding to brutal events in the nation's distant past, he clearly expects his readers to share these 'lost' memories. The solution to this paradox is, as Benedict Anderson suggests in his reading of Renan, that the community-enabling act of forgetting is not a singular event that consigns irrevocably to oblivion what would disrupt the fragile unity. Rather, the act of forgetting must be performed over and over again, and consequently what must be forgotten must also be kept in view,

---

[15] Renan's list of the various dimensions of the nation prefigures the range of criteria for national identity and nationalism resulting from the critical debate of the twentieth century. Attempting to summarise the concepts and definitions available, recent overviews typically come up with lists of complementary criteria of what constitutes a nation, including a distinct territory, a unified population, a shared culture (language, religion, symbols), collective memories (history, myth), and common law for all its members (protecting individual interests as well as shared values); see Smith, *Nationalism*, p. 124; Breuilly, *Nationalism and the State*, p. 2.

[16] Renan, 'What is a nation', pp. 10–11.

however obliquely: 'Having to "have already forgotten" tragedies of which one needs unceasingly to be "reminded" turns out to be a characteristic device in the later construction of national genealogies.'[17] In other words, the dynamics of forgetting and remembrance form an ongoing, iterative process that generates national identity. Anthony D. Smith stresses this performative quality of national identity when he defines it as 'the continuous reproduction and reinterpretation of the pattern of values, symbols, memories, myths and traditions that compose the distinctive heritage of nations, and the identification of individuals with that cultural pattern and heritage and with its cultural elements'.[18]

In early modern England, the theatre and in particular the genre of history plays provided such a performative approach to the nation's past. To be more precise, the history plays worked not only as enactments of the nation's past, they also enacted the interplay of remembering and forgetting that in fact produces both the nation and its past as a rallying point for national identity in the first place. However, I do not assume that the stage in general and history plays in particular served straightforwardly as instruments of nation building. While the theatre certainly constituted one of the early modern 'forms of nationhood', to cite the title of Richard Helgerson's important study, it was also able to reflect critically on remembering and forgetting as political practices of forging an imagined community. In other words, staging the nation's past also meant staging those perspectives that had been delegitimised, excluded and lost on the way to an imagined unity. The nationalist oblivion represented in plays like *Henry V* may well have aimed at raising a similar double consciousness in the audience. It united them in a feeling of patriotic enthusiasm that obliterated the differences of rank, religion and regional origin existing among them. Yet seeing strategic acts of forgetting displayed on stage may as well have alerted the spectators to the extent to which 'having already forgotten' was part of their own experience of nationhood and indeed 'a prime contemporary civic duty'.[19]

Henry's St. Crispin's Day speech simultaneously performs acts of commemoration and acts of erasure which together aim at constituting an imagined community, both in the play and in the theatre. The speech

---

[17] Anderson, *Imagined Communities*, p. 201.
[18] Smith, *Nationalism*, p. 18.
[19] Anderson, *Imagined Communities*, p. 200.

(as well as the play on the whole) addresses its patriotic rhetoric to two audiences, on and off the stage, seeking to unite both in a feeling of national community that joins the past with the present. Yet as we shall see, the affective and mnemonic structure of this speech is more complicated: the feats of remembering and forgetting enacted in the play-world and the playhouse, and the communities forged through them may have different, even contradictory political trajectories. One trajectory is marked by the proto-democratic rhetoric of the Saint Crispin's Day speech. Harry's insistence on brotherhood seeks to erase the divisive social hierarchy between king and common soldiers in favour of a 'band of brothers'.[20] Spilling their blood for Henry 'gentles' the common soldiers' lowly 'condition' and erases social differences that are grounded precisely on bloodlines and origin. According to Anderson, such a levelling of vertical hierarchies is one of the basic conditions for the emergence of an imagined community at national level.[21] The emphasis on male bonding and fraternal solidarity beyond social rank is strengthened by the choice of saints for this holiday: Crispin and Crispianus, the saints of shoemakers. According to Thomas Deloney's *The Gentle Craft* (1597), Crispin and Crispianus were royal twins whose mother disguised them as commoners and apprenticed them to a shoemaker in order to protect them from a tyrant's wrath. Still under the humble guise as shoemakers, the brothers rose to fame and distinction in their craft as well as on the battlefield. Their good fortune and eventual reconciliation with the king is celebrated by the shoemakers' calling out a new holiday that for one day united everybody in celebration. As Alison Chapman has shown, early modern literary and dramatic representations of the shoemaking craft associate it with the kind of social levelling Henry's speech seems to promise. This is acknowledged by its status as a 'gentle' and indeed a gentling craft, which is often played out in the

---

[20] My reading here follows Dawson's in 'The arithmetic of memory', 54–6.
Another erasure of differences crucial to national unity that this speech and the play on the whole performs, is the division between England, Wales, Scotland and Ireland which must be overcome in order to find a univocal answer to one of the play's most insistent questions, 'What ish my nation?' (3.3.61). Baldo's essay 'Wars of memory in *Henry V*' also offers a detailed reading of how the play both enacts and exposes the process of national unification through collective remembering and forgetting, but it focuses more on the question of which specific historical memories were recalled or erased by the play rather than on the mnemonic dramaturgy through which this is effected.

[21] Anderson, *Imagined Communities*, p. 7.

convivial mingling of or the exchange of social roles between shoemaker and gentleman of royal blood. Another association that is important for our purposes is the shoemakers' well-known prerogative to proclaim ad-hoc holidays. This probably goes back to the historical fact that the craftsmen were not bound to keeping the Sunday, using that day instead to sell shoes to ill-shod churchgoers, and that they were allowed to choose their own times of holiday leisure instead. This originally economic motivation emerged in the literary imagination of the early modern period as a distinctly anti-authoritarian privilege to call out holidays for the entire community. The number of literary texts on shoemakers around 1600 – among them Deloney's *The Gentle Craft* (1597), Thomas Dekker's *Shoemaker's Holiday* (1599), William Rowley's *A Shoemaker, A Gentleman* (1638) and, if only through brief references, Shakespeare's *Henry V* and *Julius Caesar* (both 1599) – attests to the contemporary popularity of this craft as the symbolic expression of a desire for social mobility and fraternal solidarity. Henry summons up these associations of levelling and holiday-making in the St Crispin's Day speech, as Chapman points out: 'Henry's image of brotherhood extends to commoner and nobleman alike, bringing all into a martial and fraternal community where social distinctions are imaginatively erased.'[22] In choosing Crispin and Crispianus as the patron saints for his holiday, Henry presents himself as a folk-king, recalling the madcap-prince of the festive popular world that was his realm in the two earlier plays and that he seems to have successfully resurrected here.

The speech, however, performs a paradoxical communicative act, which alerts us to a second trajectory of the community-forging dynamics in and of this play. It is, after all, a king's speech in which we encounter this levelling rhetoric with its subversive vision of a fraternal community. Moreover, this is the king who in *Henry IV, Part One* made a point of learning the common people's language so that he could 'command every chap in Eastcheap' when he was king (2.5.12–13); who in his first appearance in *Henry V* was resolved to be remembered as a 'Christian king', or be utterly forgotten, 'Not worshipped with a waxed epitaph' (1.2.233); who just a scene ago asserted that there was no difference between kings and common people 'save ceremony, save general ceremony' (4.1.236) – and who now seems to assert the same profound equality, but does so through the very vehicle

---

[22] Chapman, 'Whose Saint Crispin's Day is it?', 1484.

which before was revealed as the sole generator of social difference. For Harry's speech just before the battle hinges on nothing so much as ceremony: it announces a future national holiday and furnishes it proleptically with its particular rites of remembrance; and it is itself part of the ceremonial trappings of warfare which make up much of the action of this play, such as the legal justification and declaration of war (1.2.), negotiations through heralds (1.2, 2.4) and a peace treaty (5.2.). Therefore we need to acknowledge that while in Henry's public address, ceremonial remembrance is employed as a vehicle of *erasing* social difference, the private soliloquy in the previous scene depicts it as a vehicle of producing and maintaining them. When Harry complains, 'And what have kings that privates have not too, / Save ceremony, save general ceremony?' (4.1.220–1), these lines can be construed, depending on where the emphasis falls, as an argument for levelling social hierarchies – there is not much difference between kings and commoners after all – or indeed for maintaining them through ceremony. In view of the dramatic sequencing, the following scenes make the second option seem more convincing, even though this means that the very use of ceremonial language and ritual in the St. Crispin's Day Speech frames its promise of fraternity across all ranks ironically.

Another ironic frame is provided by the conflict between the soldier Williams and King Henry in disguise, which in turn directly precedes Henry's soliloquy of ceremony and is taken up again immediately after the battle in scene 4.8. As William Leahy notes, the confrontation between Williams and Henry about the military leaders' cavalier contempt for the common soldiers – a complaint that probably resonated with the contemporary discontents of soldiers serving in the Irish wars – remains unresolved.[23] When Williams later challenges Henry's stand-in, Fluellen, who wears his glove as mark of recognition, and in his response to the King's accusation of *lèse-majesté* claims 'the common humanity which lies beneath the "ceremony" of kingship',[24] the King does not even reply directly to him but buys himself off with a gold-filled glove. Fluellen tops this with twelve pence and

---

[23] Leahy, '"All would be royal": The effacement of disunity in Shakespeare's *Henry V*', 93–4. The topicality of the Irish campaign is of course not only due to its being at a height when the play was written but is also signalled by the reference to Essex's return from Ireland in the Chorus at the beginning of act 5.

[24] Mason, '*Henry V*: "the quick forge and working house of thought"', p. 185.

the patronising recommendation that 'it will serve you to mend your shoes' (4.8.67–8), adding insult to an injury that becomes even more clear when we recall that Crispin and Crispianus were the patron saints of shoemakers and, by extension, of a levelling ethos that is here betrayed. The scenes with Williams thus challenge the effacement of differences enacted in the St. Crispin's Day speech as well as in such modern criticism that insists on reading the play, if not as an unequivocal celebration of Henry as the perfect monarch, then as a successful dramatisation of national unification.[25]

An alternative way of reading the St Crispin's Day speech which would be more in keeping with the overall mnemonic policies in *Henry V* can be accessed precisely through these ironies highlighted by dramatic sequencing and framing; yet it lies not merely in the opposite of what was said. Harry is not simply lying to his soldiers, promising what he never intends to deliver. This would be a very crude interpretation, falling short of his subtle handling of memories he displays elsewhere. Rather, his promise of a soldierly community is not cancelled entirely but displaced onto the ultimate aim of a national community.[26] This second-order community is likewise forged through ceremony, but at the same time is much more in keeping with the division-stabilising properties of ceremony that Harry's earlier soliloquy emphasises. Promising his soldiers a holiday to remember their

---

[25] Leahy takes critics' evaluation of the King's treatment of Williams and his eventual response to the money offered as a test case: where Williams is discredited by being made to accept the money, the King's policy tends to be valorised and 'the disunity and disruption that the play articulates' is glossed over in a gesture of critical containment ('"All would be royal": The effacement of disunity in Shakespeare's *Henry V*', 95).

[26] Peter Womack traces a similar development: taking Shakespeare's first tetralogy as an example, Womack demonstrates how these four history plays enact the transition from a model of dynastic loyalty to a model of national allegiance, the key difference between the two being the presence of an 'idea of England' with which the audience can imaginatively identify. This 'idea of England', he claims, is eventually embodied in the King. While this may generate an 'absolutist closure' in the sense that it invokes 'the all-embracing oneness of the monarch', Womack at the same time points out that the public theatre always enacts 'two modes of address' that correspond with the status of the players as servants of a nobleman (the Admiral's Men, the King's Men) and as common people and craftsmen themselves ('Imagining communities', p. 137). Thus the double trajectory of community-forging we see at work in *Henry V* can be regarded as a structural pattern of early modern theatrical practice.

'band of brothers' by, it is ultimately the King who is to be remembered and celebrated on this new national holiday.[27] The Chorus, which has long been recognised as a mouthpiece of royalist ideology, enthuses 'Praise and glory on his head!' (Chorus, 4.0.31) and thereby unwittingly uncovers for once the true aim of Harry's mnemonic and nationalist policies: 'the near-sacralisation of the military triumphs of this young warrior king'.[28] Harry himself becomes both the instrument and the sign of the unified nation, indeed its worshipped 'idol [of] ceremony' (4.1.237).

Guy Debord has commented in a different context that in modern nations 'the spectacle appears ... as a means of unification. As a part of society, it is that sector where all attention, all consciousness converges. Being isolated – and precisely for that reason – this sector is the locus of illusion and false consciousness; the unity it imposes is merely the official language of generalised separation.'[29] This double logic of unification and separation under the guise of spectacle can usefully be recast in terms of Harry's efforts at stabilising his kingship in what retrospectively appears as an absolutist image of sovereignty. The 'gentling' of common soldiers evoked at the end of his speech is clearly dependent on creditable military service in the king's battle. It is not achieved through birth or through economic success, as was the case with the original medieval shoemaker-princes Crispin and Crispianus. This preferment-by-desert seems to belong neither to a feudal past nor a mercantile future but exists in the interstices of action, be it military or theatrical. Neither is it truly democratic in the sense that every soldier can join the band of brothers around Henry; after all, it is still the king who elects the hand-chosen 'happy few'. This discrepancy is highlighted when we note Pistol's futile attempt at gentling himself through money in the following scene: true gentility can only be conferred by the king.[30] Likewise, the promise of quasi-canonisation for each soldier implicit in the speech is no more than an empty rhetorical gesture. Harry promises that each common soldier will be grafted into the calendar as a kind of annually

---

[27] See Altman, '"Vile participation": The amplification of violence in the theater of *Henry V*', who points out the distinctly sacred aura of King Harry, especially after the battle at Agincourt.

[28] Grady, *Shakespeare, Machiavelli and Montaigne*, p. 234.

[29] Debord, *The Society of Spectacle*, p. 12.

[30] See Chapman, 'Whose Saint Crispin's Day is it?', 1486–7.

remembered saint ('he'll remember with advantages / What feats he did that day', 4.3.50–1), and he likens the English soldiers' suffering on the battlefield to the extreme agony of the martyr's body in the service of faith, witnessed by the wounds and scars received: each veteran will 'strip his sleeve and show his scars' (47). At first glance, the proposed holiday would thus commemorate the community of courage forged on the battlefield, and with it also the dependence of any military leader on his foot soldiers.[31] But as Phyllis Rackin rightly cautions, it is precisely this dependence that must be forgotten so that the king alone can be glorified. In the roll-call of the dead after the battle, the 'brothers' of the King's rousing speech have accordingly sunk back into the anonymity of others: 'None else of name, and of all other men / But five-and twenty' (4.8.106–7). Noting this as one of the 'ideologically motivated exclusions of historical writing' in early modern prose chronicles, Rackin pithily observes that Shakespeare's play not only reproduces these exclusions but also marks them, holding them up for comment and critique. Where his sources only record that 'of all other [sic] not above five and twenty persons' have died, Shakespeare's insertion 'none else of name' effectively points out their lack of an aristocratic title.[32] The end of the play reveals indeed that the martial brotherhood to be remembered ever after does in fact not even outlast the peace treaty: only a few scenes after Harry's levelling speech, the temporary brotherhood of the English army at Agincourt is given up for an aristocratic alliance with 'brother France' (5.2.2). As Baldo comments, 'A democratic sense of brotherhood or familial connection across social classes but within national boundaries yields to a rhetoric of family tied to dynastic descent and deployed to foster solidarity within a social class and across national boundaries.'[33] In retrospect, Harry's insistence on a shared English brotherhood at Agincourt serves above all to obliterate conveniently the King's own divided national loyalties as he is of both English and French descent, a fact which was laboriously proven through commemoration of genealogical lineage at the beginning of the play and which is ratified through the peace treaty and the marriage to Princess Katherine at its end, and his absolutist aspirations as the image of all Christian kings.[34]

---

[31] *Ibid.*, 1488.
[32] Rackin, *Stages of History*, p. 229.
[33] Baldo, 'Wars of memory in *Henry V*', 142.
[34] Dawson, 'The arithmetic of memory', 55.

In the light of these multiple framing scenes, and cautioned by the previous insistence that ceremony is the prop of kingship, Harry's proclamation of a national day of remembrance sends out a very different message from the levelling one it seemed to promise. As Alison Chapman has argued persuasively, 'Saint Crispin's Day as a "veteran's day", an occasion for recalling the democratic English solidarity that won a victory against the French, is quickly eclipsed by Saint Crispin's Day as a vehicle for remembering the saint-like king himself.' Through appropriating the holiday-making ability of the shoemakers in whose name Harry seems to speak here, he effectively forestalls the kind of anti-authoritarian, levelling festivity typically associated with them. Instead, he announces a holiday 'on terms that he controls', thus ensuring that it 'works primarily in his own advantage':

… by linking Saint Crispin's Day to a rhetoric of obedience, martial solidarity, and loyalty to the king, the play counters [the] image of the shoemaker who fashions subversive holidays to celebrate his own material advancement; Henry fashions a shoemaker's holiday that celebrates monarchical instead of artisanal power, and he attempts to insure that this holiday will commemorate his own apotheosis as England's saint-king rather than the transformation of shoemakers into gentlemen.[35]

From this perspective, the line 'Crispin Crispian shall ne'er go by … but we in it shall be rememberèd' points to two conflicting mnemonic trajectories and objects of remembrance, one constituted by the democratic 'we' of soldierly community, the other the royal 'we' of the pluralis majestatis, the royal spectacle that presents itself as the unifying focus for the national community. To notice the latter does not necessarily invalidate the former, however; it is rather a more inclusive view of the same phenomenon of nationalist oblivion.

Given the role of ceremony and spectacle as the ideological means of producing national unity, this raises the urgent question of the theatre's role in the process. The intermingling of statecraft and stagecraft in *Henry V* would suggest that the theatre may in fact be seen as a vehicle of nationalist oblivion. According to the Chorus at least, who functions both as the mouthpiece of ideology and at the same time provides a metadramatic commentary, the theatre reproduces the

---

[35] Chapman, 'Whose Saint Crispin's Day is it?', 1482, 1488.

rhetorical, affective and imaginative signature of nationalism, as well as its memory politics. As we shall see, the Chorus's speeches indeed enact the paradoxical interplay of attention and distraction that results in nationalist oblivion as a stage-effect. For some critics, this is an irreconcilable contradiction. Pamela Mason, for instance, sees the Chorus's metatheatrical role working firmly against the patriotic fervour and heroic glorification of war that emerges from the scenes with Henry. In her view, the Chorus at regular intervals interrupts the battle scenes and thus 'requires the audience to step back from emotional involvement to gain a perspective upon character and event'.[36] Such a view of the Chorus's function as epic narrator is premised on an at least momentarily stable opposition of historical *locus* and performative *platea*, assuming that the audience's otherwise rapt attention on dramatic action is distracted by a distancing, metatheatrical moment. Generally speaking, this can certainly be the case, one I will explore in more detail in the chapter on nostalgic spectacle in *Henry VIII*, where it is interrupted by such metatheatrical commentary. Yet in the particular instance of *Henry V*, the relation between *locus* and *platea* (as well as that between statecraft and stagecraft) is more complex.

If the Chorus may be seen as a vehicle of nationalist ideology, as Günther Walch insists it must,[37] it is not in spite of but because of its dramatic function as narrator and 'mentor' in addressing the audience (the telling phrase is Mason's). The Chorus announces the intermingling of the political and the theatrical already in the first lines of the prologue when he evokes 'A kingdom for a stage' and 'princes to act' (1.0.3). When 'war*like* Henry' is announced to appear '*like* himself' and 'assume the port of Mars' (6–7, my emphases), this creates an 'intangible slippage between the actor playing the king and the historical king fulfilling himself by playing the role of archetypal war leader', R. Scott Fraser points out.[38] Brian Walsh even suggests that these similes figure the past as fantasy, stressing that the Chorus 'cannot conceive of a way to present history that gets outside the contingencies of its telling or beyond the "like-ness" of all re-presentation'.[39] While the Chorus's prologue self-deprecatingly deplores the limitations and

[36] Mason, '*Henry V*: "the quick forge and working house of thought"', p. 180.
[37] Walch, '*Henry V* as working-house of ideology', 67.
[38] Fraser, '*Henry V* and the performance of war', 72.
[39] Walsh, *Shakespeare, The Queen's Men and the Elizabethan Performance of History*, p. 182.

contingencies of theatrical representation ('Can this cockpit hold / The vasty fields of France?', 11–12), this serves primarily as an occasion to enlist the imagination of the spectators themselves in the dramatic project of magnifying and glorifying its 'great account', the story of Henry's French campaign: 'And let us, ciphers to this great account, / On your imaginary forces work' (17–18). The theatrical spectacle, in itself nothing more than the 'crooked figure' of zero materially echoed by 'this wooden O' of the public theatre, is able to multiply its effect by 'a million' in and through the audience's imagination (15–16). When the Chorus enjoins the audience to 'Think, when we talk of horses, that you see them, / Printing their proud hoofs i'th' receiving earth' (26–7), he envisages a captivated audience whose spellbound imagination participates in producing the vivid, memorable stage pictures that are the 'purpose of playing' (*Hamlet*, 3.2.18). Throughout, the Chorus's speeches are dominated by imperatives that aim at engaging the spectators' minds and senses in the martial action: 'Suppose that you have seen' (3.0.3), 'Play with your fancies, and in them behold', 'Hear the shrill whistle', and repeatedly 'behold' (7, 9, 10, 14, 26). As Anthony B. Dawson points out with regard to a different play, 'the injunction to look generates some kind of metatheatrical consciousness which at the same time leads paradoxically to engagement'.[40] Thus when the Chorus invites members of the audience to imagine themselves being bodily swept along to war, we would be mistaken to interpret this as an invitation 'to think, judge, and assess' from a detached position, as Mason suggests.[41] Rather, calling for enthusiastic participation ('Follow, follow! / Grapple your minds to sternage of this navy, / And leave your England', 3.0.17–19) the Chorus at times resembles, in Alexander Leggatt's words, 'a recruiting sergeant' who appeals 'to the audience's pride and manhood'.[42] At the end of the Chorus that introduces act 3, dramatic narration, historical imagination and physical reality blend into each other as a cannon goes off behind the stage that signals the battle of Harfleur: 'the nimble gunner / With linstock now the devilish cannon touches, [*Alarum, and chambers go off*] / And down goes all before them' (3.0.32–4). Thus effectively collapsing historical *locus* and contemporary *platea* with

---

[40] Dawson, 'The distracted globe', p. 97.
[41] Mason, '*Henry V*: "the quick forge and working house of thought"', p. 180.
[42] Leggatt, *Shakespeare's Political Drama*, p. 124.

the play-goers' here and now, this scene provides a powerful theatrical experience which emphatically forestalls the possibility of critical distancing, offering instead a distracting spectacle that seeks to induce a state of nationalist oblivion in the audience. The Chorus's speeches enable participation in this imagined community 'precisely because the meta-theatrical allows for, even encourages, a kind of distraction (i.e. a sudden awareness of being at a play) [that] was endemic to the Elizabethan playhouse', Dawson comments.[43]

With the spectators' imagination, emotions and judgement thus engaged in what they see on stage, all the Chorus needs to do is to carry them off in the hurried sequence of events: 'Now we bear the King / Toward Calais: grant him there; there seen, / Heave him away upon your winged thoughts / Athwart the sea' (5.0.6–9). From Calais, it is a small step over the Channel to Dover and via Blackheath to London and back to France, 'so swift a pace hath thought' (15). The Chorus even announces his own oblivionating function in terms that recall Henry's memory politics: its office is to 'omit / All the occurrences, whatever chanced' that would obstruct the rapid flow of the main action, 'playing / The interim' by summing it up and 'rememb'ring you 'tis past' (5.0.40–4). Such an 'abridgement' (45) of history necessarily presents a very selective version, one that is coloured, moreover, by the nationalist patriotism that the Chorus voices throughout. In this sense, the Chorus's historical account constitutes as much an act of forgetting as of remembering. His speeches performatively bring about such nationalist oblivion in that they do not give the audience pause for thought, Leggat argues: 'The Chorus's role as patriotic spokesman is connected with his technical function of sweeping us along, filling in the gaps between acts, precisely those gaps where our questions occur'.[44] The Chorus, in other words, does not allow us to note the critical, anti-war moments interspersed throughout the play. He seeks to distract our attention from them, to direct our emotions, and to pre-empt any criticism by filling our minds with images of martial heroism.

In a sense, the entire play, with its fast-paced sequence of war scenes and its speeches of patriotic enthusiasm, could be seen as following the oblivionating example the Chorus sets. This is the

---

[43] Dawson, 'The distracted globe', p. 102.
[44] Leggatt, *Shakespeare's Political Drama*, p. 124.

position of critics who align the Chorus with Henry's political language and memory politics, seeing both engaged in the patriotic project of creating a nation. The play's nationalist thrust is punctured, however, by scenes that enable a more critical attitude to it. These are typically scenes following immediately on the Chorus's high-flung promises of military battle and heroic conduct, presenting instead treason, petty squabbles and the abuse of power. Such inconsistencies and contradictions have led some critics to accord the Chorus an ironic capacity. R. Scott Fraser, for instance, opines that the Chorus 'ironically draws attention throughout the play to the disparity between the stage action proper and his own descriptions of Henry', and even grants the Chorus the 'final ironic word'.[45] There is a difference between irony in the drama and dramatic irony, however.[46] To my mind, the Chorus nowhere betrays a sense of irony, let alone the capacity for self-irony: even the self-deprecating moments in prologue and epilogue are not genuine humility but the conventional gesture of *captatio benevolentiae*.[47] If anything, there is an inadvertent irony in the fact that the empowerment of the spectators effected through this mocking self-deprecation also encourages them to turn their critical gaze on the Chorus himself. While his speeches, read by themselves, are straightforwardly patriotic, it is the dramatic sequencing and the discrepant awareness it engenders in the audience that frame it ironically. We therefore need to account for the ways in which this play activates the audience's 'critical puissance'.

Noting the play's episodic quality, Alexander Leggatt has pointed out that *Henry V* presents an anatomy not only of its subject, war and national unification, but also of the possible responses of an audience to it. He places these responses on a continuum between unthinking patriotic enthusiasm and critical distance; which point we occupy depends on whether we are able to put the episodes of the play together and what connections we are making: 'the more we put things together, the more critical and satiric the play becomes. The patriotic reading means being swept along by the flow of the play, taking each moment as it comes; the critical reading means

---

[45] Fraser, '*Henry V* and the performance of war', 73, 81.
[46] Pfister, *Das Drama*, pp. 87–90.
[47] Womack, 'Imagined communities', pp. 91–2.

stopping and speculating, ferreting in the cracks between the scenes, noting silences and omissions.'[48] Carrying us along with the rapid war action, and having the Chorus encourage us to identify with his affirmative attitude so that we fail to register the qualifications and contradictions which the following scenes invariably present, the play itself seems to enact the Lancastrian policy of securing domestic unity by pursuing wars abroad. Stopping to note 'silences and omissions', by contrast, means to recognise the nationalist oblivion that the play both represents and resists. What breaks the play's patriotic stride is the glaring discrepancy between the nationalist rhetoric put on display by the Chorus and the dramatic sequencing of what we actually see on stage. For instance, the Chorus's depiction of England's young men united in their desire to fight and die for their nation in battle – 'Now all the youth of England are on fire' (2.0.1) – is followed by a scene of low tavern life, where we see Pistol and Nim fighting each other over the sexual favours of Mistress Quickly (2.1), the only scene of combat this seemingly militaristic play presents on stage at all. Their petty quarrel, self-aggrandisement and cowardice – the fight is carried out with words rather than swords, in an inversion of Henry's warning that the bishop's words will awake his 'sword of war' (1.2.22) – utterly demolishes the image of honour and valour the Chorus has just depicted. Their undignified squabbling is cut off only when the Boy brings news of his master's imminent death, brought about by the King's heartless rejection of his old friend ('The King has killed his heart', 1.2.84). Shared grief for Falstaff unites the men, but pious remembrance is quickly transposed into a recognition of the commercial opportunities offered by war (quite in the spirit of Falstaff himself, one might add): 'I'll live by Nim, and Nim shall live by me. / Is this not just? For I shall sutler be / Unto the camp, and profits will accrue. / Give my thy hand' (1.2.105–8). The scene ends on an uneasy note of mistrust that intermingles hopes of personal enrichment ('I shall have my noble?', 109) and misgivings about the King's treatment of his old friends ('The King is a good king, but it must be as it may', 120). The very next scene revels the treachery of Cambridge, Scroop and Grey which, as Pamela Mason insightfully points out, is necessarily coloured by the previous scene, so that 'Henry's anger at his friends' betrayal' must be read contrapuntally

[48] Leggatt, *Shakespeare's Political Drama*, pp. 121–2.

against his own betrayal of Falstaff and his later refusal to save Bardolph from hanging.[49] Whether these discrepancies are noted depends on the audience's ability to recall and compare scenes from earlier plays as well as within the play they are watching. Enabling such theatrical memories through its contrapuntal mnemonic dramaturgy, I suggest, the play itself can be read as a parody of the patriotic rhetoric voiced by the Chorus. More specifically, in drawing attention to the distraction tactics at work in the process of nation formation, the play also provides a point of resistance against them. Pitched against nationalist oblivion, the ability to recall is highlighted as an ethical, critical stance in a world characterised by a Machiavellian will to forget.[50] A small scene in act 4 articulates such a stance and, by implicating the audience, creates a moment of mnemonic resistance in the theatre.

At the beginning of 4.7, the Welsh captain Fluellen compares King Henry with Alexander the Great in what promises to be yet another occasion for enthusiastic patriotism. But the comparison is double-edged: on the surface, it seems to compliment King Henry

---

[49] Mason, '*Henry V*: "the quick forge and working house of thought"', p. 182. Mason offers more instances of what I call contrapuntal sequencing, e.g. around Henry's command to kill all prisoners of war, that 'presents a challenging and complex sequence which forces an audience to confront the uncompromising nature of the fiercely pragmatic decisions faced by both sides in war', a sequence that is rewritten onstage by Gower's (in my view rather doubtful) royalist retelling of it (*ibid.*, pp. 185–6); or the juxtaposition of Henry's threat to the Governor of Harfleur and Princess Katherine's first language lesson, whose vocabulary, by fragmenting the female body, echoes the theme of female vulnerability and prefigures her submission in marriage as a desperate strategy of survival rather than a romantic happy ending (*ibid.*, pp. 188–90). I fully agree with her that it is the structural patterning of juxtaposing heroic and anti-heroic scenes (but not, as she suggests, the Chorus's metatheatrical comments) that 'requires the audience to step back from emotional involvement to gain a perspective upon character and event. The experience of *Henry V* in performance is a process in which its audience is invited, even urged, to think, judge, and assess' (*ibid.*, p. 180).

[50] Warren-Heys comes to a similar conclusion, although she tellingly does not specify how the Chorus fits into the picture here. Drawing on Stanley Cavell's idea that the audience's ethical and political agency is suspended during performance and taken up only afterwards in recollection of and response to the play we have seen, she insists – quite rightly – that 'in *Henry V* that ethical and political imperative is given to us *during* the play as we make our memories of the interim times even while the play is being performed' ('Creating memory in Shakespeare's *Henry V*', p. 122).

as a successful military leader and to defend him against charges of cruelty after he has just ordered that all French prisoners be killed in retaliation for the French having murdered the English baggage-train boys (4.6.37). Fluellen's criticism of this proceeding as being 'expressly against the law of arms' (4.7.1–2) seems to refer to the murder of the boys only, but Gower's reply, with its rather clumsy re-scripting of 'how the sequel hangs together', opens up the possibility that he means the King's own order. With the underhand suggestion that this act of revenge was motivated by anger at the loss of his personal possessions, Gower betrays a certain scepticism concerning the King's sense of justice and honour. As always with Shakespeare, it is useful to pay attention to qualifying conjunctions. Rather than straightforwardly presenting a sequence of cause and effect (which the dramaturgy has already made impossible), Gower starts from the one fact that serves as legitimation of this breach of law – ''Tis certain there is not one boy left alive' (4.7.5) – but then continues with telling additions and prevarications, recalling Iago's famous fumbling for credible reasons why he hates the Moor: '*And* the cowardly rascals that ran away from the battle ha' done this slaughter' shifts the blame on the French soldiers themselves; '*Besides*, they have burned and carried away all that was in the King's tent' suggests an additional and rather mercenary reason for the King's wrath, an implication that is intensified by the sentence continuing '*wherefore* the King most worthily hath caused every soldier to cut his prisoner's throat' (4.7.5–10; emphases added). Gary Taylor points out in his editorial note that the conjunctive adverb 'wherefore' can be construed both in a causal and a conditional sense, with the latter undoing the neat temporal sequence suggested by the former.[51] Accordingly, Gower's conclusion 'O 'tis a gallant king' may be delivered – depending on the production – in a deeply sarcastic tone. This opening already casts a shadow of doubt over Fluellen's subsequent excuse that this act of cold-blooded policy was occasioned by the same temperamental 'rages' and 'moods' (4.7.28–9) that led Alexander to kill his friend Cleitus. Then he goes on to substantiate the comparison by recalling that just '[a]s Alexander killed his friend Cleitus, being in his ales and his cups, so also Harry Monmouth, being in his right wits and his good judgements, turned away the fat knight with the great-belly

---

[51] Taylor (ed.), *Henry V*, p. 243.

doublet; he was full of jests, and gipes, and knaveries, and mocks; I have forgot his name' (4.7.37–42). At this point, what looked like a compliment turns into pointed censure, at least for those who recall how the preceding play in the second tetralogy ended. For the comparison highlights that King Henry's rejection of Falstaff, which in the event killed the fat knight indeed, happened not in a rage but was a politic decision to forget his best friend. Fluellen's own lapse of memory here – 'I have forgot his name' – both mimics the King's deliberate forgetfulness and prompts the memory of the audience, who might have called out with Gower in recognition of the portrait: 'Sir John Falstaff!' (43). In recalling the popular hero of the prequel to *Henry V*, which many of the audience could have seen on stage only one or two seasons before, and prepared for by the carefully withheld name in the earlier episode of grief for the Boy's master (2.1), the scene reminds the audience to resort to their own historical and theatrical memory in order to withstand the force of nationalist oblivion.

The plays in which King Harry features show and to a certain extent also perform the forgetfulness by distraction which is this king's most successful political practice: caught up in the fray with him, the audience has probably forgotten about Falstaff by the fourth act of *Henry V*. In activating the audience's memory, this scene offers an opportunity to resist the flood of patriotic images, to stop and notice the discrepancy between what we see and what the Chorus tells us we should see, or the discrepancy between scenes depicting Harry as 'mirror of all Christian kings', urged to cruelty by political necessity, and those showing the cruelty of war from the perspective of its victims. In this sense, the play in performance is not only a vehicle of nationalist oblivion but also of resistant memory. Such resistance is enabled, above all, by the play's contrapuntal sequencing and the theatrical memories that audience members were clearly expected to bring to a play. This expectation of intertheatrical recollection is voiced in the Chorus's epilogue, which for once works as an anti-climactic corrective to the rhetoric of patriotic triumph when it reminds the spectators of Henry's premature death and the ensuing civil war, 'Which oft our stage hath shown' (Epilogue, 13). The epilogue alludes here to the history plays about the Wars of the Roses an audience of the 1590s would have been able to have seen, among them Shakespeare's own, and it is 'for their sake' that he bids the audience judge the success of this play. The final appeal is to the power of theatrical memory, then, not to nationalist oblivion. Yet to assume a simple opposition of stagecraft and statecraft (as Mason does) would be as mistaken as to posit an easy alignment (as Nashe did). The play's meaning cannot be determined in terms of ideology alone. Redirecting our focus on its formal features allows us instead to describe the interplay of attention and distraction generated by a pattern of contrapuntally arranged scenes, and to understand the points at which shifting the balance toward the one or the other will result in a play of containment or of subversion.

5 | Nostalgia: affecting spectacles and sceptical audiences in Henry VIII

In what is surely the best-known contemporary defence of the early modern stage, a passage from Thomas Nashe's *Pierce Pennilesse* (1592), we are also presented with an anatomy of nostalgia and its politics of memory and affect:

Nay, what if I prooue Playes to be no extreame, but a rare exercise of vertue? First, for the subiect of them (for the most part) it is borrowed out of our English Chronicles, wherein our forefathers valiant acts (that haue line long buried in rustie brasse and worme-eaten bookes) are reuiued, and they themselues raysed from the Graue of Obliuion, and brought to pleade their aged Honours in open presence: than which, what can bee a sharper reproofe to these degenerate, effeminate dayes of ours. How would it haue joyed braue *Talbot* (the terror of the French) to thinke that after he had lyne two hundred yeares in his Tombe, hee should triumphe againe on the Stage, and haue his bones newe embalmed with the teares of ten thousand spectators at least, (at seuerall times) who in the Tragedian that represents his person, imagine they behold him fresh bleeding.[1]

Nashe's defence of the stage, and of history plays in particular, is habitually quoted in critical discussions that seek to assess the role of the early modern theatre. Usually, the emphasis falls where Nashe placed it: on the straightforwardly mnemonic and didactic function of historical drama. In this reading, the theatre is a medium of national memory as well as of national identity. In resurrecting the medieval hero Talbot 'from the Graue of Obliuion', as did, for example, Shakespeare's *Henry VI, Part One*, it salvages his memory from death and forgetfulness, and gives the English audience a sense of the nation's past as well as an example for virtuous, manly conduct in the present. This goes hand in hand with an unabashedly nationalist impetus, harnessing remembrance of the past to the project of building a community in the

[1] Nashe, *Pierce Pennilesse*, pp. 86–7.

present. Admiring Talbot and mourning for him, the audience is united in a nostalgic remembrance of past glories that forges them into an 'imagined community' in the here and now of theatrical performance.

I would like to challenge this somewhat superficial reading and complicate it in two respects. First, both Nashe and his latter-day readers too easily conceive of the theatre exclusively as a medium of memory in the service of a collective identity of 'Englishness'. The constitution of a national identity, however, is just as much brought about through acts of forgetting as through acts of remembrance, as we saw in the preceding chapter. The erasure of the past, and in particular of past tragedies that would impede a peaceful co-existence as one people, is thus a precondition for nation formation. When Nashe's account chooses to remember *only* the 'valiant acts', it effectively erases the more disgraceful and potentially disruptive episodes of the nation's past. This is certainly due to Nashe's immediate aim of defending the stage as the medium of resurrecting a glorious past that may serve as a glowing example for the present. However, such a view clearly does not adequately represent the full range of historical events nor the content of the history plays with their villainous, amoral protagonists and bloodthirsty battle scenes. Nashe's strategic blindness toward this raises the interesting question of what must be obliterated from the past so that it can serve as a rallying point for present concerns of nationhood.

It seems to me, however, that nostalgic oblivion is not only a question of content in the formation and deformation of the nation's past but also a structural moment in the performative production of a passion for that past in the theatre. Thus when Nashe speaks of 'our forefathers', he presupposes an imagined community, a 'we' which actually has come about as a stage-induced effect of obliterating the social, gender, religious and regional differences among a rather heterogeneous audience. That Nashe offers 'braue Talbot, the terror of the French' as a figure of identification is a case in point: celebrating this kind of English masculine virtue excludes other subject positions and with it other, perhaps dissenting perspectives from the range of possible reactions to the spectacle on stage.

What lends authenticity and authority to this nostalgically selective version of national history, Nashe seems to claim, are its physical manifestations on and off the stage: the living, breathing body of the actor, the audience's tears embalming his 'fresh bleeding' wounds. Nostalgic representation, in the words of Linda Hutcheon, turns the absent past 'into the site of immediacy, presence, and authenticity'.[2] When Nashe obliquely acknowledges the difference between presence and representation in his reference to the figure of Talbot as 'the Tragedian that represents his person' on stage, he hints at a point I wish to foreground here: that the affective investment in the nation's past is an effect of dramatic representation.

This raises once again the issue of the role of the theatre in recreating the nation's past and a national identity. As pointed out earlier, I do not mean to imply that the early modern stage was a straightforward instrument of nation building, nor that being swept away by a passion for the past was the only response available to watching historical drama. But if nostalgic spectacle is what induces a passion for the past in the audience, if it is indeed a device for producing emotions that can unite a group of spectators, then the theatre surely is a privileged site of nation building through nostalgia. At the same time, I would contend, the open display of such passion, both on and off the stage, may threaten that very effect precisely when this passion becomes obvious *as* spectacle. This is what happens during metatheatrical moments, which, by drawing attention to the nostalgic spectacle the audience is emotionally caught up in, create an ironic distance. Opening up a space between nostalgic spectacle and affective identification, these moments reveal, if only for a moment, the memory politics of nostalgia as well as its policy of affect. In what follows, I would like to discuss how several Jacobean plays, among them Shakespeare and Fletcher's *Henry VIII; or, All is True* (1613), while undoubtedly participating in a nationalist agenda and rhetoric, at the same time offer critical insights into the political and affective workings of nostalgic spectacle. In so doing, I will pay special attention to the interplay of remembering and forgetting that actively constructs what is remembered of the past, as well as to the interplay of mimetic representation and affective identification. This double approach, I hope, challenges all-too simplistic notions of the authenticity and authority of nostalgic memories.

The word 'nostalgia' would not have been known to an Elizabethan audience. The term was probably coined in 1688 by the Swiss physician Johannes Hofer as a medical expression for a lethal kind of severe

[2] Hutcheon, 'Irony, nostalgia, and the postmodern', n.p.

homesickness. Its Greek etymology defines it in spatial and affective terms: *nostos* means 'to return home'; *algos* denotes 'pain, sadness'.[3] Although the word itself did not exist around 1600, the feeling of nostalgia was voiced in many texts that looked back, rather wistfully, to times past. While the early modern period was undoubtedly characterised by multiple departures for new shores – geographical as well as epistemological ones – it also harboured a deep longing for recovering the distant countries of the past, a desire captured by that other name for the epoch, the Renaissance. One example that springs to mind is the passage about 'The Four Ages' of the world in Arthur Golding's translation of Ovid's *Metamorphoses*, which longingly evokes the glories of the lost Golden Age from a perspective of despair about the all too brazen present. Nostalgia for the past was not only a topic for poetry but indeed its very form and function, at least according to Philip Sidney's *Defence of Poesy*, which maintained that while the natural world around us is 'brazen, the poets only deliver a golden'.[4] This longing for a Golden Age was a topos of Renaissance thought, in particular in England where the break with the past entailed by the Reformation and the dissolution of the monasteries proved particularly traumatic.[5] Indeed, for Erwin Panofsky, a 'nostalgic vision born of a sense of estrangement as well as a sense of affinity … is the very essence of the Renaissance'.[6] As appealing and, I believe, convincing as this account of nostalgia as the *zeitgeist* of the Renaissance may be, we do well to investigate the specific implications of nostalgia first so that we can see how it might work as an early modern practice of building a nation along with that nation's past.

Nostalgia, Christoper Shaw and Malcom Chase point out in their introduction to *The Imagined Past: History and Nostalgia*, is 'a protean and pervasive' concept, a cultural 'site occupied by ideas and structures of feeling which have a family resemblance'.[7] Despite its inchoate nature, two characteristic aspects can be isolated in addition to its spatial connotations: its time-structure and its affect-structure.

[3] On the etymological roots and the cultural history of nostalgia, see Starobinski, 'The idea of nostalgia', 84–6; and Muro, 'Nationalism and nostalgia', 571–3.

[4] Sidney, *The Major Works*, p. 216.

[5] Schwyzer, *Literature, Nationalism, and Memory*, p. 73.

[6] Panofsky, *Renaissance and Renascences in Western Art*, p. 210.

[7] Shaw and Chase (eds.), *The Imagined Past*, p. 2.

Nostalgia is a specific mode of connecting the past to the present. It is premised on a sense of teleological time in which past and present are clearly distinguished: there can be no longing for the past if it is not perceived as crucially different from the present. Typically, the present is seen as deficient or degraded while the past is idealised and aestheticised. This structural doubling-up of two different times, an inadequate present and an idealised past, is 'so characteristic ... of nostalgic experience that it can perhaps be regarded as its distinctive rhetorical signature'.[8] It is indeed apt to speak of a *rhetorical* signature here, since this opposition of beautiful past and grim present is above all a rhetorical effect, existing in language and in the imagination. In Linda Hutcheon's analysis, nostalgia invariably refers us to 'the past as imagined, as idealized through memory and desire. In this sense, however, nostalgia is less about the past than about the present ... the ideal that is not being lived now is projected into the past. It is "memorialized" as past, crystallized into precious moments selected by memory, but also by forgetting, and by desire's distortions and reorganizations.'[9] Trading on comfortable and conveniently reassuring images of the past, nostalgia at the same time suppresses both its variety and its negative aspects. In other words, nostalgia remembers and simultaneously forgets the past.

While this is true for the constitution of memory in general, nostalgia is special in that it connects memory with affect. As a 'historical emotion',[10] it provides us with a sense of time passing just as it allows us to register that very fact emotionally. Nostalgia is predominantly an affective or, as Shaw and Chase put it, an 'affectionate' mode of connecting past and present.[11] This emotional attitude can take different forms: a dissatisfaction with the present situation which motivates nostalgia in the first place; a longing for past glories which distances one from the present; an elation triggered by remembering former feats which authenticates the imagined past as 'true'. Indeed, Hutcheon stresses, it is above all 'its visceral physicality and emotional impact' that lends nostalgia its power. Nostalgia seems to touch one immediately, on a very personal, even bodily, level as is testified by its original, medical meaning

---

[8] Davis, *Yearning for Yesterday*, p. 16.
[9] Hutcheon, 'Irony, nostalgia, and the postmodern', n.p.
[10] Boym, *The Future of Nostalgia*, p. 10.
[11] Shaw and Chase (eds.), *The Imagined Past*, p. 2.

of homesickness. While it is primarily an effect of language and the imagination, as noted above, its emotional and physical impact makes it feel authentic. Nevertheless we should be aware, Hutcheon cautions us, that nostalgia does not describe the quality of the past itself, but rather ascribes a certain quality to one's response to the past. It is what one feels when two temporal moments, past and present, come together: 'It is the element of response – of active participation, both intellectual and affective – that makes for the power' of nostalgia.[12]

Taken together, nostalgia's signature time- and affect-structure can help us understand its psychic as well as social functions. As a specific form of memory, nostalgia is a very personal experience as well as a deeply social emotion. As such, 'it derives from and has implications for our lives as social actors': a distinctive way of negotiating the difference between past and present, it performs 'the never ending work of constructing, maintaining, and reconstructing our identities'.[13] Furthermore, it offers consolation: the reason for nostalgia is usually found in dissatisfaction with the present situation, and this dissatisfaction is typically counter-balanced by an image of the past that offers 'a consolation for the [perceived] loss of status and power'.[14] Related to this is the function of a critique of the present, which draws legitimacy and authority from the idealised past as a counter-image. The imagined past also provides a rallying-point for the dissatisfied, enabling them to form an imagined community of their own. The element of emotional and intellectual response, which Hutcheon considers so crucial for nostalgia, becomes indeed a formative element of personal and group identity. Nostalgia thus fuses not only memory and affect but also 'affect and agency, or emotion and politics': it articulates a selective memory of the past, charges it emotionally and, through this, enables agency and authorises political stances.[15]

By the same token, nostalgia is not innocent. We therefore need to recognise and examine the politics of nostalgia, that is, the vested interests which are both served and disguised by its seemingly natural, authentic 'visceral physicality'.[16] As so often, the question 'who is speaking?' is a reliable hermeneutic method for scrutinising the

---

[12] Hutcheon, 'Irony, nostalgia, and the postmodern', n.p.
[13] Davis, *Yearning for Yesterday*, pp. vii, 31.
[14] Shaw and Chase (eds.), *The Imagined Past*, p. 3.
[15] Hutcheon, 'Irony, nostalgia, and the postmodern', n.p.
[16] *Ibid.*

political uses of nostalgic rhetoric. In keeping with the longing for past glories, it is likely that individuals or groups who have lost their place in a territory (exiles or migrants) or in history (empires or classes on the decline) will develop nostalgia. Nostalgia can also emerge in sovereign nations that cultivate admiration for group traits of their ancestors and feel the need to live up to a glorious past.[17] This suggests that the political valence of nostalgia is per se undetermined, that it is 'transideological' – if never unideological – in the sense that it can be made 'to happen by (and to) anyone of any political persuasion'. In other words, nostalgia is a tool that can be seized for very different political purposes. On the one hand, nostalgia is 'fundamentally con-servative in its praxis, for it wants to keep things as they were – or, more accurately, as they are imagined to have been'.[18] By providing consolation for the frustration suffered over the loss of prized values, nostalgic feeling, much like a safety valve, thus also manages to sta-bilise a disappointing present situation.[19] On the other hand, nostalgia can trigger revolutionary political programmes advocating the restor-ation of political kingdoms, traditional lifestyles, religious beliefs, and so on.[20] The one constant factor in both cases, I think, is its ability to forge imagined communities through an imagined past.

Nostalgia is therefore a powerful tool of nationalism in that it offers a selective, idealised vision of the distant past and charges it with a deeply nationalist, patriotic sentiment.[21] In so doing, nostalgia does not simply manipulate the nation's past but actually produces both the nation and its past in the same act of remembering and forgetting. The idealising and sentimentalising rhetoric of nationalist nostalgia provides the nation, above all, with an image of past unity. David Lowenthal argues that nostalgia conjures up 'a past that was unified and comprehensible, unlike the incoherent, divided present' and that 'what we are nostalgic for is the condition of having been'.[22] This vision of national unity can only be achieved through an act of for-getting, as Ernest Renan insisted, for while the past usually has been

---

[17] Muro, 'Nationalism and nostalgia', 575.

[18] Hutcheon, 'Irony, nostalgia, and the postmodern', n.p.

[19] Davis, *Yearning for Yesterday*, p. 99.

[20] Muro, 'Nationalism and nostalgia', 576.

[21] Davis, *Yearning for Yesterday*, p. 98; Muro, 'Nationalism and nostalgia', 574.

[22] Lowenthal, 'Nostalgia tells it like it wasn't', p. 29.

just as 'incoherent' and 'divided' as the present, this fact must be forgotten if one wants to forge unity in the present and for the future. As a selective form of remembering and hence also a form of forgetting, nostalgia is a specific way of connecting the past with the present, which usually serves as an instrument or technique for creating and expressing a 'désir d'intégration',[23] resulting in what we might term, in response to Benedict Anderson's work, an 'affective community'.

Nostalgia is not only a tool of national unification, however. It can also run counter to the dominant propaganda of unity, for as a desire to return to an idealised past it also casts an unfavourable light on the present as somehow deficient. This was especially the case with a body of Jacobean history plays that looked back longingly to the Elizabethan reign as a golden era. Staging desire for Elizabeth, they also upstaged the 'deliberate attempts of the Stuart kings to define their rule of reunited Britannia as the fulfilment of all past history'.[24] In the changed context of the Stuart reign, Elizabeth, far from being a locus of national unity for England, was in fact a potentially destabilising memory, at least for her successor, as Jonathan Baldo and others have argued convincingly.[25] From the very beginning of his reign James I was troubled by the memory of his Tudor predecessors. In particular, Queen Elizabeth's posthumous status as the heroine of a militant Protestantism was at odds with James's own ecumenical, conciliatory policy, and hence needed to be regulated. The broad range of his attempts at controlling the memory of the Tudors through historiography, ritual and political as well as popular discourse testifies to the scope and depth of his anxiety.[26] For example, James dissolved the Society of Antiquaries in 1607 and prevented its revival in 1614, fearing that recent political history might be written in his disfavour. When Fulke Greville wanted to write a history of Elizabeth's reign in 1610, he was denied access to state papers necessary to his research. James attempted to control the memory of his predecessor not only by

---

[23] Paul Zumthor qtd. in Harris, *Untimely Matter*, p. 69.
[24] Grant, 'Drama Queen', p. 125.
[25] Baldo, 'Forgetting Elizabeth in *Henry VIII*', p. 145; see also Dobson and Watson, *England's Elizabeth*, pp. 46–50.
[26] The traumatic memory of his mother's death and the fact that he succeeded the woman who was responsible for her execution seem to have haunted King James beyond a measure accountable for by reasons of state policy and legitimation only (Baldo, 'Forgetting Elizabeth in *Henry VIII*', pp. 134–6).

suppressing its articulations, however; he also actively sought to shape it by commissioning William Camden to continue writing his history of Elizabeth's reign, with the stipulation that it include a sympathetic account of the life and death of his own mother, Mary Stuart, and buttress James's own authority by presenting his reign as a continuation of Elizabethan policy.[27] In 1606, he apparently ordered that Elizabeth's corpse be removed from the altar under the chapel built by Henry VII in Westminster Abbey and reburied in the same vault as her half-sister Mary Tudor. The Henry VII Chapel constitutes a highly symbolic place in the historical narrative of the Tudors: it functioned as a space that materialised and commemorated what became known much later as the central trope of early modern monarchy and historiography, the Tudor myth. The Tudor rose, symbol of the united houses of Lancaster and York, is the recurrent *leitmotif* of the Chapel's stained glass and the carvings. Henry VII is buried there with his queen, Elizabeth of York, beside him, 'stressing the physical union of the Lancasters he represented with the Yorks he displaced, making concrete the indisputable claim of their descendants'.[28] To bury Elizabeth in the same vault meant to position her as central to that claim and to present her as the crowning figure of the Tudor dynasty.[29] By the same token, when three years later her successor James Stuart had her body removed from that symbolic place and reburied, 'isolated in the dark north aisle of the chapel, her body lying on top of her Catholic half-sister Mary, to whom she erected no monument during her reign', this amounted to a strategic attempt at manipulating her place in the country's political memory.[30]

---

[27] While Camden's measured Tacitean account in Latin (1615) presents Elizabeth as an eminently politic ruler – prudent, wise but also devious and cold – who could hardly give rise to nostalgic feelings, the translators of his work into English (1625, 1629, 1630 and 1635) transmuted his cool appraisal of Elizabeth into a glittering panegyric (see Collinson, 'William Camden and the anti-myth of Elizabeth').

[28] Walker, *The Elizabeth Icon*, p. 17.

[29] Her own father, Henry VIII, was buried with all the honours of a heraldic funeral in a vault in St. George's Chapel at Windsor, and while both Edward VI and Mary Tudor rest in the Henry VII Chapel in Westminster Abbey, no tomb was built specifically for them (Woodward, *The Theatre of Death*, p. 132).

[30] In Julia Walker's account, this relocation of the Queen's grave meant that her memory was shoved aside along with her physical remains, laying her into a 'grave of oblivion' (*The Elizabeth Icon*, p. 15). This is hardly the case, given the rather grand funeral tomb James erected for her at that site, even though

Despite these concerted efforts at laying the memory of Elizabeth to rest, the first decade after James's accession to the throne saw an upsurge of nostalgia for Elizabeth. It was articulated across a wide range of popular culture media including stained-glass windows, prints, pictures, verse and monuments.[31] Most relevant to my topic, however, is a number of history plays that staged the reign of the Tudor monarchs: Samuel Rowley's *When You See Me You Know Me* (1604), Thomas Heywood's two-part *If You Know Not Me, You Know Nobody* (1604/05), Thomas Dekker's *The Whore of Babylon* (1607) and *Henry VIII; or, All is True*, written by Fletcher and Shakespeare in 1613.[32] These plays present the Tudors, and especially Elizabeth as the model Protestant princess, in a nostalgic light that casts a dubious shadow on the monarchical abilities and confessional affiliations of James and his Catholic queen. They all call for a topical reading that highlights the analogies as well as the differences between the history staged and contemporary politics. Titles like *If You Know Not Me, You Know Nobody* and *When You See Me You Know Me* alert the audience to use their knowledge of current political figures and discover who is behind the mask of the persona. This highlighted topicality corresponds with nostalgia's time- and affect-structure: an imagined past, 'idealised through memory and desire', invariably casts a bleak light on the present that is perceived as inadequate.[33] Desire for Elizabeth, in other words, articulated dissatisfaction with James. Moreover, the glorification of the Elizabethan past ran counter to the mnemonic policy of the current monarch, James I.[34]

it is indeed 'plainer and less sumptuous that that of Mary Queen of Scots' (p. 27). In somewhat more measured tones, Dobson and Watson point out that the reorganisation of the Abbey effectively marked the Tudor monarchs since Henry VII as a mere digression and carved out a material as well as discursive space in which James could represent himself as the true heir of the Tudors' founding father instead (*England's Elizabeth*, p. 46).

[31] Doran and Freeman, *The Myth of Elizabeth*, p. 8.

[32] The Dekker-Webster play *Sir Thomas Wyatt* (pr. 1607) is often included in this canon but will not receive any attention here because its early form, the two-part play of 1602, *Lady Jane*, was already written before Queen Elizabeth's death, and no substantial changes were made to the printed version afterwards.

[33] Hutcheon, 'Irony, nostalgia, and the postmodern', n.p.

[34] Curtis Perry also discusses 'an oppositional critical strain of Elizabethan nostalgia' that indeed had serious political repercussions, as the later example of Oliver Cromwell shows. Cromwell based his concept of parliamentary freedom on an inaccurate, idealised notion of Elizabeth's governmental

Given this tension between royal mnemonic policy and popular nostalgic commemoration, the question of the politics of nostalgia for Elizabeth is a vexed one, as many critics have noted. Curtis Perry, for example, cautions that far from being univocally critical of James, depictions of Elizabeth stand in a variety of relationships to Jacobean orthodoxies. He suggests that particular texts from the beginning of his reign rather tended to stress the continuity between the 'queen of famous memory' and her successor, using the appeal of the queen's memory to ratify King James's policies. Moreover, the uses of Elizabethan nostalgia in Jacobean England varied according to the milieus in and for which they were produced, and to the interests that they served. And finally, Perry notes, the social implications of this nostalgia changed and developed over time. In the beginning, comparison with Elizabeth helped to articulate contemporary notions about the role of the monarch and to set expectations against which James's style and policies were judged. Only later did it become a conventionalised vehicle for expressing dissatisfaction with the government of James and, still later, of his son Charles.[35]

While Perry's revisions of the nostalgia for Elizabeth are apt, they bear some revision themselves. For one, I do not quite agree with his assessment of nostalgia as a straightforward celebration of continuity, because the idea of continuity is itself at odds with the basic impetus of glorifying the past, namely discontent with the present.[36] This is precisely why James was so wary of the nostalgia for Elizabeth and sought to by-pass or redeploy memory of the Tudors rather than encourage it. Praise for James in these texts should accordingly be read rather as a cautious bowing to authority, since criticising a king is a risky business at best. In fact, such praise for the present ruler may indeed be seen as a fully integral part and tactical aspect of the nostalgic mode, at least in the case of such a pronounced tension between royal policy and popular memory. It is this discrepancy in interests served by nostalgia that motivates

---

practice, a nostalgic notion that was an element in the climate of opinion that made the seventeenth-century Civil War possible (Perry, 'The citizen politics of nostalgia: Queen Elizabeth in early Jacobean London', 110–11).

[35] *Ibid.*, 90–2, 109–11.

[36] This does not mean that popular nostalgia is necessarily subversive either; in its desire to return to the way things were, or were imagined to have been, it is essentially conservative (Kamps, *Historiography and Ideology in Stuart Drama*, p. 67).

my second revision of Perry's reading: where he, in spite of his essay's title, 'The citizen politics of nostalgia', holds only the divergent interests of King James and Prince Henry responsible for different images of Elizabeth, I would include the common citizens (who, after all, constituted the majority of spectators in the public playhouses) in the picture. While the audience surely got caught up in the patriotic enthusiasm that is so typical of nostalgia and that so effectively covers up its vested interests, their perspective may also provide a critical angle on the royal politics of remembering and forgetting at work in the representation of history. As Gordon McMullan has noted, the nostalgic history plays of the Jacobean stage invite 'the members of its audience to interpret their own history, giving them the choice of seeing the play either as a celebration of Stuart power or a questioning of the state of the Reformation ten years into James's reign'.[37] I would add that nostalgic plays even of a later date did not necessarily deteriorate into a mere 'conventional tool' for criticising James, as Perry claims,[38] but self-critically examined the mnemonic and affective politics of nostalgic spectacle.

None of the plays under discussion here depicts the Elizabeth who would have been most readily remembered by contemporaries, as Dobson and Watson point out: 'the ageing, parsimonious, debt-ridden, step-motherly queen of the 1590s, stalemated in the long endgame of the succession crisis'. Rather, 'the process of selectively remembering Good Queen Bess was at the same time a process of selective forgetting'.[39] Popular memory of Elizabeth as elderly queen needed to be emptied out before it could be recharged with new meaning and before Elizabeth could function as an icon in the nostalgic semiotics. According to German literary critic Renate Lachmann, such a process of evacuating and charging a cultural sign with new meaning can be usefully described as, in her words, the 'designification' and 'resignification' of signs. The nostalgia for Elizabeth can be conceptualised, in her semiotic perspective, as the result of a process of designification, through which a cultural sign loses the semantic and pragmatic value it had while circulating within a cultural system and its institutions, and resignification that occurs when the devalued sign is brought back into the circulation of culturally validated,

[37] McMullan, 'Introduction', p. 93.
[38] Perry, 'The citizen politics of nostalgia', 109.
[39] Dobson and Watson, *England's Elizabeth*, p. 45.

meaningful signs but charged with a different meaning.[40] This difference can also be seen as a form of cultural forgetting, and nostalgia
is one of the forms it takes.

Samuel Rowley's *When You See Me You Know Me* enacts the first
step of such a designification of the icon of Elizabeth. Set in the 1540s
at the court of Henry VIII, it depicts the machinations of Cardinal
Wolsey to win the papal throne, as well as his intrigue against the
King's Lutheran queen, Catherine Parr; King Henry's legendary noc-
turnal excursion into the city in disguise; and the birth and education of Prince Edward. Elizabeth is notably absent from this play,
except for a letter in which she offers theological advice to her brother
Edward and which he reads out on stage (sc. 12, ll. 2410–18). This
scene establishes Elizabeth as the mouthpiece of a pure, uncorrupted
Protestantism, and it is precisely because she is absent from the action
of the play that her figure remains uncompromised by any personal
involvement in the political intrigues depicted. Produced within less
than a year of Elizabeth's death, Rowley's play undertakes to erase the
memory of the old, compromised Queen and begins to recreate instead
a memorable image of the young Protestant princess.[41]

The imaginative space carved out by such semiotic erasure was filled
by other plays over the years following. They recharged the icon of
Elizabeth with new meaning and enacted the re-scripted memory of
her reign. In so doing, they shaped the topoi of what would become the
early seventeenth-century cult of Elizabeth: her tribulations under the
reign of Queen Mary; her coronation entry of 1559; her special relationship with the citizens of London; her providential escape from Catholic
attempts on her life; and the triumph over the Spanish Armada in 1588.
These episodes of her life were already part of cultural memory by the
time of her death, yet the Jacobean stage turned them into a nostalgic
spectacle by taking them out of their historical contexts and presenting
only a selection of what would quickly become quasi-mythical topoi.

In Heywood's two-part *If You Know Not Me You Know Nobody*,
the topoi of nostalgia for Elizabeth (as well as their topical function
of criticising her successor James) are already in place. The first part
shows the plight of the young princess Elizabeth under the reign of her
half-sister, which she suffers with exemplary meekness and patience

---

[40] Lachmann, 'Kultursemiotischer Prospekt', p. xviii.
[41] Dobson and Watson, *England's Elizabeth*, p. 51.

until the death of Mary saves her from her dire fate. Her greatest support is her steadfast Protestant faith as well as the sympathy of the common people. Both come together in the grand finale whose preliminary dumb show dramatises Elizabeth's coronation entry into the city of London, where the Lord Mayor presents her with an English Bible. In a magnificent gesture that announces her unwavering allegiance to the Protestant faith as well as to the commoners, she kisses the Bible and declares it to be 'the Iewell that we still loue best' (l. 1582). With this scene, nostalgic enthusiasm for Elizabeth undoubtedly reached one of its first peaks, catering as it does to a sense of collective Protestant identity as well as to the patriotic pride of the common citizens that would console them for the overbearing disregard in which James held them. The extreme popularity of the first part of *If You Know Not Me* testifies to this appeal: it was immediately pirated and went through at least eight editions before 1639. On the stage, it was quickly followed by a second part and continued to be a house-filling success well into the reign of Charles II. As late as 1667 the well-known 'sad story of Queen Elizabeth' was still able to draw tears from the audience, in spite or because of its having been 'sucked in … from the cradle', as Samuel Pepys wrote in his diary.[42]

The bulk of the second part deals with the life of the wealthy merchant Thomas Gresham, who built the London Royal Exchange in 1570. Elizabeth herself appears only on three occasions: the naming of the Royal Exchange (sc. 8), her escape from Dr Parry's alleged assassination attempt (sc. 15) and the victory over the Armada (sc. 17, 18). Both parts of *If You Know Not Me* articulate an anxiety about a possible strengthening of the Catholic faith in Jacobean England. It was fuelled by the negotiations for a marriage between Prince Henry and the Spanish Infanta Anna, which was to crown the peace treaty between England and Spain in 1604, as well as by the Gunpowder Plot of 1605.[43] James's leniency toward English recusants and the fact that he had a wife who was most probably Catholic seemed to put the Church of England into danger.[44] The play gives voice to such anti-Spanish, anti-Catholic feelings through Queen Mary's marriage to Prince Philip of Spain in the first part, and the conspiracy of the Catholic physician Parry in the second. Elizabeth's glorious triumph

---

[42] Grant, 'Drama Queen', pp. 120–1.   [43] *Ibid.*, p. 130.
[44] Kamps, *Historiography and Ideology*, pp. 72–3.

in the two final scenes, however, exorcises these fears and restores
an ideal of militant Protestantism. Dramatising the triumph over
the Spanish Armada in 1588, they provide a point of critical comparison with James by pitching Elizabeth as a champion of militant
Protestantism against his appeasing and ecumenical policies. The queen
enters at scene 17 and famously delivers her speech to the troops at
Tilbury (l. 2630–9). Apart from employing the rhetoric of patriotism
and militarism, Elizabeth's speech is remarkable for recalling another
stage-address to English troops, Henry's speech before the battle of
Agincourt. Like Henry, Elizabeth permits all soldiers 'that loue vs not,
or harbour feare ... to leaue our Campe / Without displeasure'; like
him, she is willing to shed her blood 'with the meanest here', stressing
the equality between herself and her 'noble soldiers', 'loving countrey-
men, / Subjects, and fellow-soldiers' (l. 2686–7); and like Henry, she is
careful that the tale of their triumph shall be commemorated properly:

> And give commandment to the Deane of Powles [St. Paul's]
> He not forget in his next learned Sermon,
> To celebrate this conquest at Powles Crosse:
> And to the Audience in our name declare.

> (l. 2679–82)

These intertheatrical echoes link Elizabeth and Henry, with the latter
acting as the patron saint of patriotic pride implicitly invoked and
commemorated in this address. In so doing, the scene can also be read
as a metadramatic moment that highlights the extent to which nostalgic remembrance is a theatrical effect, produced through speech and
spectacle, and 'declare[d] to the Audience'. Henry's promise that the
'Feast of Crispian' be kept as annual holiday on which the heroes
of the battle would be 'remembered, with advantages' had not been
made good by later times and existed, after all, only in the theatre (*H5*,
4.3.40, 50). This theatrical nature of nostalgia also goes some way to
explain Elizabeth's rare and rather formulaic appearances on the stage
of *If You Know Not Me, Part Two*. They are neither due to diminish-
ing interest in her person, nor to the lack of dramatic finesse that critics have often charged this play with. Rather, this dramatic structure
enacts the nostalgic practice of idealising the past: in order to preserve
the image of Elizabeth as the pure Protestant princess uncompromised
by unpopular decisions taken by the queen, Heywood 'must silently
suppress all the topics which might produce dramatic conflict within

Elizabeth and her court', Dobson and Watson explain. The play's aim is not to dramatise Elizabeth as a character, but to show her as a figure, not to interrogate royal history, but to restore a royal icon.[45]

While engaging its audience in patriotic enthusiasm and tearful nostalgia, Heywood's play offers at the same time a critical analysis of the forgetfulness this involves and the self-serving policies behind it. Just before the triumphant climax in part 1, the playwright has inserted a curious retarding moment that allows him to examine critically the mechanisms and politics of nostalgia. In scene 21 we see Elizabeth in fear for her life when the news of Mary's death reaches her and she realises, shocked, that she is now saved, and Queen. Three courtiers try to outrun each other to be the first to hail her with cries of 'God save the Queen, God save Elizabeth' (l. 1436). When she rewards the first messenger with titles and pensions, hope of preferment rather than loyalty is ironically foregrounded as the true reason for this enthusiasm. The following, penultimate scene shows the common people's response, embodied by two clowns, one of whom says:

> Come, neighbor, come away, euery man his faggot,
> And his double pot, for ioy of the old Queenes death,
> Let bells ring, and children sing,
> For we may have cause to remember,
> The seauenteenth of November.

> (l. 1472–7)

But on their way to hail the new queen, they are held up by the courtier Lord William Tame, who severely rebukes them for so easily forgetting the dead. He reminds them that they had loved Mary, just as they did her father and her brother: 'Yet once departed, ioyfully you sung, / Runne to make Bone-fires, to proclaime your loue / Vnto the newe, forgetting still the old' (ll. 1492–4). When he points out the suitable rites of mourning – 'Now she is gone, how you mone for her, / Were it not fit a while to mone her hearse, / And dutifully there reioyce the tother[?]' (ll. 1495–7) – his admonitions are shrugged off with the mocking compliment: 'By my fayth my masters, he speakes wisely' (l. 1503). In spite of Tame's rebuke, the street-wise clowns resolve to spend yet another half-penny on a faggot, 'rather then the newe Queene shall / Want a Bone-fire' (ll. 1507–8).

---

[45] Dobson and Watson, *England's Elizabeth*, p. 55.

This complaint about callous forgetfulness strikes an odd note in a play dedicated to the remembrance of a late sovereign. Tame's complaint of the populace's will to forget even 'the wisest and the louingst Prince, / That euer swayd a Scepter in the world' (ll. 1498–9) is in stark contrast to the nostalgia for Elizabeth which this play caters to. One possible reading could argue that in keeping with the contrast between Mary and Elizabeth that the play employs throughout, this forgetfulness may be seen as what is due to the unloved Catholic queen and what certainly won't happen to the beloved Elizabeth. This is contradicted, however, by the fact that, according to Tame, this forgetfulness was the fate also of Henry and Edward, both popular Protestant heroes. The scene thus seems to imply that, almost by historical default, the old sovereign, however well loved while alive, is quickly and deliberately forgotten in favour of the new one. Seeking to give this rather dreary message a positive spin, Teresa Grant suggests that the scene might in fact offer a consolation to James: even 'the wisest and louingst Prince' must sink into oblivion, no matter whether he is loved of feared, 'For after death, there's none continues it' (ll. 1501–2). In Grant's view, these lines rescue Heywood 'from a complaint that he is too much addicted to the memory of Elizabeth since they admit the impossibility of a dead prince, no matter how extraordinary, outshining a living one'.[46] But this reading sits oddly with the fact that the entire play, after all, represents nothing so much as the very possibility that a dead prince may indeed outshine a living one, as Elizabeth outshone James.

What the scene does, I would argue instead, is to highlight the element of forgetfulness that is constitutive of nostalgia, as well as the political uses of such forgetfulness. The scene as a whole works as a retarding moment in the glorification of Elizabeth: interpolated between the scenes that show her receiving the news of her half-sister's death and her official coronation, it carves out a space in which the workings of remembrance and oblivion are brought to the audience's attention. The clown articulates this dynamic as the perpetual pattern of history: in the present, the ceremonial celebration of Elizabeth displaces the ceremonial commemoration of Mary; in the future, a national holiday will commemorate her accession rather than her precursor's demise. New holidays are constituted at the expense of old

---

[46] Grant, 'Drama Queen', p. 131.

ones, effacing the memories those were meant to convey into posterity.[47] Yet such forgetfulness is not due to the callousness of the common people, as Tame seems to claim. The clown slyly answers Tame's rebuke with a proverb that acknowledges this forgetfulness not only as a long-established response to a sovereign's death – the king is dead, long live the king – but moreover as an expedient policy: 'do not you know the old prouerbe, / We must liue by the quicke, and not by the dead' (ll. 1477–8). This pragmatic adjustment of popular memory is not a self-serving act, as was the case with courtiers in the scene before. It is rather a self-preserving policy that is acknowledged in the end even by Tame: 'I blame you not, nor do I you commend, / You will still the strongest side defend' (ll. 1509–10). In delaying the spectacle of the final scene, this moment holds up a mirror to the audience, giving it pause to regard its own acts of nostalgic commemoration and to find a necessary policy of forgetfulness at its very heart. It interrupts the process of affective identification with the fate of Queen Elizabeth and, by extension, with a glorified version of the English nation's past that by the time Pepys was writing apparently found an almost automatised expression in a flood of nostalgic tears. In contrast with the following dumb show of Elizabeth's triumphant entry into the city that removes the veil of language between the spectacle on stage and the audience's feelings, this small scene spells out the political and affective investments of nostalgia and reflects on the role of theatrical spectacle in inciting a passion for the past.

The reduction of the dramatic action to a spectacular *tableau vivant* presented either in dumb shows or in episodic series is another device of stage-nostalgia that characterises all the plays under discussion

---

[47] The Queen's Accession Day did in fact replace another holiday, that of St Hugh who had been celebrated on 17 November. As Alison Chapman points out, the royal appropriation of religious holidays fulfilled a definite socio-political function: a unified memorial practice brings about social cohesion and unified consciousness, and the commemorative celebration of the monarch provides a stabilising focus for the national community. To judge by the institutionalisation of her Accession Day as a national holiday (to say nothing of the carefully stylised cult surrounding her person), Elizabeth was aware of this – as was her successor James I, who in his turn abolished 17 November as a day commemorating Elizabeth and restored St Hugh as the proper saint of that holiday: in the King James Bible of 1611, St Hugh's name is listed, while Queen Elizabeth's is erased from the calendar (Chapman, 'Whose Saint Crispin's Day is it?', 1479–81 and 1491, n. 41).

here. A particularly striking example is provided by Thomas Dekker's *The Whore of Babylon* (1607), which opens with a dumb show of the allegorical figure of Truth being awakened at the funeral of a Queen (Mary I) by the entrance of her successor (Elizabeth) and ends with the spectacle of the popish Whore of Babylon's despair at the destruction of the Armada, offered to the Queen and her court by Time. The acts in between are episodic set-pieces of Elizabeth's reign, in each of which she is presented as championing the Protestant cause, ranging from the marriage question over the support of Protestants in the Netherlands, the rebellion in Ireland and the Lopez plot (only one of several plots to assassinate her in the course of the play), to culminate once again in Elizabeth's Tilbury speech and the triumph over the Spanish Armada.[48] As was the case with Heywood's play, the episodic structure allows the dramatist 'to concentrate on building up to this refurbished visual image of Elizabeth as supreme championess of militant Protestantism'.[49] Disregarding chronology as well as causality, Dekker's allegory effectively takes the figure of Elizabeth out of history and into myth. This is an intended effect: the playwright announces in the preface that 'I write as a Poet, not as an Historian, and that these two doe not liue under one law.'[50] The allegorical character of the play is signalled already by its title: the Whore of Babylon and her fight against the Truth of the Protestant Reformation was a central topos of militant Protestant discourse. It was made popular through theological tracts and sermons, but also in texts of Protestant historiography like John Foxe's *Actes and Monuments*, religious plays like John Bale's *King Johan* and epic poems like Edmund Spenser's *The Faerie Queene*.[51]

In Dekker's play, the thinly veiled allegorical figure of Titania, standing for Elizabeth and, by metonymic extension, for England, struggles against the machinations of the Whore of Babylon, doubling as the Church of Rome and a supranational Popish Empire. Each scene is developed through the stark contrast between the glorious protagonist and her devious antagonist, between English patriotism and

[48] Gasper, *The Dragon and the Dove*, pp. 80–96.
[49] Dobson and Watson, *England's Elizabeth*, p. 60.
[50] Dekker, *The Whore of Bablyon*, p. 497, ll. 23–4.
[51] On the Protestant apocalyptic tradition in England and on the Continent that forms the context for Dekker's play, see Gasper, *The Dragon and the Dove*, pp. 62–80.

Popish imperialism, between plain dealing and painted faces, between pure Protestant faith and the courtly arts of flattery, between chastity and sexual promiscuity.[52] While the iconography and dramaturgy are unabashedly celebratory, the topical undertow of remembering Elizabeth seems more equivocal. In spite of the playwright's assertions to the contrary, *The Whore of Bablyon* is full of topical references to the historical Elizabeth's reign as well as to that of her successor James I. Dobson and Watson claim that supplying her with a negative female counterpart allowed for a wholly idealised image of Elizabeth to emerge: the dualistic contrast makes all problematic aspects of the historical Elizabeth's reign (from the fact of her female sex to her unpopular political decisions such as the execution of Mary Queen of Scots) dwindle into insignificance and saves her as the heroine of the play.[53] In keeping with the praise for Elizabeth, the pattern of contrast would also have served as a vehicle of discouraging King James's Catholic sympathies and of inviting him to take up the cause of militant Protestantism, as Curtis Perry claims, a reading with which Julia Gasper concurs when she sees 'political frustration' as the message of the play with regard to the events of King James's reign.[54] But also with regard to that of Elizabeth, Gasper cautions that 'idealisation is a form of implied criticism': scenes like the enthusiastic support for the cause of Protestants in the Netherlands, shown in act 2, might just as well have triggered the recollection that the historical Elizabeth was 'neither so warm nor so prompt in embracing the principles of international solidarity and interventionism', just as the recurrent references to that champion of militant Protestantism, the Earl of Essex, and his execution can be seen as a critique of Elizabeth for harming the cause of the True Church.[55]

It is impossible to decide whether Dekker intended his play as straightforwardly celebratory or as implicit critique of either monarch. On the whole, the polemic tone and the pattern of stark contrasts suggest the first. This is reinforced, in my view, by the dramaturgic frame of two spectacles at the beginning and end of the play, which are emphasised by the absence of language and the presence of on-stage

[52] Perry, 'The citizen politics of nostalgia', 103.
[53] Dobson and Watson, *England's Elizabeth*, p. 60.
[54] Perry, 'The citizen politics of nostalgia', 100; Gasper, *The Dragon and the Dove*, pp. 96–108.
[55] Gasper, *The Dragon and the Dove*, pp. 83–96.

spectators respectively. The opening dumb show is introduced by a Prologue casting a 'Charm of silence' over the audience and calling for 'attention' fitting its elevated subject matter (1.0.1–4). In terms that recall those of the prologue to *Henry V*, the spectators' imagination is enlisted to 'piece out [the] imperfections' of the stage (*H5*, 1.0.23): 'You must fetch backe [winged Time] and here imagine still hee stands' (*Whore of Babylon*, 1.0.12–14). 'These Wonders sit and see', Dekker's Prologue promises: 'vpon this narrow floore / Swell vp an Ocean, (with an Armed Fleete,) / And lay the Dragon at a Doues soft feete' (17–19). In contrast to *Henry V*, however, it is not the spectators' patriotic passions but their 'Iudgment' (21) that is elicited as the appropriate mood to receive the following play. Thus prepared, the allegedly silent, attentive audience watches the dumb show, whose description nevertheless highlights it as an emotionally appealing scene of mourning and despair changed into joyful hope. We see the allegorical figure of Truth 'in sad abiliments; vncrowned; her haire disheueld, and sleeping on a Rock', with her father Time watching and mourning over her (27–31). A funeral procession attended by a queen's entourage crosses the stage, upon which Truth suddenly awakes and 'shews (with her father) arguments of Ioy' (35). Having withdrawn briefly to put on a bright, shining costume and a crown, Truth proceeds to draw the veils of superstition and ignorance from the eyes of the dead Queen's councillors. This sets the stage for 'Titania the Farie Queene: vnder whom is figured our late Queene Elizabeth': she enters, is presented a book by Truth and Time, kisses it and shows it to those around her, who drawing their swords vow 'to defend her and that booke'.[56] This is a memorable stage picture that a contemporary audience would have been likely to recall, for example, from the triumphant finale of Heywood's *If You Know Not Me*. Then 'those Cardinals, Friers &c. (that came in before) with Images, Croziar statues &c.' (48–9) are driven over and finally off the stage in a shameful spectacle that allegorises the eviction of superstition and idolatry from the realm of England. The dumb show culminates in the return of 'graue learned men' from their Marian exile on the continent with 'great signes of gladnesse' (51), in which the audience was certainly expected to join, in spite of the Prologue's appeals to dispassionate judgement.

[56] Dekker, *The Whore of Babylon*, p. 496 and 1.0.42–5.

The final scene presents the English victory over Catholicism in another memorable stage picture. Accompanied by Truth, and elevated aloft with her councillors, Titania/Elizabeth witnesses the dismay of the Whore of Babylon and her scheming cardinals and kings as they watch in turn the destruction of the Armada. The spectacle is sponsored by the figure of Time, who, in a remarkable piece of stage-management of historical time, rewinds to the moment of the fleet's destruction for the Queen's and the theatre audience's benefit. By doubling the act of watching on stage, this scene presents us with a self-reflexive image of nostalgic spectacle in the theatre: like Father Time, the stage replays scenes of the past for the benefit of the spectators; while this past is idealised, it purports to be presented and presided over by Truth. Metatheatrical self-reflexivity does not always create critical distance and sceptical awareness, however, as we saw in the previous chapter concerning the Chorus in *Henry V*. There the Chorus, by 'abridging' time and decking the play's action in mythical and heroic terms ('war-like Harry' as another 'Mars'), exposed the theatre's stage mechanisms in order to involve the audience imaginatively and emotionally in the spectacle. Dekker's play takes this myth-making to an extreme, since its ideological affiliation to militant Protestantism and apocalyptic allegory is not relieved by the presence of any scenes that would set the reality of war against such martial rhetoric. This does not mean that dramaturgic devices such as dumb shows and choric figures per se invite an uncritically nostalgic attitude in the audience. The contrary can be the case, as my following analysis of Shakespeare and Fletcher's *Henry VIII; or, All Is True* will show.

In ironic contrast to its subtitle, Shakespeare and Fletcher's play about Henry VIII evinces a profound scepticism toward the purported truth of nostalgic spectacle.[57] Covering similar chronicle ground as Rowley's earlier play, it presents the downfall of Cardinal Wolsey, the divorce trial of Queen Catherine, the coronation of Queen Anne and the birth of Princess Elizabeth. Despite its subject matter, *Henry VIII* does not so much cater to nostalgic spectacle but critically interrogates the politics

---

[57] This scepticism is one reason why Rudnytsky identifies *Henry VIII*, despite its use of 'the romantic elements of masque and spectacle', as 'Shakespeare's final history play' ('*Henry VIII* and the deconstruction of history', 45); I follow his assessment, yet will show in the following pages that it is precisely through – and not in spite of – the conspicuous use of masque and spectacle that the play articulates its sceptical stance.

of remembering and forgetting it entails.[58] This preoccupation is already signalled by the play's original title, *All Is True*. Recalling titles such as *When You See Me You Know Me* and *If You Know Not Me, You Know Nobody*, which draw attention to the fact that looking is not seeing,[59] *All Is True* invites the spectators to question their own perception of nostalgic spectacle: Are we meant to take what is shown on stage as the truth? Does the play fulfil the promise of delivering historical truth, or does it critically comment on such expectations? In other words, if *all* is true then does this not suggest that '*any* interpretation of the past may be true if one thinks it so'?[60] Critical readings of the play so far have tended, quite rightly, to focus on the tension between truth and representation.[61] I would like to add a concern with the passions that are evoked in performance to make the represented truth feel authentic and authoritative. This play, that so insistently reflects on history as a stage-managed spectacle, has a lot to tell us about how emotions are stage-managed to make that spectacle authoritative.

The relation between theatrical spectacle, truth and nostalgic feeling is already addressed by the Prologue. At the very outset of the play, he sets the frame of mind as well as the emotional attitude with which the audience should receive the show:

> I come no more to make you laugh: things now
> That bear a weighty and a serious brow,
> Sad, high and working, full of state and woe,
> Such noble scenes as draw the eye to flow,
> We now present.

                                                                (1.0.1–5)

The Prologue then proceeds to outline expected motivations for the audience to see this play; some come to indulge their emotions, some seek for historical truth, others merely an entertaining spectacle:

> Those that can pity here,
> May, if they think it well, let fall a tear:
> The subject will deserve it. Such as give
> Their money out of hope they may believe

---

[58] Baldo, 'Forgetting Elizabeth', p. 141.
[59] Grant, 'History in the making', p. 230.
[60] Rudnytsky, '*Henry VIII* and the deconstruction of history', 46.
[61] For an overview see McMullan, 'Introduction', pp. 57–106.

May here find truth, too. Those that come to see
Only a show or two and so agree
The play may pass, if they be still and willing
I'll undertake may see away their shilling
Richly in two short hours.

(1.0.5–13)

Ending with a description, or perhaps rather: a prescription of acceptable responses, the Prologue emphasises that nostalgic spectacle takes
a tearful (as well as rather gullible) audience to unfold the authority
of its 'chosen truth' (18), or at least one prepared to accept it 'still
and willing[ly]' (11). In Dekker's *Whore of Bablyon*, the Prologue's
injunction to silence and dispassionate judgement in the face of what
is glorified a priori as Truth inadvertently stands in ironic contrast to
the polemic rhetoric and emotional scenes of the play. In an inverted
scenario, the Prologue to *Henry VIII* calls for a suspension of disbelief
and affective involvement, a kind of audience attitude that the play
itself does not encourage, however. The Prologue links the affective and
mnemonic workings of nostalgia with the issue of producing national
memory as a selective version of history, which only an audience in a
certain emotional state can accept as truth: in order 'To make that only
true we now intend' (21), the audience needs to 'Be sad as we would
make ye' (25). The means to achieve this is, in another intertheatrical
echo to the prologue of *Henry V*, imaginative and emotional involvement in a fast-paced sequence of events:

> Think ye see
> The very persons of our noble story
> As they were living; think you see them great,
>   …; then, in a moment, see
> How soon this mightiness meets misery.

(0.25–30)

What would ruin the nostalgic effect as well as its ideologically unifying effect, by contrast, is a noisy, disrespectful audience 'That come[s]
to hear a merry, bawdy play' (14), such as Rowley's *When You See
Me*, revived earlier that year, would have attracted.[62] In making these
distinctions, the Prologue also articulates a subtle politics of class

---

[62] Rowley's play presented Henry VIII in the 'bluff King Hal' tradition as a

that is interesting for our topic. For it is not the uneducated ground-lings that constitute the ideally gullible, emotional audience for nos-talgia, but those that can afford the more expensive, genteel seating bought at the price of 1 shilling (12). The lower-class spectators, by contrast, who mix up 'our chosen truth with such a show / As fool and fight is' (18–19), 'Will leave us never an understanding friend' (21), the word 'understanding' referring to both the cognitive cap-acity and the physical location of the lower-class groundlings who stand under the raised stage.[63] This comment hints at the possibility of a part of the audience being resistant to, or at least unaffected by, nostalgic spectacle.

At the climax of the play, the christening of Princess Elizabeth and Cranmer's prophecy of England's glorious future under her reign and that of James I, we are presented with such a noisy audience. Fittingly, we do not see but hear the '*Noise and tumult within*', as the Porter is trying to keep an excited crowd from storming the palace out of sheer joy at the arrival of an heiress. The unruly multitude outside, composed of 'brazier[s]', 'haberdasher's [wives]' and 'youths that thunder at a playhouse' (5.3.38, 43, 55) is associated with popular festivities and spectacles such as the bear- and bull-baiting going on at Paris Garden in the immediate vicinity to the Globe, the May Day celebrations, or the militia training at Moorfields. These offered rival spectacles to the royally sponsored ritual of the christening nostalgically staged by the play. In fact, the Porter scene interrupts a series of ceremonial shows that constitute the final act of *Henry VIII*, the trial of Cranmer and the christening of Elizabeth. The celebratory mood is bracketed here for a moment in order to present a very different attitude to what will be nostalgically remembered as a glorious event in the nation's past. While the unseen rabble in the Porter scene might serve merely as a

swaggering, jovial ruler, with scenes of 'fool and fight' (*H8*, 1.0.19) that show Henry moving in disguise among his subjects or getting into brawls and even being arrested, inviting the kind of rumbustious audience reaction rejected here. Since the play is set in the time of Prince Edward's birth and education, the topical comparisons invited tend to be between Henry VIII and James I, Queen Catherine Parr and James' Queen Anne, as well as the princes Edward Tudor and Henry Stuart, with the nostalgic emphasis falling on the Protestant fervour of Prince Edward and the Lutheran Catherine, as Teresa Grant has shown in 'History in the making'.

[63] *Henry V*, ed. by McMullan, note to Epilogue line 21. Stern comments on the alternative term 'understander' in *Making Shakespeare*, p. 28.

negative foil to a more appropriate response, it nevertheless could also remind the audience at the Globe that reactions other than nostalgic tearfulness and obedient acceptance of what is presented as truth are possible.

Another response that would also spoil the nostalgic mood is not mentioned at all in the Prologue, but rather enacted several times throughout the play: a sceptical, ironic distance toward the spectacle of history. As in *Henry V*, where the martial rhetoric of the Chorus is counteracted by the scenes depicting war as a messy and thoroughly un-heroic business, so is the Prologue's aligning of nostalgic spectacle, truth and affective identification in *Henry VIII* punctured by scenes that separate truth from spectacle and thus carve out a space for ironic distance. This deconstruction of historical truth already begins with the opening scene. It presents us with Norfolk's report of the historical events on the Field of the Cloth of Gold, where the kings of England and France meet to sign a peace treaty. Norfolk's description focuses on the splendour this encounter entailed, which he witnessed and now retails with admiration:

> Today the French,
> All clinquant, all in gold like heathen gods,
> Shone down the English; and tomorrow they
> Made Britain India. Every man that stood
> Showed like a mine.

(1.1.18–22)

Only a few lines on, the sartorial competition of 'two kings, / Equal in lustre' (28), is revealed as a mere show, however: the pact is quickly broken, and the peace did 'not value / The cost that did conclude it' (88–9). What could be seen on the field that day was precisely not 'all true', but even if one saw through the spectacle, one could not say so openly: 'no discerner durst wag his tongue in censure' (33). As Lee Bliss – one of the first critics to recognise the discrepancy between truth and spectacle as a structural feature of the play – remarks: 'In the beginning all had seemed true to Norfolk and, in his report, to us; only in retrospect can we see how false, how truly unstable ... that appearance was.' While Norfolk initially confessed himself a 'fresh admirer' of the spectacle (1.1.3), we are quickly made to see that his admiration 'did not signify wonder in the sense of approbation, but rather an ironic sense of amazement at the disparity' between spectacle and truth.[64] This disillusionment with spectacle is arrived at only by hindsight, a cautionary tale that seems out of place with a nostalgic play that operates by idealising the past in retrospect. It is in keeping, however, with a reading of this play as a critical inquiry into nostalgic spectacle and the truth it serves to obfuscate.

Such a reading is offered by Jonathan Baldo, who argues that, despite its insistence on the visual of costume drama, the play above all 'draws attention to that which is not given view. Some of *Henry VIII*'s most noticeable features are its omissions.' Even the persons and events it does include are primarily used to highlight their eventual 'omission or deletion from the pageant of history': in presenting the downfall of the Duke of Buckingham, Queen Katherine and Cardinal Wolsey, and their eventual deletion from the dramatic narrative that goes on to celebrate the memory of the King, the play dramatises the process of history-making 'under monarchical control as a process of obliteration'. With the representatives of alternative accounts of history silenced, what remains in the end is the 'univocal and undivided' version of official royal historiography.[65] I would add that this process of obliteration and adjustment of popular to official memory is not only staged but also upstaged by the play, as the spectacle of nostalgic truth is punctured again and again by alternative, contradictory perspectives.

The scene immediately following Wolsey's demise furnishes an illustrative example. Two nameless gentlemen standing in the crowd watching Queen Anne's coronation procession comment on what they – and the audience in the playhouse – see represented as an elaborate pageant on the stage. The First Gentleman identifies the members of the procession and their position at court to the Second Gentleman. Obviously unfamiliar with the inner circle of the royal household, as the common audience at the playhouse would have been too, the Second Gentleman is nevertheless not dazzled by the spectacle but proves a rather cynical, savvy observer. He reacts to the sight of Queen Anne with what might easily be mistaken as a paean to her beauty, were it not for the recurrence of a catchword that recalls the opening-scene with its critical

[64] Bliss, 'The wheel of fortune', 3.
[65] Baldo, 'Forgetting Elizabeth', pp. 132, 141, 142.

dissection of royal shows. 'Our King', the Second Gentleman states, 'has all the Indies in his arms, / And more, and richer, when he strains that lady' (4.1.45–6). Again, the riches of India are evoked in order to describe a victory that might have come at too great a price. Just as the costly peace with France was quickly broken, so Anne's status as queen already seems precarious: her star and those of her ladies have risen quickly, yet those may 'sometimes [be] falling quickly', as the First Gentleman insinuates. The sexual pun on 'falling' fits into a pattern of innuendos about Anne's chastity throughout the play, suggesting that her display of modesty, godliness and saintliness at the coronation is again nothing more than a stage-managed spectacle (71–86). The dangerous truth of this insinuation may be measured by the Second Gentleman's warning reply: 'No more of that' (56).

The pageant is followed by a report of the coronation ceremony itself, structurally recalling the opening scene in that the subject is again a ceremonious occasion whose splendour comes to us as a second-hand historical narrative. It even contains a direct textual reference to the ability of spectacle to render the participants indistinguishable in the eyes of the spectators, just as was the case with the kings on the Field of the Cloth of Gold. Now a Third Gentleman describes how Queen Anne put herself on display 'some half an hour or so / In a rich chair of state', and how 'the beauty of her person' excited such passion in the people that 'No man living / Could say "This is my wife" there, all were woven / So strangely into one piece [of cloth]' (4.1.66–81). In Jonathan Baldo's view, what is most remarkable about this scene is that '[n]o one challenges the veracity of the Third Gentleman's report or the accuracy of his memory', and he takes this as evidence that memory is now entirely under the king's control.[66] This is apposite as far as the memory politics *in* the play are concerned. When we shift attention to the memory politics *of* the play, however, a different mnemonic effect emerges: in recalling the rhetoric and the structure of the opening scene, the audience may also recall that some scepticism about the truthfulness of spectacle is in order. No figure on stage voices that scepticism, for this role has now been shifted to the audience itself. Moreover, the scene draws our attention to the dynamic of forgetting and remembering that underpins this royal spectacle. The Third Gentleman's report closes with the information that, after the

[66] *Ibid.*

ceremony, the new queen withdrew to 'York Place, where the feast is held', when the First Gentleman cuts in:

> Sir,
> You must no more call it 'York Place' – that's past;
> For since the Cardinal fell, that title's lost.
> 'Tis now the King's, and called 'Whitehall'.

(4.1.94–7)

'I know it', the Third Gentlemen concedes, 'But 'tis so lately altered that the old name / Is fresh about me' (98–9). This brief moment of forgetfulness, which is in actual fact motivated by an inability to forget the established name and remember a new one, highlights how popular memory has to adjust to new political and material circumstances, as did the scene between Lord Tame and the Clowns in *If You Know Not Me*. Where such adjustment is not accomplished, it creates a tension with official royal memory and may offer a critical perspective on it. Reviving the paradoxical pattern we already observed in *Henry V*, a moment of conspicuous forgetfulness on stage alerts the audience that the spectacle they are watching is not a straightforward representation of historical truth, however authentic it may appear or feel.

Henry VIII is one of the few Shakespearean plays of which actual spectator reports exist. Sir Henry Wotton's description of the play and the fire that destroyed the Globe during a production in the summer of 1613 is famous for giving us a view of the early modern stage through the eyes of a contemporary. It also suggests that at least some of the audience took their cue from the critical on-stage spectators discussed above. Instead of being reduced to pity and tears by the 'Pomp and Majesty' of the nostalgic spectacle, or dazzled into an easy acceptance of it as historical truth, Wotton notes that the play presents quite another truth about royalty, 'sufficient ... to make greatness very familiar, if not ridiculous'.[67] In keeping with this sentiment, his report of the fire – an event of potentially tragic stature – closes on a farcical note when the burning breeches of one spectator are doused with a bottle of ale, collapsing the 'sad, high' matters of 'state and woe' (1.0.3) into a 'merry, bawdy' (14) show indeed. What this eye-witness report of one of the first performances of *All is True* lacks utterly,

---

[67] Wotton, *The Life and Letters of Sir Henry Wotton*, vol. II, p. 32.

however, is the kind of awed submission to the spectacle of nostalgia the Prologue claims so confidently and comprehensively. This contemporary report affirms rather that while its subject matter makes *Henry VIII* qualify as a nostalgic play, this is self-reflexively and effectively qualified by the play itself as it repeatedly makes the issue of theatrical spectacle – and its fraught relation to historical truth and nostalgic feeling – its subject. In so doing, it provides those who care to look and see with a disillusioning insight into the mnemonic and affective politics of nostalgia that, as Wotton's report suggests, endows them with the authority to discern 'sufficient truth' not to succumb to its appeal.

Conclusion: Shakespeare's mnemonic dramaturgy

This study has examined Shakespeare's historical drama with a view to exploring how these plays engage with the English nation's past and the historical consciousness of their audiences. In particular, my aim was to demonstrate that this engagement takes the shape of a dynamic interplay between remembering and forgetting through which the collective memory is formed and transformed. It bears pointing out that it was also *performed*, in the literal sense of recreated on the stage, for it is only when we acknowledge this theatrical dimension that we can fully understand the process of making memory and of creating a historical consciousness to which the early modern stage contributed so significantly. We need to acknowledge how in early modern England 'history [was] understood according to the structures and dynamics of theatre', as Brian Walsh also claims.[1] In order to do so I have not only discussed Shakespeare's histories in the light of what memories they recall or erase, but also sought to identify the specifically theatrical devices of rhetoric, imagery, dramaturgy and acting through which they do so. These devices do not occur only in one play, creating one specific form of remembering and forgetting, but are part of Shakespeare's dramaturgic repertoire that he developed over the course of his career. Employing different dramaturgic devices in different constellations results in different mnemonic effects, especially when we take into account that individual performances may make more or less use of particular elements. While the mnemonic dramaturgy of each play (and each production) is thus specific, the devices from which it is composed engender connections between the histories and beyond to other plays, recalled and reconfigured with those presented on stage, turning the public playhouse into a memory theatre indeed.

---

[1] Walsh, *Shakespeare, the Queen's Men and the Elizabethan Performance of History*, p. 5.

The elements of Shakespeare's mnemonic dramaturgy can be usefully distinguished according to the level on which they operate.
Beginning at the lexical and semantic level, verbal echoes constitute
micro-mnemonic devices that recall a specific rhetoric and imagery –
of lament, for example, or of ritual – but that can also be redeployed
and turned into vehicles of obliterating memories, as we saw with the
forms of traditional lament in *Richard II*, or emptied of significance
through mocking repetition, as was the case with Falstaff's parodied
catechism on honour. Puns are a specific form of lexical mnemonic
devices, as they turn on the simultaneous presence and absence of
alternative meanings: while one is present, the other must be recalled
for the pun to work, replacing in turn the original meaning represented
by the word. Falstaff's word-plays, which he employs most often in
order to distract his on-stage audience from inopportune memories,
thus follow and reinforce the same pattern of erasure and substitution,
forgetting and remembering, that is embodied by this figure.

The use of objects and stage properties forms another level of
mnemonic devices, to which a recent study by Lina Perkins Wilder
is dedicated: they constitute 'the materials of memory', including the
space of the stage and the actors' bodies.[2] As we have seen, objects
like the gloves in *1 Henry IV* or *Henry V* can serve as duplicitous
'favours': they are marks of remembrance by which the identity of
a person is recalled, but at the same time they can serve to disguise
or erase that identity, substituting a go-between or another object of
remembrance instead. In a similar way, in *Richard II* the symbols of
kingship or of sainthood are evoked (and, in production, materially
present as props) in order to erase one identity and replace it with
another. The mirror which Richard destroys on stage is an important device that symbolises the self-destruction of his former image
as king and manages at the same time to recall to the audience the
memory of the Reformation's iconoclasm, both acts of forgetting that
are being remembered in this moment. Falstaff's lethargic body is an
example for an embodied mnemonic device that is theatrically created.
In one sense, he is 'a sweet creature of bombast', a word that refers to
both his inflated language and the cotton stuffing used to create his
corpulence.[3] In another, this figure is theatrically created in that his

---

[2] Wilder, *Shakespeare's Memory Theatre*, p. 1.
[3] *Ibid.*, p. 89.

protean character and shape-shifting performances are the result of a dramatic appropriation of a historical figure, a 'shameless transform-ation' (1.1.44) of former identities that Falstaff's fat, sweating, lethargic body recalls and defers endlessly.

Memorable stage pictures created through pageants, *tableaux vivants* and ceremonial scenes are a staple of history plays, as Janet Dillon has pointed out. They are emphatically mnemonic devices in the traditional sense of the *ars memorativa*, creating vivid images that are deposited in the memory environment of the stage as well as our collective imagery: who would not immediately recognise the image of Hamlet holding a skull, or of Cleopatra with the asp at her breast? These images have become icons of Western culture, and as such form part of the deep-structure of our cultural memory. Yet striking stage images can also serve as screens that divert our attention away from what is really happening, Dillon cautions with regard to the opening pageant in *Henry VIII* where 'court ceremony is always a front to distract the people from the true import of the events thus ceremoni-alised'. Ceremony is a particularly apt mnemonic device, congenial to the theatre because of their shared attention to costume, props, set-ting and tempo. Moreover, in both the sacred and the profane, cere-mony 'forms a crucial element in the way history is constructed and remembered, since it furnishes striking and memorable visual images and sensory experiences'.[4] The formative mnemonic role of ceremony also includes, as we have seen, acts of forgetting. The scenes with the weeping queens in *Richard III*, for example, offer highly ritu-alised tableaux of grief which are, however, constantly interrupted and rendered ineffective by Richard of Gloucester; these instances of 'maimed rites' (*Hamlet*) become memorable in the playhouse precisely because they fail to complete their mnemonic work in the play-world. Ceremony can also itself become a vehicle for erasing memories, as we saw with regard to the inversed ritual of divestiture in *Richard II* through which the King demolished his image as mon-arch only to re-create an image of Christ-like martyr and saint in its stead, or the ceremonial epitaph Prince Hal speaks for Hotspur on the battlefield through which the memory of rebellion in the name of honour is erased.

---

[4] Dillon, *Shakespeare and the Staging of English History*, pp. 22, 54.

Beyond the dynamic of remembering and forgetting enacted by such stage pictures, these memorable scenes are themselves part of a mnemonic pattern across a play's overall dramatic structure. Such 'scenic memory' is activated through the repetition of stage pictures and 'units of action' (the terms are Dillon's). Richard's rehearsal of abdication in act 3 of *Richard II*, for instance, prefigures and is recalled by the actual abdication scene in act 4, just as the recurring scenes of mourning for Gloucester's murdered victims take on a nightmarish quality that culminates in the procession of ghostly memories haunting Richard III before the battle of Bosworth. Another important device of mnemonic dramaturgy at the level of scenic memory is the framing of scenes, which we saw at work, for example, in *Richard III* or *Henry VIII*. In both plays, scenes that are addressed to on-stage audiences and aim at implanting future memories – the election of Richard at Baynard Castle, or Queen Anne's coronation procession – are framed by other scenes that offer the theatrical audience a different perspective, warning them against taking the memory image offered at face value. The three ceremonial scenes shown in *Henry VIII* (the meeting of kings on Field of the Cloth of Gold, the crowning of Queen Anne, the christening of Princess Elizabeth) form a nostalgic triptych that the audience is supposed to remember – along with the Gentlemen's choric comments that sceptically puncture such memorable spectacles. In a markedly different way, the Chorus of *Henry V* is implicated in the ideological manufacturing of memories intended to sweep the audience along on a wave of nationalist enthusiasm, so that it falls to other figures and scenes to provide counter-memories and counter-images. Following this pattern of 'contrapuntal sequencing', as I have called it, the audience is actively involved in questioning the very patterns of remembering and forgetting that the plays enact.

Scenic memory is complemented by intertheatrical memory: lines, scenes or figures remembered from other plays. Thus the audience is clearly expected to be familiar with the development of Prince Hal from madcap prince to the mirror of all Christian kings across the *Henriad*; and as the Epilogue to *Henry V* makes clear, the playwright also counted on an audience that had seen the plays of the first tetralogy when it refers to the Wars of the Roses as a conflict 'which oft our stage hath shown' (13). The cyclical structure of the two tetralogies in fact enables a movement back and forth against the chronological order of events, clearly privileging intertheatrical memory over historical memory and inviting the audience to acknowledge the formative role the plays perform in re-enacting the past. Spaces, too, are invested with memories that can carry over from play to play or even beyond the play. Thus the Blackfriars Theatre at which *Henry VIII* was also performed was the original site, back in the days when it was still a monastery, of the historical trial against Queen Katharine, and her dramatic speeches in the play repeat almost verbatim her own defence before the court. For an audience familiar with the historical records as well as the history of the place, this mnemonic substratum of the place would have been activated in performance.[5]

The figure of Falstaff is perhaps the most explicit instance of a dramatic character that calls on the intertheatrical memories of the spectators, as the scenes of forgetting Falstaff only develop their (tragi-) comic and mnemonic potential when the audience members bring their memories of him to the theatre. In the case of Falstaff, intertheatrical recollection is complemented by intertextual relations of recall, erasure and substitution between play-text and the texts of the prose histories that add further mnemonic substrata to this figure: memories of the Lollard rebel, the proto-Protestant martyr and the grotesque parody of Puritan hypocrisy are all activated in his shape-shifting performances only to be subsumed again by the overwhelming presence of the fat knight. Generally speaking, the relations between chronicle histories and history plays are an important aspect of Shakespeare's mnemonic dramaturgy, though not in the sense of static source study (what is taken up, what is left out) but rather in the sense that for those audience members familiar with other mediations of history, deviations and omissions would have alerted them to the ways in which dramatic performance can actively transform historical memory.

The audience's collective memory is also crucial for enabling the interplay between the dramatic text performed on stage and its non-dramatic contexts. If the Globe theatre is a mnemonic site, it can work only in concert with the memories brought to it by the spectators (as well as, of course, the playwrights and actors). The reconstruction of the past as well as its cognitive and affective reception during performance, are informed by the constraints and conditions of the present. Historical memories can trigger topical references and vice

---

[5] See Schwyzer, 'Shakespeare's art of reenactment: Henry at Blackfriars, Richard at Rougemont'.

versa, thus extending the memory environment created in performance beyond the playhouse to include the social environment. In turn, the conditions of contemporary culture – the socio-political situation, the dawning of commercial capitalism, the spread of literacy and print culture, the discourses and practices of religion, nation, ethnicity and gender – determine what can be remembered, or what counts as a valid memory, in any case. But as I hope to have demonstrated throughout, we also need to take into account the specific mnemonic devices of theatrical dramaturgy as another formative condition that enables not simply *what* is remembered or forgotten on the early modern stage, but *how*.

Bibliography

Adrian, Gregory, *The Silence of Memory: Armistice Day 1919–1945* (Oxford: Berg, 1994).

Agnew, Jean-Christophe, *Worlds Apart: The Market and the Theater in Anglo-American Thought, 1550–1750* (Cambridge University Press, 1986).

Althusser, Louis, 'Ideology and ideological state apparatuses [1968]', in J. Rivkin and M. Ryan (eds.), *Literary Theory: An Anthology* (Oxford: Blackwell, 1998), pp. 294–304.

Altman, Joel B., '"Vile participation": The amplification of violence in the theater of *Henry V*', *Shakespeare Quarterly*, 42:1 (1991), 1–32.

Anderson, Benedict, *Imagined Communities: Reflections on the Origin and Spread of Nationalism*. Revised edition (London and New York: Verso, 1991).

Anderson, Thomas P., *Performing Early Modern Trauma from Shakespeare to Milton* (Aldershot: Ashgate, 2006).

Assmann, Aleida, *Cultural Memory and Western Civilization: Functions, Media, Archives* (Cambridge University Press, 2011).

'Formen des Vergessens', in N. Diasio and K. Wieland (eds.), *Die sozio-kulturelle (De-)Konstruktion des Vergessens: Bruch und Kontinuität in den Gedächtnisrahmen um 1945 und 1989* (Bielefeld: Aisthesis Verlag, 2012), pp. 21–48.

'The battle of memories in Shakespeare's histories', in A. Assmann, *Cultural Memory and Western Civilization: Functions, Media, Archives* (Cambridge University Press, 2011), pp. 53–78.

Assmann, Jan, *Das kulturelle Gedächtnis: Schrift, Erinnerung und politische Identität in frühen Hochkulturen* (München: Beck, 1992).

Bacon, Francis, *Of the Advancement and Proficiencies of Learning ...* (London: 1640).

Baldo, Jonathan, '"A rooted sorrow": Scotland's unusable past', in N. Moschovakis (ed.), *Macbeth: New Critical Essays* (London and New York: Routledge, 2008), pp. 88–103.

'Exporting oblivion in *The Tempest*', *Modern Language Quarterly*, 56:2 (1995), 111–44.

'Forgetting Elizabeth in *Henry VIII*', in E. Hageman and K. Conway (eds.), *Resurrecting Elizabeth I in Seventeenth-Century England* (Madison, NJ: Fairleigh Dickinson University Press, 2007), pp. 132–48.

Memory in Shakespeare's Histories: Stages of Forgetting in Early Modern England (New York: Routledge, 2012).

'Shakespeare's art of distraction', *Shakespeare*, 10:2 (2014), 138–57.

'Wars of memory in *Henry V*', *Shakespeare Quarterly*, 47:2 (1996), 132–59.

Barber, C. L., *Shakespeare's Festive Comedy: A Study of Dramatic Form and Its Relation to Social Custom* (Princeton University Press, 1959).

Barish, Jonas, 'Remembering and forgetting in Shakespeare', in R. B. Parker and S. P. Zitner (eds.), *Elizabethan Theater* (Newark: University of Delaware Press, 1996), pp. 214–12.

The Antitheatrical Prejudice (Berkeley: University of California Press, 1981).

Batman, Stephen, *Batman Uppon Bartholome* (London: Thomas East, 1582).

Bawcutt, Nancy W., *The Control and Censorship of Caroline Drama: The Records of Sir Henry Herbert, Master of the Revels 1623–1672* (Oxford: Clarendon Press, 1996).

Beecher, Donald, 'Introduction: The crisis of memory', in D. Beecher and G. Williams (eds.), *Ars Reminiscendi: Mind and Memory in Renaissance Culture* (Toronto: Centre for Reformation and Renaissance Studies, 2009), pp. 17–24.

Bevington, David, 'Introduction', in D. Bevington (ed.), *King Henry IV, Part One*. The Oxford Shakespeare (Oxford University Press, 1987), pp. 1–110.

Bliss, Lee, 'The wheel of fortune and the maiden phoenix in Shakespeare's *King Henry the Eighth*', *English Literary History*, 42 (1975), 1–25.

Bolzoni, Lina, *The Gallery of Memory: Literary and Iconographic Models in the Age of the Printing Press*. Transl. by Jeremy Parzen (University of Toronto Press, 2001).

Boym, Svetlana, *The Future of Nostalgia* (New York: Basic Books, 2001).

Breuilly, John, *Nationalism and the State* (Manchester University Press, 1993).

Bruster, Douglas, *Drama and the Market in the Age of Shakespeare* (Cambridge University Press, 1992).

Cahill, Patricia, *Unto the Breach: Martial Formations, Historical Trauma, and the Early Modern Stage* (Oxford University Press, 2008).

Calhoun, Craig, *Nationalism* (Minneapolis: University of Minnesota Press, 1997).

Carlson, Marvin, *The Haunted Stage: The Theatre as Memory Machine* (University of Michigan Press, 2003).

Carroll, William C., '"The form of law": Ritual and succession in *Richard III*', in L. Woodbridge (ed.), *True Rites and Maimed Rites: Ritual and Anti-Ritual in Shakespeare and His Age* (Urbana and Chicago: University of Illinois Press, 1992), pp. 203–19.

Carruthers, Mary, *The Book of Memory: A Study of Memory in Medieval Culture*. 2nd edn. (Cambridge University Press, 2008).

Cavanagh, Dermot, Stuart Hampton-Reeves and Stephen Longstaffe (eds.), *Shakespeare's Histories and Counter-Histories* (Manchester University Press, 2006).

Chapman, Alison, 'Whose Saint Crispin's Day is it? Shoemaking, holiday making, and the politics of memory in early modern England', *Renaissance Quarterly*, 54:4 (2001), 1467–94.

Charnes, Linda, *Notorious Identity: Materializing the Subject in Shakespeare* (Cambridge, MA: Harvard University Press, 1993).

Chartier, Roger, 'Jack Cade, the skin of a dead lamb, and the hatred for writing', *Shakespeare Studies*, 34 (2006), 77–89.

Chernaik, Warren, *The Cambridge Introduction to Shakespeare's History Plays* (Cambridge University Press, 2007).

Clare, Janet, *'Art Made Tongue Tied by Authority': Elizabethan and Jacobean Dramatic Censorship* (Manchester University Press, 1990).

Clegg, Cyndia Susan, *Press Censorship in Elizabethan England* (Cambridge University Press, 1997).

Cohen, Derek, *Searching Shakespeare: Studies in Culture and Authority* (University of Toronto Press, 2003).

Cohen, Stephen, 'Between form and culture: New Historicism and the promise of a historical formalism', in M. D. Rasmussen (ed. and introd.) and R. Strier (afterword), *Renaissance Literature and Its Formal Engagements* (New York, NY: Palgrave, 2002), pp. 17–41.

Cohen, Stephen (ed.), *Shakespeare and Historical Formalism* (Aldershot: Ashgate, 2007).

Collinson, Patrick, 'William Camden and the anti-myth of Elizabeth: Setting the mould?', in S. Doran and T. S. Freeman (eds.), *The Myth of Elizabeth* (Basingstoke: Palgrave Macmillan, 2003), pp. 79–98.

Connerton, Paul, *How Societies Remember* (Cambridge University Press, 1989).

'Seven types of forgetting', *Memory Studies*, 1:1 (2008), 59–71.

Corbin, Peter and Douglas Sedge (eds.), *The Oldcastle Controversy: Sir John Oldcastle, Part I and The Famous Victories of Henry V* (Manchester University Press, 1991).

Craik, T. W., 'Introduction', in *King Henry V*, ed. by T. W. Craik. Arden Third Series (London and New York: Routledge, 1995), pp. 1–111.

Davis, Fred, *Yearning for Yesterday: A Sociology of Nostalgia* (New York: The Free Press, 1979).

Dawson, Anthony B., 'The arithmetic of memory: Shakespeare's theatre and the national past', *Shakespeare Survey*, 52 (1999), 54–67.

'The distracted globe', in A. B. Dawson and P. Yachnin (eds.), *The Culture of Playgoing in Shakespeare's England: A Collaborative Debate* (Cambridge University Press, 2001), pp. 88–107.

Dawson, Anthony B. and Paul Yachnin, *The Culture of Playgoing in Shakespeare's England: A Collaborative Debate* (Cambridge University Press, 2001).

Day, Gillian, '"Determinèd to prove a villain": Theatricality in *Richard III*', *Critical Survey*, 3:2 (1991), 149–56.

de Sousa, Geraldo U., 'The peasants' revolt and the writing of history in *2 Henry VI*', in D. Bergeron (ed.), *Reading and Writing in Shakespeare* (Newark: University of Delaware Press, 1996), pp. 178–93.

Debord, Guy, *The Society of Spectacle* [1967]. Transl. by Donald Nicholson-Smith (New York: Zone Books, 1994).

Dekker, Thomas, *The Whore of Babylon* [1607], in *The Dramatic Works of Thomas Dekker*, vol. II, ed. by Fredson Bowers (Cambridge: Cambridge University Press, 1955).

Diehl, Huston, *Staging Reform, Reforming the Stage: Protestantism and Popular Theatre in Early Modern England* (Ithaca, NY: Cornell University Press, 1997).

Dillon, Janette, *Shakespeare and the Staging of English History* (Oxford University Press, 2012).

Dobson, Michael and Nicola Watson, *England's Elizabeth: An Afterlife in Fame and Fantasy* (Oxford University Press, 2002).

Dobson, R.B., *The Peasant's Revolt of 1381*. 2nd edn. (London: Macmillan Press, 1983).

Doran, Susan and Thomas S. Freeman, *The Myth of Elizabeth* (Houndmills, Basingstoke: Palgrave Macmillan, 2003).

Döring, Tobias, *Performances of Mourning in Shakespearean Theatre and Early Modern Culture* (Houndmills, Basingstoke: Palgrave Macmillan, 2006).

'Shadows to the unseen grief? Rituals of memory and forgetting in the history plays', paper given at the International Shakespeare Conference, Brisbane, July 2006, Panel Session *Cultural Memory in Shakespeare – Shakespeare in Cultural Memory*. Unpublished lecture manuscript.

Downame, John, *The Second Part of the Christian Warfare* (London: 1611).

Dubrow, Heather, 'Guess who's coming to dinner? Reinterpreting formalism and the country house poem', *Modern Language Quarterly*, 61:1 (2000), 59–77.

Dubrow, Heather. *A Happier Eden: The Politics of Marriage in the Stuart Epithalamium* (Ithaca: Cornell University Press, 1990).

Duffy, Eamon, *The Stripping of the Altars: Traditional Religion in England, c. 1400 – c. 1580* (New Haven, CT: Yale University Press, 1992).

Dutton, Richard, *Licensing, Censorship and Authorship in Early Modern England* (Basingstoke: Palgrave, 2000).

Mastering the Revels: The Regulation and Censorship of English Renaissance Drama (London and Basingstoke: Macmillan, 1991).

Eco, Umberto, 'An ars oblivionalis? Forget it!', *PMLA*, 103:3 (1988), 254–61.

Engel, William, *Death and Drama in Renaissance England* (Oxford University Press, 2002).

Engel, William E., 'The decay of memory', in C. Ivic and G. Williams (eds.), *Forgetting in Early Modern English Literature and Culture: Lethe's Legacies* (London: Routledge, 2004), pp. 21–40.

Mapping Mortality: The Persistence of Memory and Melancholy in Early Modern England (Amherst: University of Massachusetts Press, 1995).

Engle, Lars, 'Who pays in the Henriad?', in L. Engle, *Shakespearean Pragmatism: Market of His Time* (University of Chicago Press, 1993), pp. 107–28.

Erne, Lukas, *Shakespeare as Literary Dramatist* (Cambridge University Press, 2003).

Fischer, Sandra K., '"He means to pay": Value and metaphor in the Lancastrian tetralogy', *Shakespeare Quarterly*, 40:2 (1989), 149–64.

Fitter, Chris, 'Historicising Shakespeare's *Richard II*: Current events, dating, and the sabotage of Essex', *Early Modern Literary Studies: A Journal of Sixteenth- and Seventeenth-Century English Literature*, 11:2 (2005), http://extra.shu.ac.uk/emls/11–2/fittric2.htm, last accessed 13.02.2015, no pagination.

'"Your captain is brave and vows reformation": Jack Cade, the Hacket Rising, and Shakespeare's vision of popular rebellion in *2 Henry VI*', *Shakespeare Studies*, 32 (2004), 173–219.

Fitzpatrick, Joan, *Food in Shakespeare: Early Modern Dietaries and the Plays* (Aldershot: Ashgate, 2007).

Foakes, R. A., 'Review of Wells, Stanley; Taylor, Gary. The Complete Works, original-spelling edition', *Modern Language Review*, 84:2 (1989), 438–9.

Fraser, R. Scott, '"The king has killed his heart": The death of Falstaff in *Henry V*', *SEDERI*, 20 (2010), 145–57.

Frow, John, *Genre*. New Critical Idiom Series (New York: Routledge, 2006).

'Toute la mémoire du monde: Repetition and forgetting', in J. Frow, *Time and Commodity Culture: Essays in Cultural Theory and Postmodernity* (Oxford: Clarendon Press, 1997), pp. 218–46.

Garber, Marjorie, *Shakespeare's Ghost Writers: Literature as Uncanny Causality* (New York and London, Methuen: 1987).

Gasper, Julia, *The Dragon and the Dove: The Plays of Thomas Dekker* (Oxford: Clarendon Press, 1990).

Goldberg, Jonathan, 'The commodity of names: "Falstaff" and "Oldcastle" in *1 Henry IV*', in J. Crewe (ed.), *Reconfiguring the Renaissance: Essays in Critical Materialism* (Lewisburg: Bucknell University Press; London and Toronto: Associated University Press, 1992), pp. 76–88.

Goldmann, Stefan, 'Statt Totenklage Gedächtnis: Zur Erfindung der Mnemotechnik durch Simonides von Keos', *Poetica*, 21 (1989), 43–66.

Goodland, Katherine, *Female Mourning in Medieval and Renaissance English Drama* (Aldershot: Ashgate, 2005).

Gosson, Stephen, 'Playes Confuted in Five Actions [1582]', in *Markets of Bawdrie: The Dramatic Criticism of Stephen Gosson*, ed. by Arthur F. Kinney (Salzburg: Institut für Englische Sprache und Literatur, 1974), pp. 138–200.

'The School of Abuse [1587]', in *Markets of Bawdrie: The Dramatic Criticism of Stephen Gosson*, ed. by Arthur F. Kinney (Salzburg: Institut für Englische Sprache und Literatur, 1974), pp. 69–120.

Grady, Hugh, 'Falstaff: Subjectivity between the carnival and the aesthetic', *The Modern Language Review*, 96 (2001), 609–23.

Shakespeare and Impure Aesthetics (Cambridge University Press, 2009).

Shakespeare, Machiavelli and Montaigne: Power and Subjectivity from Richard II *to* Hamlet (Oxford University Press, 2002).

Grant, Teresa, 'Drama queen: Staging Elizabeth in *If You Know Not Me You Know Nobody*', in S. Doran and T. S. Freeman (eds.), *The Myth of Elizabeth* (Basingstoke: Palgrave Macmillan, 2003), pp. 120–42.

'History in the making: The case of Samuel Rowley's *When You See Me You Know Me* (1605/06)', in T. Grant and B. Ravelhofer (eds.), *English Historical Drama, 1500–1660: Forms Outside the Canon* (Houndmills, Basingstoke: Palgrave Macmillan, 2008), pp. 125–57.

Gratarolus, Gulielmus, *The Castel of Memorie*. Transl. by William Fulwood. London: Rouland Hall, 1562.

Greenblatt, Stephen, *Hamlet in Purgatory* (Princeton, NJ and Oxford: Princeton University Press, 2001).

'Murdering peasants: Status, genre, and the representation of rebellion', *Representations*, 1 (1983), 1–29.

Renaissance Self-Fashioning: From More to Shakespeare (University of Chicago Press, 1980).

Greene, John [*see also* I. G.], *A Refutation of the Apology for Actors* (London: W. White, 1615).

Grene, Nicolas, *Shakespeare's Serial History Plays* (Cambridge University Press, 2002).

Gurr, Andrew, 'Introduction', in *Richard II*, ed. by A. Gurr. The New Cambridge Shakespeare (Cambridge University Press, 2003), pp. 1–60.

The Shakespeare Company, 1594–1642 (Cambridge University Press, 2004).

Hadfield, Andrew, *Literature, Politics and National Identity: Reformation to Renaissance* (Cambridge University Press, 1994).

Hageman, Elizabeth H. and Katherine Conway (eds.), *Resurrecting Elizabeth I in Seventeenth-Century England* (Madison, NJ: Fairleigh Dickinson University Press, 2007).

Haigh, Christopher, *English Reformations: Religion, Society and Politics under the Tudors* (Oxford: Clarendon Press, 1992).

Halbwachs, Maurice, *Les Cadres Sociaux de la Mémoire* (Paris: Libraire Félix Alcan, 1925).

Hall, Edward, *The Union of the Two Noble Houses of Lancaster and York* (London, 1550).

Hammer, Paul, 'Shakespeare's *Richard II*, the play of 7 February 1601, and the Essex Rising', *Shakespeare Quarterly*, 59:1 (2008), 1–35.

Hampton-Reeves, Stuart, 'Staring at Clio: artists, histories and counter-histories', in D. Cavanagh, S. Hampton-Reeves and S. Longstaffe (eds.), *Shakespeare's Histories and Counter-Histories* (Manchester University Press, 2006), pp. 1–12.

Harmon, A. G., 'Shakespeare's carved saints', *Studies in English Literature*, 45:2 (2005), 315–31.

Harris, Jonathan Gil, *Untimely Matter in the Time of Shakespeare* (Philadelphia: University of Pennsylvania Press, 2008).

Hattaway, Michael, 'The Shakespearean history play', in M. Hattaway (ed.), *The Cambridge Companion to Shakespeare's History Plays* (Cambridge University Press, 2002), pp. 3–24.

Helgerson, Richard, *Forms of Nationhood: The Elizabethan Writing of England* (Chicago and London: University of Chicago Press, 1992).

Hertel, Ralf, *Staging England in the Elizabethan History Play: Performing National Identity* (Farnham: Ashgate, 2014).

Heywood, Thomas, 'An Apology for Actors [1612]', *English Renaissance Literary Criticism*, ed. by Brian Vickers (Oxford: Clarendon Press, 1999), pp. 474–501.

If You Know Not Me You Know Nobody, Parts I and II [1605]. 2 vols., ed. by W. W. Gregg (Oxford: The Malone Society Reprints, 1934).

Higden, Ranulf, *Polycronycon* (Westminster: Printed by William Caxton, 1482).

Hillman, David, '*Homo clausus* at the theatre', in B. Reynolds and W. N. West (eds.), *Rematerializing Shakespeare Authority and Representation on the Early Modern English Stage* (Basingstoke: Palgrave Macmillan, 2005), pp. 161–85.

Hiscock, Andrew, *Reading Memory in Early Modern Literature* (Cambridge University Press, 2011).

Hobgood, Allison P. *Passionate Playgoing in Early Modern England* (Cambridge University Press, 2011).

Höfele, Andreas, 'Making history memorable: More, Shakespeare and Richard III', *REAL: The Yearbook of Research in English and American Literature*, 21 (2005), 187–203.

Holderness, Graham, *Shakespeare: The Histories* (Houndmills, Basingstoke: Palgrave Macmillan, 2000).

Shakespeare's History (Dublin: Gill and Macmillan, 1985).

Holinshed, Raphael, *Holinshed's Chronicles of England, Scotland, and Ireland* [1586], ed. by Vernon F. Snow. 6 vols. (New York: AMS Press, 1976) [= facsimile reprint of the 1807–8 edition printed for J. Johnson, London.]

Holland, Peter, 'On the gravy train: Shakespeare, memory and forgetting', in P. Holland (ed.), *Shakespeare, Memory, and Performance* (Cambridge University Press, 2006), pp. 207–34.

Howard, Jean E., 'Shakespeare, geography, and the work of genre', in S. Cohen (ed.), *Shakespeare and Historical Formalism* (Aldershot: Ashgate, 2007), pp. 49–67.

Howard, Jean and Phyllis Rackin, *Engendering a Nation: A Feminist Account of Shakespeare's English Histories* (New York: Routledge, 1997).

Hutcheon, Linda, 'Irony, nostalgia, and the postmodern' (1998), www. library.utoronto.ca/utel/criticism/hutchinp.html#N26, last accessed 15.02.2015, no pagination.

I. G. I[ohn] G[reene], *A Refutation of the Apologie for Actors* [1615], ed. by Richard H. Perkinson (New York: Scholar's Facsimiles and Prints, 1941).

Ivic, Christopher, 'Reassuring fratricide in *1 Henry IV*', in C. Ivic and G. Williams (eds.), *Forgetting in Early Modern English Literature and Culture: Lethe's Legacies* (London and New York: Routledge, 2004), pp. 99–109.

Ivic, Christopher and Grant Williams (eds.), *Forgetting in Early Modern English Literature and Culture: Lethe's Legacies* (London and New York: Routledge, 2004).

James I., *The Political Works of James I*. Introd. by Charles Howard McIlwain (New York: Russell & Russell, 1965).

Joughin, John J., 'Shakespeare's memorial aesthetics', in P. Holland (ed.), *Shakespeare, Memory and Performance* (Cambridge University Press, 2006), pp. 43–62.

Joughin, John J. and Simon Malpas (eds.), *The New Aestheticism* (Manchester University Press, 2003).

Jowett, John, 'Introduction', in *The Tragedy of King Richard III*, ed. by J. Jowett. The Oxford Shakespeare (Oxford University Press, 2000), pp. 1–132.

Kamps, Ivo, *Historiography and Ideology in Stuart Drama* (Cambridge University Press, 1996).

Kerrigan, John, *Motives of Woe: Shakespeare and 'Female Complaint'* (Oxford: Clarendon Press, 1991).

Revenge Tragedy (Oxford: Clarendon Press, 1996).

Kewes, Paulina, 'The Elizabethan history play: A true genre?', in R. Dutton and J. E. Howard (eds.), *A Companion to Shakespeare's Works*, vol. II: *The Histories* (Oxford: Blackwell, 2003), pp. 170–93.

Kewes, Paulina (ed.), *The Uses of History in Early Modern England* (San Marino, CA: Huntington Library Press, 2006).

Kinney, Daniel, 'The tyrant being slain: Afterlives of More's *History of King Richard III*', in N. Rhodes (ed.), *English Renaissance Prose: History, Language, and Politics* (Tempe, AZ: Arizona State University, 1997), pp. 35–56.

Knowles, Ronald, 'Introduction', in *King Henry VI, Part Two*, ed. by R. Knowles. Arden Shakespeare Third Series (London: Cengage, 1999), pp. 1–141.

Shakespeare's Arguments with History (Houndmills, Basingstoke: Palgrave, 2002).

Krämer, Sybille, 'Das Vergessen nicht vergessen! oder: Ist das Vergessen ein defizienter Modus von Erinnerung?', *Paragrana*, 9:2 (2000), 251–75.

Lachmann, Renate, 'Kultursemiotischer Prospekt', in A. Haverkamp and R. Lachmann (eds.), *Memoria: Vergessen und Erinnern* (München: Fink, 1993), pp. xvii–xxvii.

Laroque, François, 'Shakespeare's "Battle of Carnival and Lent": The Falstaff scenes reconsidered', in R. Knowles (ed.), *Shakespeare and Carnival: After Bakhtin* (New York: Macmillan, 1998), pp. 83–96.

Leahy, William, '"All would be royal": The effacement of disunity in Shakespeare's *Henry V*', *Shakespeare-Jahrbuch*, 138 (2002), 89–98.

Lees-Jeffries, Hester, *Shakespeare and Memory*. Oxford Shakespeare Topics (Oxford University Press, 2013).

Leggatt, Alexander, 'Killing the hero: Tamburlaine and Falstaff', in P. Budra and B. Schellenberg (eds.), *Part Two: Reflections on the Sequel* (University of Toronto Press, 1998), pp. 53–67.

Shakespeare's Political Drama: The History Plays and the Roman Plays (London and New York: Routledge, 1988).

Levy, Fritz J., *Tudor Historical Thought* (San Marino, CA: Huntington Library Press, 1967).

Liebler, Naomi C., 'The mockery King of Snow: *Richard II* and the sacrifice of ritual', in L. Woodbridge and E. Berry (eds.), *True Rites and Maimed Rites: Ritual and Anti-Ritual in Shakespeare and His Age* (Urbana and Chicago: University of Illinois Press, 1992), pp. 220–39.

Linton, David, 'Shakespeare as media critic: Communication theory and historiography', *Mosaic*, 29:2 (1996), 1–21.

Long, Zachariah, '"Unless you could teach me to forget": Spectatorship, self-forgetting, and subversion in antitheatrical literature and *As You Like It*', in C. Ivic and G. Williams (eds.), *Forgetting in Early Modern English Literature and Culture: Lethe's Legacies* (London and New York: Routledge, 2004), pp. 151–64.

Lopez, Jeremy, *Theatrical Convention and Audience Response in Early Modern Drama* (Cambridge University Press, 2003).

Low, Jennifer A. and Nova Myhill, *Imagining the Audience in Early Modern Drama, 1558–1642* (Houndmills, Basingstoke: Palgrave Macmillan, 2011).

Lowenthal, David, 'Nostalgia tells it like it wasn't', in C. Shaw and M. Chase (eds.), *The Imagined Past* (Manchester University Press, 1989), pp.18–32.

The Past is a Foreign Country (Cambridge University Press, 1985).

'Preface', in A. Forty and S. Küchler (eds.), *The Art of Forgetting* (Oxford and New York: Berg Publishers, 1999), pp. xi–xiii.

Machiavelli, Niccolò, *The Prince*, ed. by G. Bull (London: Penguin, 2003).

Marche, Stephen, 'Mocking dead bones: Historical memory and the theater of the dead in *Richard III*', *Comparative Drama*, 37:1 (2003), 37–57.

Marshall, Peter, *Beliefs and the Dead in Reformation England* (Oxford University Press, 2002).

Mason, Pamela, '*Henry V*: "the quick forge and working house of thought"', in M. Hattaway (ed.), *The Cambridge Companion to Shakespeare's History Plays* (Cambridge University Press, 2002), pp. 177–93.

Maus, Katharine Eisaman, *Inwardness and Theater in the English Renaissance* (University of Chicago Press, 1995).

Mazzola, Elizabeth, *The Pathology of the English Renaissance: Sacred Remains and Holy Ghosts* (Leiden: Brill, 1998).

McMullan, Gordon, 'Introduction', in *King Henry VIII*, ed. by G. McMullan. Arden Shakespeare Third Series (London: Cengage, 2000), pp. 1–199.

Meek, Richard, Jane Rickard and Richard Wilson (eds.), *Shakespeare's Book: Essays in Reading, Writing and Reception* (Manchester University Press, 2008).

Melchiori, Giorgio, 'Dying of a sweat: Falstaff and Oldcastle', *Notes and Queries*, 34 (1987), 210–11.

Melchiori, Giorgio (ed.), 'Introduction', in *The Second Part of King Henry IV*. New Cambridge Shakespeare (Cambridge University Press, 1989), pp. 1–73.

Montrose, Louis, *The Subject of Elizabeth: Authority, Gender and Representation* (University of Chicago Press, 2006).

More, Thomas, *The Complete Works of St. Thomas More*. ed. by Richard S. Sylvester (New Haven, CT: Yale University Press, 1963).

Muir, Edward, *Ritual in Early Modern Europe* (Cambridge University Press, 1997).

Mullaney, Steven, *The Place of the Stage: License, Power and Play in Renaissance England* (University of Chicago Press, 1988).

Muro, Diego, 'Nationalism and nostalgia', *Nations and Nationalism*, 11:4 (2005), 571–89.

Murphy, Andrew (ed.), *A Concise Companion to Shakespeare and the Text* (Oxford: Blackwell, 2007).

Nashe, Thomas, *Pierce Pennilesse, his Supplication to the Divell*, ed. by G. B. Harrison (Edinburgh University Press, 1966).

Neill, Michael, *Issues of Death: Mortality and Identity in English Renaissance Tragedy* (Oxford: Clarendon Press, 1997).

Northbrooke, John, *A Treatise wherein Dicing, Dauncing, Vaine Playes or Enterluds ... are Reproved* (London: H. Bynneman for George Byshop, 1577).

Orgel, Stephen, 'The play of conscience', in E. Kosofsky Sedgwick and A. Parker (eds.), *Performativity and Performance* (New York: Routledge, 1995), pp. 133–51.

Panofsky, Erwin, *Renaissance and Renascences in Western Art* (New York: Harper & Row, 1972).

Passerini, Luisa, 'Memories between silence and oblivion', in K. Hodgkin and S. Radstone (eds.), *Memory, History, Nation: Contested Pasts* (New Brunswick, NJ and London: Transaction Publishers, 2006), pp. 238–54.

Paster, Gail Kern, 'Melancholy cats, lugged bears, and early modern cosmology: Reading Shakespeare's psychological materialism across the species barrier', in G. K. Paster, K. Rowe and M. Floyd-Wilson (eds.), *Reading the Early Modern Passions: Essays in the Cultural History of Emotion* (Philadelphia: University of Pennsylvania Press, 2004), pp. 113–29.

Patterson, Annabel, *Censorship and Interpretation: The Conditions of Writing and Reading in Early Modern England* (Madison: University of Wisconsin Press, 1994).

'Sir John Oldcastle as symbol of Reformation historiography', in D. B. Hamilton and R. Strier (eds.), *Religion, Literature and Politics in Post-Reformation England, 1540–1688* (Cambridge University Press, 1996), pp. 6–26.

Pendleton, Thomas A., '"This is not the man": On calling Falstaff Falstaff', *Analytical and Enumerative Bibliography*, 4 (1990), 59–71.

Perry, Curtis, 'The citizen politics of nostalgia: Queen Elizabeth in early Jacobean London', *Journal of Medieval and Renaissance Studies*, 23.1 (1993), 89–111.

Pfister, Manfred, *Das Drama*, utb 580 (München: Fink, 1977).

'Shakespeare's memory: Texts – images – monuments – performances', in J. Kamm and B. Lenz (eds.), *Shakespearean Culture – Cultural Shakespeare* (Passau: Stutz, 2009), pp. 217–40.

Philippy, Patricia, *Women, Death and Literature in Post-Reformation England* (Cambridge University Press, 2002).

Plato, *Collected Dialogues*, ed. by E. Hamilton and H. Cairns (Princeton University Press, 1961).

Platter, Thomas, *Travels in England* [1599], ed. by C. Williams (London: n. pub., 1937).

Pollard, A. F., 'The making of Sir Thomas More's *Richard III*', in R. S. Sylvester and G. P. Marc'hadour (eds.), *Essential Articles for the Study of Thomas More* (Hamden, CT: Archon Books, 1977), pp. 421–33.

Poole, Adrian, 'Laughter, forgetting and Shakespeare', in M. Cordner, P. Holland and J. Kerrigan (eds.), *English Comedy* (Cambridge University Press, 1994), pp. 85–99.

Poole, Kristen, 'Saints Alive! Falstaff, Martin Marprelate, and the staging of Puritanism', *Shakespeare Quarterly*, 46:1 (1995), 47–75.

Pugliatti, Paola, '"More than history can pattern": The Jack Cade rebellion in Shakespeare's *Henry VI, 2*', *Journal of Medieval and Renaissance Studies*, 22:3 (1992), 451–71.

Shakespeare the Historian (New York: St. Martin's Press, 1996).

Rabkin, Norman B., *Shakespeare and the Problem of Meaning* (University of Chicago Press, 1981).

Rackin, Phyllis, *Stages of History: Shakespeare's English Chronicles* (London and New York: Routledge, 1990).

Ralegh, Walter, *The Works of Sir Walter Ralegh*. Vols. II–VII: *The History of the World* [1614] (New York: Burt Franklin, 1965) [= reprint of the facsimile edition of the 1829 *Works*, Oxford University Press].

Rankins, William, *A Mirrour of Monsters* (London: I.C. for T.H., 1587).

Rasmussen, Mark David (ed. and introd.) and Strier, Richard (afterword), *Renaissance Literature and Its Formal Engagements* (New York: Palgrave, 2002).

Renan, Ernest, 'What is a nation? [1882]', in H. Bhabha (ed.), *Nation and Narration* (London and New York: Routledge, 1990), pp. 8–22.

Richards, Michael, *A Time of Silence: Civil War and the Culture of Repression in Franco's Spain, 1936–1945* (Cambridge University Press, 1999).

Rowley, Samuel, *When You See Me You Know Me* [1605], ed. by F.P. Wilson (Oxford: The Malone Society Reprints, 1952).

Rudnytsky, Peter L., '*Henry VIII* and the deconstruction of history', *Shakespeare Survey*, 43 (1991), 43–58.

Ruiter, David, *Shakespeare's Festive History: Feasting, Festivity, Fasting and Lent in the Second Henriad* (Aldershot: Ashgate, 2003).

Schmidt, Gabriela, '"To set some colour vpon ye matter": Thomas More's *History of King Richard the Third* zwischen humanistischer Vergangenheitskonstruktion und autoreflexiver Skepsis', in F. Bezner and K. Mahlke (eds.), *Zwischen Wissen und Politik: Archäologie und Genealogie frühneuzeitlicher Vergangenheitskonstruktionen* (Heidelberg: Winter, 2011), pp. 161–82.

Schneider, Manfred, 'Liturgien der Erinnerung, Techniken des Vergessens', *Merkur*, 41:2 (1987), 676–86.

Schoenfeldt, Michael C., *Bodies and Selves in Early Modern England: Physiology and Inwardness in Spenser, Shakespeare, Herbert, and Milton* (Cambridge University Press, 1999).

Schwyzer, Philip, *Literature, Nationalism, and Memory in Early Modern England and Wales* (Cambridge University Press, 2004).

'Shakespeare's art of reenactment: Henry at Blackfriars, Richard at Rougemont', in A. Gordon and T. Rist (eds.), *The Arts of Remembrance in Early Modern England: Memorial Cultures of the Post Reformation* (Aldershot: Ashgate, 2013), pp. 179–94.

Shakespeare, William, *The Norton Shakespeare*, ed by Stephen Greenblatt et al. (New York: W.W. Norton & Co, 1997).

Sharpe, Kevin, *Reading Revolutions: The Politics of Reading in Early Modern England* (New Haven, CT: Yale University Press, 2000).

Shaw, Christopher and Malcolm Chase (eds.), *The Imagined Past: History and Nostalgia* (Manchester University Press, 1989).

Sidney, Sir Philip, *The Major Works*, ed. by Katherine Duncan-Jones. Oxford World's Classics (Oxford University Press, 1989).

Simpson, James, *Under the Hammer: Iconoclasm in the Anglo-American Tradition* (Oxford University Press, 2011).

Smith, Anthony D., *Nationalism: Theory, Ideology, History* (Cambridge: Polity Press, 2001).

Smith, Helen, '"A man in print?" Shakespeare and the representation of the press', in R. Meek, J. Rickard and R. Wilson (eds.), *Shakespeare's Book: Essays in Reading, Writing and Reception* (Manchester University Press, 2008), pp. 59–78.

Starobinski, Jean, 'The idea of nostalgia', *Diogenes*, 54 (1966), 84–103.

Stern, Tiffany, *Making Shakespeare: From Stage to Page* (London and New York: Routledge, 2004).

Stewart, Frank (ed.), *Silence to Light: Japan and the Shadows of War* (Honolulu: University of Hawai'i Press, 2001).

Stow, John, *The Annales; or, General Chronicle of England* ... (London, 1615).

A Survey of London [1603], ed. by Charles Lethbridge Kingsford, 2 vols. (Oxford: Clarendon Press, 1908).

Strohm, Paul, *England's Empty Throne: Usurpation and the Language of Legitimation, 1399–1422* (New Haven, CT and London: Yale University Press, 1998).

Sullivan, Garrett A. Jr., 'Lethargic corporeality on and off the early modern stage', in C. Ivic and G. Williams (eds.), *Forgetting in Early Modern English Literature and Culture: Lethe's Legacies* (London: Routledge, 2004), pp. 41–52.

Memory and Forgetting in English Renaissance Drama: Shakespeare, Marlowe, Webster (Cambridge University Press, 2005).

Summit, Jennifer, 'Reading reformed: Spenser and the problem of the English library', in C. Ivic and G. Williams (eds.), *Forgetting in Early Modern English Literature and Culture: Lethe's Legacies* (London: Routledge, 2004), pp. 165–78.

Sylvester, Richard S., 'Introduction', in *The Complete Works of Sir Thomas More, vol. II*, ed. by Richard S. Sylvester (New Haven, CT and London: Yale University Press, 1963), pp. 1–151.

Takada, Shigeki, 'The first and second parts of *Henry IV*: Some thoughts on the origins of Shakespearean gentleness', in Y. Takahashi (ed.), *Hot Questrists After the English Renaissance* (New York: AMS Press, 2000), pp. 183–96.

Taylor, Gary, 'The fortunes of Oldcastle', *Shakespeare Survey*, 38 (1985), 85–100.

Taylor, Gary (ed. and introd.), *Henry V* (Oxford University Press, 1982).

Tillyard, E. M. W., *Shakespeare's History Plays* [1944]. Revised edition (London: Chatto and Windus, 1969).

Tribble, Evelyn, *Cognition in the Globe: Attention and Memory in Shakespeare's Theatre* (Houndmills, Basingstoke: Palgrave Macmillan, 2011).

Walch, Günter, 'Henry V as working-house of ideology', *Shakespeare Survey*, 40 (1987), 63–8.

Walker, Julia, *The Elizabeth Icon: 1603–2003* (Houndmills, Basingstoke: Palgrave Macmillan, 2004).

Walsh, Brian, *Shakespeare, the Queen's Men and the Elizabethan Performance of History* (Cambridge University Press, 2009).

Warren-Heys, Rebecca, ' "[R]emember, with advantages": Creating memory in Shakespeare's *Henry V*', *Journal of the Northern Renaissance*, 2:1 (2010), 111–27.

Weimann, Robert, 'Performance, game, and representation in *Richard III*', in R. Weimann and D. Bruster (eds.), *Shakespeare and the Power of Performance: Stage and Page in the Elizabethan Theatre* (Cambridge University Press, 2008), pp. 42–56.

Shakespeare und die Tradition des Volkstheaters (Berlin: Henschel Verlag, 1967).

Weinrich, Harald, *Lethe: Kunst und Kritik des Vergessens* (Munich: Beck, 1997).

West, William N., 'Intertheatricality', in H. S. Turner (ed.), *Early Modern Theatricality* (Oxford University Press, 2013), pp. 151–72.

Whitehead, Anne, *Memory*. Routledge New Critical Idiom (New York: Routledge, 2010).

Whitney, Charles, 'Versions of Sir John', in C. Whitney, *Early Responses to Renaissance Drama* (Cambridge University Press, 2006), pp. 73–122.

Wilder, Lina Perkins, *Shakespeare's Memory Theatre: Recollection, Properties, and Character* (Cambridge University Press, 2010).

Wiles, David, *Shakespeare's Clown* (Cambridge University Press, 1987).

Williams, Raymond, *Marxism and Literature* (Oxford University Press, 1977).

Willis, John, *Mnemonica; Or, the Art of Memory, Drained out of the Pure Fountains of Art & Nature* [Lat. 1618] (London, 1661).

Womack, Peter, 'Imagining communities: Theatres and the English nation in the sixteenth century', in D. Aers (ed.), *Culture and History, 1350–1600: Essays on English Communities, Identities and Writing* (Detroit, MI: Wayne State University Press, 1992), pp. 91–145.

'Henry IV and epic theatre', in N. Wood (ed.), *Henry IV, Parts One and Two* (Buckingham: Open University Press, 1995), pp. 126–61.

Womersley, David, 'Why is Falstaff fat?', *Review of English Studies*, 47 (1996), 1–22.

Woodward, Jennifer, *The Theatre of Death: The Ritual Management of Royal Funerals in Renaissance England, 1570–1625* (Woodbridge: Boydell, 1997).

Woolf, Daniel, *The Social Circulation of the Past: English Historical Culture,*
    1500–1730 (Oxford University Press, 2003).

Wotton, Henry, *The Life and Letters of Sir Henry Wotton*, ed. by Logan
    Pearsall Smith. 2 vols. (Oxford: Clarendon Press, 1970).

Yachnin, Paul, 'The powerless theater', *English Literary Renaissance*, 21
    (1991), 49–74.

Yates, Frances, *The Art of Memory* [1966] (London: Pimlico, 1996).

Index

Abelin, Johann Philipp
  Theatrum Europaeum, 1–3
Act of Uniformity, 65
Agnew, Jean-Christophe, 95
Althusser, Louis, 107
Anderson, Benedict, 13, 16, 135, 137
André, Bernard
  Vita Henrici VII, 52
antitheatrical writings, 33
  food metaphors in, 90–2
  forgetfulness in, 90–2
Aquinas, Thomas, 38
ars memorativa, 4, 5, 13, 38, 39, 185
Assmann, Aleida, 8, 13
Assmann, Jan, 68
audience, 164
  mnemonic task of, 26, 29–31, 33,
    34, 57, 180, 187
  sceptical audience, 35, 60–1

Bacon, Francis, 37
Baldo, Jonathan, 20, 30, 131, 142,
    179, 180
Bale, John, 51
  King Johan, 171
Bliss, Lee, 178

Cade, Jack
  in *Henry VI, Part 2*, 41, 45, 46
  historical figure, 46–7
  as Lord of Misrule, 51
Camden, William, 161
Carlson, Marvin, 27
Carruthers, Mary, 38
censorship, 10, 11, 15, 114, 121
ceremony
  in *Henry IV, Part 1*, 83–9
  in *Henry V*, 134, 139
  as mnemonic device, 185
  mnemonic role of, 134

parody of, 86–9
  in *Richard II*, 72–82
  in *Richard III*, 62–5
Chapman, Alison, 137–8, 143
Charnes, Linda, 95
Chase, Malcolm, 156, 157
Chernaik, Warren, 22
Cicero, 5
Cohen, Stephen, 21
Connerton, Paul, 134
Craik, T. W., 120
Cromwell, Thomas, 131

Daniel, Samuel, 37
Dawson, Anthony B., 93,
    123, 145
Day, Gillian, 58
de Sousa, Geraldo, 42
Debord, Guy, 141
Dekker, Thomas
  The Gull's Horn-Book, 96
  The Shoemaker's Holiday, 138
  The Whore of Babylon, 162,
    170–4, 176
Deloney, Thomas
  The Gentle Craft, 137
Diehl, Huston, 68–9
Dillon, Janet, 31, 32, 185
distraction
  as ideological tool, 34, 125
  as performance effect, 25, 124–5
  in the playhouse, 123–4
Dobson, Michael, 164, 172
Döring, Tobias, 184
dramatic vocabulary, 32
Drayton, Michael, 37
Duffy, Eamon, 78

Eco, Umberto, 4–5, 44
Edward VI, 17, 50